SAMSON'S HAIR IS GROWING AGAIN.

Barry Manson

Dedication

To Linda, who, like Jesus, never gave up on me. Thank you.

ISBN: 978-0-244-18711-8

© Barry J Manson, May 2019.

All rights reserved. No part of this book may be reproduced, stored in a retrieval system, or transmitted, in any form or by any means, electronic, mechanical, photocopying, recording or otherwise, without the prior permission of the author.

Bible quotations from the following sources;

The Holy Bible, Today's New International Version (TNIV), Copyright © 2001, 2005 by International Bible Society.

New Revised Standard Version of the Bible, © 1989 by the Division of Christian Education of the National Council of the Churches of Christ in the United States of America.

The Holy Bible, English Standard Version, © 2001, 2006, 2011, 2016 by Crossway Bibles, a division of Good News Publishers.

King James Version, Public Domain

The Message: The Bible in Contemporary Language, © 2002 by Eugene Peterson.

Acknowledgements

I am very grateful to Sonia Perez and Lauren Dunning for proofreading the manuscript and offering insightful corrections.

Thank you Chris Pick for the design of the front and back cover. You did a magnificent job.

Joshua Tiplady, you made me look good with the photo on the back page, thank you.

Dave Mansfield, thank you for your immense help in preparing the book for publishing.

Endorsements

"Barry has been one of the most influential people in my Christian walk as pastor, mentor and friend. We met nearly 30 years ago at King's Centre, Sheffield and I was captivated by his revelation of the Word and dynamic preaching style. Over those years I have had the honour of walking with Barry through some of his toughest times and seen how the Lord's grace has captivated his heart. Barry's life is an intricate symphony declaring that grace. His story will inspire you to endure no matter the circumstances".

Fabiano Altamura, Dean, Bethel Conservatory of the Arts, Bethel Church, Redding, Cal. USA.

"Barry is a man of grace and truth. His understanding of the power of God's amazing grace is not described as an abstract theory, but earthed here in the story of his life. It has made him the man that he has become; a man I can call my friend. Barry's warmth and vulnerability are evident throughout this book which will encourage you that God hasn't finished with you yet".

Jonathan Dunning, Pastor, Meadowhead Christian Fellowship, Sheffield.

"I count it a privilege to have Barry and Linda as two of my closest friends. From our days together in Amsterdam and India until now, I have seen the grace and provision of God at work in their lives. In his book Barry shares his life journey with openness, honesty and humour as he uncovers both the triumphs and struggles in his journey with God. If you want to know and experience the outrageous grace, love and power of God in your life, then I highly recommend this book".

Geoff Walvin, Pastor, Harvest Christian Centre, Woodham, U.K. Former Missionary Church planter to India and Nepal.

"Life is a journey and Barry's life certainly exemplifies that! It was 25 years ago that we first met. There are some people who come into our lives for a brief season, and others with whom we share the ongoing journey and camaraderie in the fight. This has been the case with Barry and myself. We have shared pulpits and many vacations together with our wives. I found it fascinating to read Barry's story as there were many things that I had not previously heard. I recommend this book as a fascinating story of searching and finding the Saviour. It is also refreshing how open and vulnerable Barry is in recounting his history before and after conversion. We all struggle but we do not always talk about it. I commend him for his openness. This book has the potential to inspire its readers to experience for themselves, Samson's hair growing again. It is a book filled with hope for those who desire to follow Jesus".

Errol Faulkes, Former Pastor, Heights Vineyard Church, Albuquerque. Co-Founder, New Life City Albuquerque. USA. Global Awakening Instructor, Christian Healing Certificate Programme.

"I am proud to call Barry Manson my best friend. Over the past 25 years, we have developed a strong friendship and have shared many ups and downs together. He has been a rock for me in my winter season and I have been privileged to be there for him. This book is a wonderful read and reveals the story of a man who against all the odds dramatically changed his life to allow God to work through him to change thousands of lives. He is honest, warm, funny, authentic and personifies mental resilience. He may have once been a ragamuffin, but he is now a father to many. I've heard Barry preach countless times and there is a tangible presence of God when he does. My wife Julie and I love Barry and Linda to bits and look forward to spending many years eating, laughing and sharing life (and ribs) together".

John Dabrowski, International speaker, Mental Resilience expert and author of 'Off the Wall – How to Develop World Class Mental Resilience'. jdmindcoach.com

"One of the terms Barry applies to himself in this book is "Ragamuffin". It's the kind of word someone who sees only the superficial might use, but it's a good starting point for a man

God took by the "scruff of his neck", or by his long hair, and dragged into the Kingdom. The adventures Barry shares in this account of his journey will be a great encouragement to many, especially to those who think they are beyond God's reach. Barry discovered the hard way how extraordinary is the grace of God, and how limitless is His love for us".

Vic Whittaker, Co-Founder of Open Kingdom, UK, and TLC Restoration & Renewal Prayer & Retreat Centre in Turkey.

"Get ready for a good read! This book will share some of Barry's real world experiences. Read this book and allow Barry's authentic and down to earth approach encourage you. Enjoy the stories of his travels from a life truly transformed by the power of our Living Christ. From a real-life rocker who found the Rock of ages, unveiling destiny and identity; spiritual truths that lead to actual life lessons that will help you in your real world journey".

Lester Sumrall, third generation minister and visionary. President LSI, www.lestersumrall.com

"I count Barry as a friend and fellow life traveler, always there to support, no matter what the battle. This book tells the story of God's immense grace in Barry's own life. It champions a simple but timeless truth, that no matter how bad things get, and no matter how much we mess up, there is always a way back to the one who redeems. Barry and Linda are living examples of how, even in the darkest times, we can look to a redemptive and transforming God, who always gives hope".

Ian Mayer, Author of "Are We Brave Enough?" 2019, Instant Apostle. ISBN 9781909728974

"One can never tell where a chance meeting will finally end up, and this was true for myself and Pauline when we met Barry and Linda up in the Himalayas, Mussoorie, India to be exact. There are not many who can say that Barry Manson cut their hair, however I was grateful for him to use his latent hairdressing skills, to tidy me up. It all happened while they were working with Floyd and Sally McClung at "Dilaram House" in Delhi, dealing with the great "hippy flow" that made their way to that place. Some were a bit "past it" and eventually we agreed for a "Home for the Helpless" to be established with us at The Firs Fellowship, in the quiet and cool of The Firs, in Landour, Musssoorie. We are grateful to those who took on this ministry, and the results for good that followed. We were glad of the friendship of Barry and Linda, and were happy to share our heart for world mission, something that has remained in their hearts.

The years pass, and then another chance meeting at the Booksellers Convention in the UK, brought our lives together again. It's quite a story, but as an Elder at Sheffield House Church, it led to him and Linda being introduced to the late Peter Fenwick leader of the Fellowship.

Do read the book, as all that resulted in a very on going way, is recorded. The introduction eventually brought Barry and Linda to Sheffield, where they still live. Today, from time to time, we still enjoy a "cuppa",[1] together, and recall the goodness of the Lord, over all these years. You'll enjoy the book".

Geoffrey and Pauline Williams. Missionary Statespeople.
GAP Ministries and The Partnership Trust.
Sheffield. S. Yorks. England.

"I met Barry when he came to take over the leadership of a Church in Sheffield and subsequently we became good friends. His ministry was very much respected but, as he shares in this book, due to the pressure and busyness of church work, he hit the lowest point in his life. In a time of recuperation, Barry discovered a fresh revelation of the grace of God. He now preaches with fresh grace and anointing wherever he goes. This book is a great read, and a very powerful and accurate version of Barry and Linda's life story. it will challenge and encourage you. I recommend it to you".

Ray Booth, Church Father, Christian Minister, Sheffield.

---

[1] cup of tea.

"I have known Pastor Barry Manson since 2004. He is a man full of love and passion for God, and has been to our church in Bangalore, India and preached in all 6 services continuously without a break. I see so much richness of God's deposit which rests in him to be gleaned by thousands.

He has written this book [in] black and white which reveals the power of Grace. I believe this book will not only strengthen and build every reader in their walk with Christ, but also their faith and confidence in God. This is a book to be reread and treasured for its rich and real content gathered from life's experience, to challenge your life's dangers, toils and snares. Shiby and I love Barry and Linda very dearly and cherish their friendship".

Samson Arthur Paul, Apostolic Pastor, Grace Gospel Church, Bangalore, India

Foreword by Alan Hawkins.

Like Abraham, many of us have heard the voice of God calling us to go without telling us where we are going. He just says that He will show us. The voice is more compelling than all of our fears. Something in the sound assures us that we will not be alone. My friends Barry and Linda heard that voice back in the early days of sex, drugs and rock and roll. We were all very distracted but the promise in that voice overcame every other sound and they obeyed.

If Jesus had told us everything that was in store we could not have said yes so readily. However, when you follow a carpenter with nail scars right through His hands you cannot expect to journey unscathed. Barry tells a story of leaving everything to follow. The hymn singer recollects that it is a story of dangers, toils and snares. My friend opens his life in a way that beckons to hear.

When we met, Barry was the envy of pastors; a growing church, international travel, acclaim, and all the markers of professional and personal success. We became easy friends. His story was such an inspiration. But life is measured by what we are when the dreams are shattered and the glory is gone. This book is hewn out of the ashes of that story. The beauty is that on every page he veils the crushing of the grapes and offers the new wine. He writes with the ease of one who directs the play knowing the story will resolve well. He writes to tell us that the one who called us is going to get us safely home.

The letter to the Hebrews is written to encourage us that if we hear God's voice we must not delay. Barry is testifying with that great cloud of witnesses that we were made to overcome every obstacle and that we too can run with endurance the race that lies ahead. I am grateful to know this friend of God and to be strengthened by his story.

Alan Hawkins, Senior Pastor, New Life City, Albuquerque, New Mexico, USA.

Foreword by Dave Gilpin.

Barry Manson will always be a legend in my eyes as well as God's eyes. He's done the hard yards of ministry and not only got the t shirt, he's spent his years handing out t shirts made to measure to all who hear him preach or share, whether it be in America, India, Ireland or England.

If that's not enough, he's also done the impossible yards of picking himself from a 'perfect storm' that few survive from. He's lived a full life that is still marked by a hunger to see more, go more and be more. We salute him.

 He's interesting. He's brotherly. He's experienced. He's seasoned. He's Barry Manson: the likes of which are rare, just as God intended. This is his story.

Go and put the kettle on, find a comfortable place to relax and let this book take you away to places both known and unknown. You'll love it for sure.

Dave Gilpin, Senior Pastor, Hope City Church, Sheffield.UK. hopecity.church Author of 'Sacred Cows Make Great BBQs'. Authentic Publishing. ISBN 1860247583.

Foreword by David Mansfield.

I have known, and loved Barry and Linda Manson for over 35 years. Their friendship and love have outlasted all others save my eldest daughter and the Lord Himself! I have walked with these guys, seen them up close and personal, walked with them through their highs and lows and can tell you, they are the real deal. This book has been a while in the writing and a lifetime in the making. You will laugh, you may cry, but you will certainly see a story of amazing grace unfold as you make your way through these pages. This book is open, honest, gritty and gracious. You may just find your own life changed a little as you read it!

David F Mansfield, Senior Minister, The Haven Church, Nottingham, author and teacher, Barry's mate.

Foreword by Dave Andrews.

This book is not just a book by Barry, this book is Barry. Reading this book is like visiting Barry after ages; catching up, having lots of cuppas and a long chat about his life. Its full of classic Barry jokes, quotes, anecdotes and asides; references to his favourite places, people, movies and music; reflections on the good times and bad times he has gone through as the 'Lone Ranger' with his faithful companion, Linda, by his side; and orations, homilies and sermons, in praise of grace, without which, in my experience, no conversation with Barry is complete. I finished the book feeling Barry's gratitude for the love he has found in the life he has lived.

Dave Andrews, Brisbane, Australia. Author of 'Not Religion But Love'. Wipf and Stock Publishers. ISBN 13:978-1-61097-851-4.

Foreword by John Herbert.

I have thoroughly enjoyed this book and been encouraged by it. This is partly because his story includes moments when our lives have intersected, or where it describes times and places familiar to me -- the search for the meaning of life and the discovery of how we are relevant and loved by God, the hippy trail to the East, and participation in a Christian community in Holland. But he also looks perceptively at his experiences in church leadership, what he sees as an adventure, and he includes with honesty the hiccups on the way. Barry outlines his personal journey into and within faith in Jesus, with plenty of stories and anecdotes. For anyone who has had discouragements in church leadership this book speaks reassuringly. But I would recommend anyone to read this book. He has learned that mysterious thing, that ultimately all our skills, plans and experience seem slight when we grasp that God truly does love us.
John Herbert, The Earl of Powis. Ex hippie, former Professor of English Literature. Currently running a prayer house on top of a small mountain.

Gratitude.

A friend loves at all times. Proverbs 17:17.

On my journey I found some wonderful helping hands. If I missed you out, it was not intentional, there are so many of you.

Peter Fenwick, my spiritual Dad, always believed in me no matter what. We'll talk again in Heaven.

Ken McGreavy, my spiritual mentor, and very special friend, taught me just about everything I do well today. You never gave up on me. We will also talk again and laugh in Heaven.

Steve Henry, thank you so much for introducing me to a gracious Jesus.

Frans and Martha Vellema, bedankt voor je onvoorwaardelijke acceptatie van een lamme en hem naar Jezus te leiden, (Thank you for your unconditional acceptance of a ragamuffin and leading him to Jesus).

Floyd McClung, your visionary leadership inspired me.

Dave and Ange Andrews, your radical commitment to Jesus has always inspired me. You also showed us true friendship and you still do. Thank you for introducing India to us.

Geoff and June Walvin, great friends, thank you for your encouragement, side splitting funny phone conversations, and affirmation always. We should have another 'shopping' trip in Asia!

Geoff and Pauline Williams, you gave me a missions world view. How are the camels doing?

Dave Mansfield, thank you for being a great friend; for leading and travelling the world with me. Our motto is still, "We *stand at the front and smile because we have no idea what is going on"*.

Dr. David Petts, thank you for your teaching and your critique on my Masters essay. *"You have clearly understood the subject, and have the ability to write well..."*. Those words inspired me to write this book; more than you will ever know.

John and Julie Dabrowski, thank you for your faithful friendship, and inspiration. 'Damons' will always be our favourite place!

Dave Gilpin, I will always remember you stood with me in my '*perfect storm*'. Always thankful.

Peter Birtles, my friend, advisor and defender. Thank you.

Wendy Holmes, we'll never forget your generosity. Thank you.

Terence and Michael Clark, thank you for reaching out to me in my lostness.

Patrick and Mia Cheadle, Thank you for your support and belief in this book.

A Special mention.

My Sheffield church family, Charis Church International. Your support over the years has been outstanding and greatly appreciated. Keep soaring like the eagle.

The Far Pavilions - India.

Samson and Shiby Paul. Your friendship and welcome to Grace Gospel Church and the Garden City of Bengaluru, India, always makes me feel at home.

Across the Pond

Errol and Brenda Faulkes, all time friends and coconspirators, doing life together. We still have more mountains to climb. Our motto...Blessed are the flexible.

Alan and Gail Hawkins, you became and remained my friends when I had nothing to offer you. I owe you a debt of love that I can never repay.

To my other church family, New Life City, Albuquerque, your warm welcome always refreshes my heart. I am at home with you.

To all of you, my gratitude is more than words can express.

<u>My Family</u>

Zara and Tim, Kyrie, Amber and Chris and of course Gus, I am so glad we found you. My four adorable granddaughters, you always make my heart smile, I love you to the moon and back.

All of you are my life, and my reason at times for never giving up.

<u>Most importantly</u>

Linda, my rock and steadfast companion for forty-six years. You never gave up, you held me up when I couldn't hold myself up. I would not have achieved anything without you. I love you.

Introduction

This book is about my life, my circumstances, failure, success and everything in between. A roller coaster ride in fact. From my upbringing in Northern Ireland to rock band days in Dublin. To drugs and bad trips, to Holland, then India, and my questions, in particular;

1. Who am I?

2. What is the meaning of life?

These questions drove my motivation to find answers. It reminds me of the story I once heard of the young man who walked through a city centre with a sign around his neck stating "*boy am I konfused*". When someone told him *"you don't spell confused with a K"*, he replied, *"you don't know how konfused I am"*.

That was my state of mind in those early days. I was reading an old King James Bible, which I had been given, listening to Hare Krishna music, taking LSD[2] and smoking Pot[3]...all at the same time. I was '*konfused*', but at least I was searching for an answer. My journey continues today, only now I have a clear certainty of those two questions. I've seen those questions answered, followed by success, then failure and restoration. From the lowest point in my life I discovered that, 'Samson's hair was growing again'.[4] Read on to discover the powerful truth of these words.

*Some names in the book have been changed for privacy reasons.

---

[2] Lysergic Acid Diethylamide is an hallucinogenic drug, also known as Acid.

[3] Hashish is the resin from the Cannabis plant. Marijuana comes from the dried leaves, flowers, seeds, and stems of the cannabis plant. Both can be smoked.

[4] Judges 16:22

Contents

Part 1. Setting Out on Life.   23

Chapter 1. Celtic Roots   23
The wee town in County Down.   25
Keeping up appearances.   26
Breaking the Spirit of poverty.   27
Only child syndrome.   28
Vagabond of the Western World.   28
Dreaming beyond the Horizon.   29
Hi Yo Silver, away!   31
Nagging Negatives.   33
Spiritual values and religious dogma.   34
School days, negative identity.   36
Devastation, definitely not the teacher's pet!   37
Words can Break your Heart.   37
Is this a private fight?   38

Chapter 2. Travelling Man   41
Short back and sides!   41
Down on the Island.   41
Rock n' roll Days: The rocky road to Dublin.   43
First big break.   45

Know the Author, know the meaning behind the words.	48
The rocky road to Hell.	48
The windmills of my mind.	50
Light begins to shine, but slowly.	51
The wild rover returns.	54
Gotta get back to the garden.	56
Our Princess arrives.	56
Divine directional detour.	57

Part II. New Adventures. 59

Chapter 3. Going Dutch. 59

A new beginning.	59
Desperation, and more divine appointments.	60
The day my Life changed forever.	61
God steps in again and again.	62
Coffee bar hang out.	63

Chapter 4. Down on the Farm 67

From the Ark to the Farm.	67
Houseboat church.	68
A fresh vision	69
DIY = Destroy it yourself!	70
Bell ringing for beginners.	71

Leading with humility.	72
A heritage from the Lord.	75
India calling.	76
He supplies all our needs.	77
God knows your phone number	78
Chapter 5. The Far Pavilions	**81**
Incredible, mysterious India.	81
It ain't half hot here!	82
Hope for Hippies.	83
When the cupboard is bare.	85
Overland to Afghanistan.	87
Learning to love in Kabul.	90
Blocked at the Border.	92
Medieval Kathmandu trip.	93
Destiny unfolds. Summer in Mussoorie, India.	95
Chapter 6. Culture Shock in Reverse.	**99**
We're going home.	99
In the land of smiles.	99
Out of the mouth of babes.	100
Re-entry.	100
The Amber glow.	102
Finding a home.	102

New wine, old wine!	103
Faith, lost and found.	103
God gave me a Church to train me.	105
Better caught than taught.	106
Elastic walls.	109

Chapter 7. Called to God's Own Country. — 111

God's agenda.	111
Sheffield steel.	112
Rebuilding what has been broken.	113
God's healing presence.	114
Limping junkie.	115
Toronto comes to town.	116
How the mighty have fallen.	117

Part III. Light Shines in the Darkness. — 121

Chapter 8. The End is Just the Beginning. — 121

The darkest hour is just before the dawn.	121
His light shines in my darkness.	122
God handles Real Estate.	124
When your Brook dries up.	124
Bringing light to persecuted believers.	125
Return to the 'Far Pavilions'	126
Grace upon Grace.	127

Radicalised by Grace	128
Goin' back in time. Lost and found.	130
A lovely Christmas tale: by Gus Moore.	132

Chapter 9. Learning to Love Again: Who Loves ya Baby.   133

Code word 'Kokolat'.	133
Loved forever.	134
The answer to Kojak's question.	135
How long does everlasting last?	137
Passion leads to vision. 'The greatest is love'.	140
From Ragamuffin to Royalty.	142

Chapter 10. Come Away With Me.   145

Rest and recuperation.	145
Dealing with the performance Trap.	147
From the mountaintop to the valley of Achor.	148
Deal with it.	149
Learning to get away.	150
Be sure to wear some flowers in your hair.	151
Rest for your soul.	153

Chapter 11. Samson's Hair is Growing Again.   157

The roots are still there.	157
Believing your own publicity.	158

'With you', Lessons from the rugby field.	159
Begin to reign.	160
Restorer of Antiques.	161
Redesigned by the Master.	162
A bruised reed.	162
Failure is not the last word.	163
Second chances and new beginnings.	164
Ring your bell of freedom.	165
Chapter 12. Dreams and Adventures	**169**
Duke City.	169
Bengaluru, dreams realised.	170
A Child realises he is a Son.	171
Friends in high places	172
Dream again, only bigger.	173
A new season begins.	174
And finally.	175

Part 1.
Setting Out on Life.

Chapter 1. Celtic Roots

The Ragamuffin Arrives

Ragamuffin runnin' round and round,
Your feet never touch the ground,
With the longest red hair in the world,
Man it looks like it's been curled,
And tattered jeans all falling apart,
A picture of your broken heart.

"You have a baby boy and he has beautiful golden hair" the nurse said to my mum as she presented me to her in the hospital ward. I was the third child born to Mary Manson; my two older siblings had been stillborn, so I entered the world by Caesarean section. Obviously to the delight of my Mum and Dad and a gift from God who she had believed and prayed for, (somewhat like Hannah of old),[5] to ease her loss.

Edinburgh, my birth city gave me my Celtic birthright. My hair colour, 'golden' as Mum always maintained (though more red really), gave me the hallmark of a Scottish Irish heritage. My Mum let my hair grow because she loved it so much. It was somewhat curly and dropped into ringlets as it grew longer. I recall as a little boy, folk would tousle my hair and jokingly call me a 'ragamuffin'. I found out when I was older what a ragamuffin really meant, I looked it up in the dictionary.

---
[5] 1.Samuel 1:9ff

Ragamuffin: *"A child who is dressed in rags and is usually dirty and poor"*.[6]

It was never meant that way and outwardly it was never the case, but as I grew up that description began to settle in my heart subconsciously.

Mum was Scottish by birth as was my Dad, but Mum was from Irish stock and grew up in Northern Ireland, so I grew up with that status in my heart and mind. She was so proud of her Irish heritage, and often stated that she was proud to be Irish and proud to be British. Her Father who was born in Belfast had red hair and an adventurous outlook on life. I was often told I shared his hair colour and temperament. As a young man he lied about his age in order to join the British army and fight in the Boer war in South Africa. I heard many stories of my relatives' adventures as I grew up. They were exciting and affirmed my own aspirations for adventure and travel in my developing years.

My father told me a story once about my great uncle who went to the theatre in Edinburgh one night. A lady sat down right in front of him wearing a very elaborate hat with long feathers protruding on both sides. The hat restricted his view of the stage so he politely asked her to remove the offending item. She refused several requests by my uncle so he took out his penknife, cut off the feathers from her hat and handed them to her. Quite an uproar followed with the manager of the theatre being called upon. Fortunately, the manager took my uncle's side and the lady had to sit with her feathers in her hand, no doubt fuming about the affront to her dignity, not to mention her hat!

So I grew up with the folklore of my grandfather, uncle and other adventurous impetuous relatives. My Celtic temperament and heritage, both positive and negative was being nurtured from a very early age.

---

[6] Webster's Dictionary

The wee town in County Down.

At the tender age of two and a half years my parents moved to a small town in Northern Ireland where Mum had spent her early years. Rathfriland, in County Down (in Gaelic it's named, Ráth Fraoileann), is built on a hill. The remains of an old castle dating back to the Middle Ages still dominates the skyline. The Magennis Family ruled the area. From Castle Hill there is a great view towards the majestic Mourne mountains in the south and Knock Hill lies several miles north. It was obviously a very strategic military location.

All around my hometown were rolling hills and green fields, as well as the awesome and mysterious Dark Mournes, which became an amazing outdoor playground for myself and my young friends. My childhood summer days were spent out in the fields playing 'cowboys and Indians', which was probably the result of watching too many adventures of cowboy heroes at the Saturday afternoon cinema matinees. Sometimes we'd walk down to 'Dan Burns' river, which was actually a small stream on the edge of the town. We always took our jam jars[7] with the intent of trying to catch and take home tadpoles. One of our most exciting summer activities included riding our bicycles to the Mournes where a river ran down from the mountains. We brought our swimming shorts and spent all day splashing in the river or climbing the 'Hen' mountain which was one of the smallest of the Mournes. The scenery there is outstanding with the mountains, hills, river and a wonderful tapestry of green fields. It's true what they say that Ireland is the land of the forty shades of green. Those summer days are forever etched in my memory. The scenery, the colour, and the scent of the countryside can easily be recalled even today. They were carefree days of adventure and fun. God was instilling in me even back then the sense of wonder and adventure that has stayed with me throughout the years, though I didn't realise it at the time.

---

[7] Glass containers with lids

Our first home in Rathfriland looked straight out to those magnificent Mourne Mountains. My mother often told me, *"Americans would pay thousands of dollars to have a view like that outside their front door"*. It was something I didn't truly appreciate till later in my life.

Percy French, the famous Irish songwriter, and artist penned a well-loved song entitled 'The Mountains of Mourne'. It's the sad tale of a young man who leaves his Irish home by the mountains and seaside to find his fortune in London. Failing to discover that fortune, French laments the young man's nostalgia for his sweetheart and native home. That seaside town is Newcastle in County Down where the dark Mournes sweep down to the sea. The song always draws me back to special memories of carefree days growing up.

Keeping up appearances.

I recall in my early years, thinking we weren't well off. Our first home in Rathfriland was pleasant with great views and the big plus was a bathroom. However, not long after our arrival, my great aunt offered us a bigger, two storey house which she owned. It was right in the centre of the town and had two great, ground floor, shop units. One for my father's hairdressing business and the other would become a confectionary shop, run by my mum.

The downside of the 'new' house was that it only had an outside toilet. I recall this left me with a feeling of embarrassment and shame if any of my friends came to see me. As well as the outside 'loo', I also remember we had a tin bath which was pulled into the living room when it was bath time. We did eventually put a bathroom suite in the house but by then I believe that a poverty spirit was already within me. As I look back, I realise that an outside loo or tin bath wasn't that uncommon in the area in those days.

Breaking the Spirit of poverty.

I discovered much later in life that a spirit of poverty can pervade your soul if you allow it space in your head. In general, the spirit of poverty is the fear of not having enough, causing you to hold onto what you do have. Two things can happen when you have this attitude

i. You resign yourself to never having.

ii. You resolve to never giving.

These attitudes are the product of a poverty spirit. It may not be necessarily true but if you believe it then a poverty spirit can manifest itself in these ways.

In the story of Elijah and the widow we see this 'spirit' emerging. During a time of famine, the widow was afraid to give Elijah food as she had so little flour and oil in her jar. The prophet's response was *"Don't be afraid...make a small cake of bread for me from what you have and then make something for yourself and your son"*.[8] As she did there was always enough oil and flour for both of them.

The lesson I learned later in life was to trust God with myself and my resources. I discovered that He would always provide all of my needs. Much more importantly than that was that my heart changed. Proverbs 11:24 says, *"One man gives freely yet gains even more, another withholds unduly but comes to poverty"*. Giving is not so much something you do in a meeting, it's a lifestyle of generosity. When I began to understand and apply this principle in my life, the spirit of poverty and shame began to break down over me, but that was much later.

---

[8] 1. Kings 17:8-16.

Only child syndrome.

There was also this only child thing, I would get taunted from time to time by my peers that I was spoiled. I didn't understand this at the time, though in truth I must have been in some way because I was an only child. The loss of my two older siblings at birth must have had a huge impact on how my parents treated me in my early years. To be fair, my mother in particular was quite strict with me and a firm believer in the verse *"folly is bound up in the heart of a child but the rod of correction will drive it far from him".*[9] I have quite a few memories of being told to bend over the end of the couch and receive the rod of correction to the seat of my understanding!

Vagabond of the Western World.

In my early twenties I became friends with a great Irish rock band called Thin Lizzy. Phil Lynott, the lead singer wrote a terrific song called 'Vagabond of the Western World'. It was about a playboy vagabond searching for riches and fame. I saw something of myself in the song. I'll tell you more about Thin Lizzy later on.[10]

The name, 'vagabond' lends itself romantically to an adventurous, roguish, loveable kind of person, but the reality is much different. Here is the definition of "vagabond" from Webster's Dictionary.

Vagabond: *"Leading an unsettled, irresponsible, or disreputable life".*

I later became that vagabond in heart and lifestyle.

I grew up with both Irish and Scottish accents in our house. Mum having a strong Northern Irish accent and Dad truly Scottish. I sometimes felt I was caught between two accents

---

[9] Proverbs 22:7.

[10] Chapter 2. See under, Know the author, know the meaning behind the words.

and two worlds. As I grew up, at times I wasn't sure where I belonged. That, along with being an only child, having a poverty spirit and enduring negative experiences at senior school, (which I will share later,)[11] left me, I believe, with deep insecurity, and a hostile attitude which eventually led to my rebellious 'vagabond' lifestyle.

I wanted to be 'normal' like everyone else but I felt 'less than normal' for some reason. Outwardly that would not have been obvious in my early life, but as I grew, I developed this inner restlessness, aggression and soul poverty. It would become a longterm negative hook in my life even though I was able to compensate for it most of the time, hiding it beneath my strong outgoing personality. Nevertheless, it became a stronghold, always watching for an opportunity to dominate me.

Dreaming beyond the Horizon.

Despite the negatives in my life as a boy there were some wonderful adventurous times as well. Dreams and adventures helped me escape my deep-rooted insecurities and developing low self-image.

As well as the mountains, the seaside was the other great adventure playground for me. As I grew older, summer days were all about getting the local bus to Newcastle and spending the day on the beach and having fun in the sand dunes. Other times it was almost mystical to stand on the seashore and stare at the vastness of the Irish Sea, trying to visualise beyond the horizon to far off distant shores.

These feelings settled down deep in my heart and have remained. God has given us this wonderful gift of imagination. It is so incredible. It opens up your future world and moves you beyond the average to the amazing. I am aware that the New Age has made use of "imagining", but Christians need to realise that they stole it from God and try to reclaim it. The devil never has an original thought. He steals from God and uses it for

---

[11] Chapter 1. See under, School Days, Negative Identity.

destructive purposes. The church sometimes seems to be unaware of this and so anything to do with the imagination is apparently frowned upon. However, God had it first! You can call it perception if you prefer. It is seeing from within your spirit. We know and perceive things in our spirits that our souls can take time to comprehend.

Paul told us in Ephesians 3:20 that God will give to us more than we can ask for or 'imagine'. From this I believe we can understand that to imagine is a good and God given thing. It is how we 'see' beyond the natural limitations to the limitless possibilities which God intends for us. We do, however, need to discern between vain imagination and God given imagination.

I believe dreaming is an essential part of envisioning our future in God. Childhood dreams can become God ordained realities as we allow Him to shape all that He imparts to us. Young men are supposed to have visions and older men dreams.[12] I like to think we all can have both. As a young man Joseph also had dreams which were God inspired, but it took some shaping before they became a reality. Dreams and visions are what shape the plans God puts in our hearts. As we grow in Him we learn to allow Him to shape those dreams into the actuality of His destiny for our lives.

Back in those early days, I was beginning to imagine and dream about the great adventures life has to offer. I didn't know, back then, that God was orchestrating expectations in my heart for the future.

Some years ago, while visiting Albuquerque, New Mexico, USA, I found a postcard in a bookshop which caught my attention. The card showed a photo of a lovely green pasture with the following words.

Passion.

> "There are many things in life that will catch your eye, but only a few will catch your heart... Pursue those".

---

[12] Acts 2:17.

It struck a resonating chord in my heart. I bought it and still look at it from time to time on my study wall, reciting the words to myself.

We should never give up dreaming. Joseph got a hostile reception to his first dream; undeterred he dreamt again.[13] He never gave up on his dreams and eventually they came to pass.

What has captured your heart? Take those God ordained dreams, the things you imagine for your future, and as you lie in bed at night, allow them to flourish. As I have discovered, if you keep believing and nurturing them, they will grow, and in due course they will come to pass.

Hi Yo Silver, away!

I have to confess, as a boy I dreamed of being 'The Lone Ranger'. There was always something about being a hero and a rescuer within me and I would go to bed at night and dream of being that hero. Although it may sound childish and even silly, I look back and believe that God was using external stimulus, yes perhaps even 'The Lone Ranger', to awaken spiritual desires He had placed within me before my birth that would be refined one day.

I truly believe God develops our spiritual DNA within us before we are born. It's like a seed planted deep within us awaiting the right conditions to blossom into life. Then as we grow up He begins to awaken what He has placed within us.

Some of those dreams may have just been childhood fantasies, but God still works within us in our mother's womb, preparing us for the things He wants us to do in life. Over time, the fantasy dreams evaporate but the God ordained dreams remain and become more focused and mature. These are the deeply rooted desires of our heart that won't go away.

---

[13] Genesis. 37:5,9.

At the right time Father God speaks and calls forth the dream He instilled in our heart so long ago in order for us to fulfil His divine destiny for our lives. Jeremiah discovered this when, at the appropriate moment, God said to him: *"Before I formed you in the womb I knew you, before you were born I set you apart; I appointed you as a prophet to the nations".*[14]

As I grew up something inside me kept reminding me that there was some kind of purpose to my life but, as a boy, I didn't understand what that meant. I know now that we are not born as an accident or without a destiny on this planet. We have all been called from our mother's womb. We are not only called but also uniquely gifted, perhaps to be a teacher, a carpenter, a doctor, a musician, a business person, an electrician, a builder, a magician perhaps, or a helper, (now that's a very Biblical one).[15] It's tucked in there between some other seemingly superior gifts, but the others don't function very well without this important gift of helping. Gifts and calling are not limited to this short list, it is almost endless. I added magicians to make the point that whatever we have a desire to do in the natural can usually be transformed into God's call. For instance, apart from a desire to do tricks, magicians are usually preoccupied with mystery, the mystical and even the supernatural. So if those people turned to Christ they may become prophets with ministries marked by the miraculous. Paul was a terrorist who was 'radicalised' by Christ and became an amazing risk-taking, freedom-fighting disciple for Jesus. Just imagine the untapped desires lying in your heart that could be unlocked and released by God's grace just as it happened to Paul.

God uses a variety of apparently natural or circumstantial issues in life to get us ready for the ultimate adventure of serving His purposes. We are His workmanship.[16] The Greek word for workmanship here also means 'poem'. A poem is the work of a creative individual. Therefore, I believe we are designed in our core being by God's creative artistry.

---

[14] Jeremiah 1:5.

[15] 1. Corinthians 12:28.

[16] Ephesians 2:10.

To change the imagery for a moment, we sometimes have to spend time on the potter's wheel until the potter shapes us correctly, which can be the painful part of the preparation process! God always has in mind the work He has already prepared for us to do, even before we were born. All that preparation is never wasted, although we sometimes wonder what is going on in our lives. Looking back on my life I can see how God had been singing His song over me as He shaped me for the work He would call me to do. The potter will not be satisfied until the pot He has 'thrown',[17] or the poem He has sung over us,[18] is crafted properly and uniquely for the work He prepared way back in eternity past for us to achieve.[19]

Nagging Negatives.

Even though my early growing up years were filled with dreams, fun and adventure, the poverty spirit and a feeling of poor self-image stayed with me like a nagging voice in the back of my mind. Perhaps it was indeed that Scottish parentage in a totally Irish setting where I sometimes felt the odd one out, though that was hardly ever spoken of. It may have been that I thought we were poorer than other folks because we only had that outside toilet and no proper bathroom. Maybe the 'only child' syndrome affected me. Whatever it was it stuck with me as I grew up. I felt inferior, the odd one out, a displaced ragamuffin. I hid it well due to my personality but inside those nagging negatives kept eroding my confidence as I started to believe those lies about myself. Years later, God healed my heart and I became deeply aware of His everlasting love,[20] but it would be quite some time before that happened.

---

[17] Jeremiah 18:1-4.

[18] Zephaniah 3:17 NIV.

[19] Ephesians 2:10b.

[20] Jeremiah 31:3.

Spiritual values and religious dogma.

For a small town, Rathfriland produced some interesting characters. One of the more famous people to preach in the area in years gone by was Patrick Brontë, the father of the famous Brontë sisters, Charlotte, Emily and Anne. A more infamous resident was Andrew George Scott, alias Captain Moonlight. He was born in Rathfriland in 1842 in a house on Castle Hill. His father was an Anglican clergyman who wanted his son to join the priesthood, but it would appear he was not able to bring him up to follow in his father's spiritual footsteps. Scott travelled to Australia where he became a notorious Australian bushranger. In my more light-hearted moments I consider the impact that small village had on these two very different people and how it may have affected my life.

My Mum was very keen for me to go to Sunday school as a young boy. I discovered much later in life that she had a very profound faith though she didn't go to church when I was small. So in my early years I was sent to the local Church of Ireland Sunday school, the Irish equivalent of the Anglican or Episcopalian church.

I learned all the classic stories of Noah and the Ark, Abraham the man of faith and friend of God, Jacob whose name was changed after an amazing encounter with God, Joseph and his coat of many colours, Moses and the parting the Red sea, Joshua the warrior leader, David and Goliath, Samson and Delilah, and of course I also learned about Jesus. Those stories formed a deep and positive impression on my mind as a child and remained with me. I often dreamt of being like those Bible heroes of the faith, a big step up from the Lone Ranger! I imagined overcoming impossible obstacles, winning battles, rescuing people, doing exploits and enjoying the presence and favour of this great big God.

However, in my early years I also went to some other church meetings with a childhood friend. His father would take us to Sunday evening 'gospel' services where the message was one laced with themes of hellfire and condemnation. I found out later in life that the word gospel means good news, something that I have no recollection of hearing at those meetings. The preachers used to frighten me with their condemning message that lacked any good news or remembrance of a God who loved me.

I was once invited to see a Christian film shown in our town centre. It was a film organised by a visiting evangelistic society and told the story of a family that stopped going to church. The only thing that I remember about it was that the father preferred to play golf on Sundays rather than attend church. As the story unfolded, his daughter became ill and eventually died. The moral of the story for me was that if you don't go to church someone you love will die. Now I may have misunderstood, but in my mind God was an angry ogre who would cause you harm if you didn't toe the line and I found it all very frightening.

I grew up with a great measure of confusion in my heart. On the one hand I learned of a God who loved imperfect people and used them to do amazing things, but on the other hand I heard of an angry God who was out to destroy you if you didn't measure up. It would take a long time to get things straight in my heart and have that religious dogma and frightening legalism leave me.

During my late teens and twenty-somethings vagabond wanderings, when I had written off the Christian church because of those very legalistic and condemnatory meetings, I began dabbling with different religions. Even with my negative reaction to religion, the good memories of my Sunday School days would come back into my thoughts. They were most likely the saving element for me so I would not forget completely the Bible stories of God's love so well told by my Sunday School teachers. Looking back now I realise it is so important to teach our children the good news of the love that God has for us. The writer of Proverbs wrote, *"Train up a child in the way that he should go and when he is old he will not depart from it".*[21] It seems to me, that back in my youth, the good news was lost and replaced by an angry God message, which in my opinion

---

[21] Proverbs 22:6.

has nothing to do with the Grace news of Jesus. Sadly I think that still happens today. Who knows what difference there was between captain Moonlight and the Brontë sisters' spiritual upbringing and how their lives unfolded. I can only speculate on that with reference to my own life, but more of that later.

School days, negative identity.

I enjoyed primary school, it seemed to be mostly a fun memory for me. Moving up to senior school was another thing altogether! Getting extra tuition in order to pass my qualifying exam to go to the prestigious 'grammar'[22] school in the next town was a big deal for my parents who wanted me to excel academically. As for me, I just wanted to have fun.

However I surprisingly passed the exam and went to Banbridge Academy grammar school, a place I never settled into. I felt out of place and wasn't interested in study. It was a very strict school with rules and regulations that seemed irrelevant to me. One of these rules was that all the students had to wear their school cap or beret as they walked along the long avenue to and from the school. If you were caught without your head-gear on you got detention. Perhaps it was a good discipline, but not for me. I was always in trouble! Years later someone said in passing that I was never one to conform to the status quo. My rebellious spirit was obviously in evidence way back then.

The only things I enjoyed and gave myself to willingly were rugby and cricket. I did quite well at both, playing for the school teams. After leaving school I went on to play rugby for Banbridge town for a few seasons which I thoroughly enjoyed. Back at school however, my academic studies were not up to par. I just didn't seem to be able to concentrate or absorb the information being taught. Frankly I was neither motivated nor interested in learning, but perhaps I would have thrived better in a different teaching environment, something which I did discover some years later.

---

[22] In the UK a state secondary school to which pupils were admitted on the basis of academic ability.

Devastation, definitely not the teacher's pet!

I had done so badly in my end-of-first-year exams that it was decided to keep me back in the entrance class, while my peers were moved up to the next year class. This was announced in front of my classmates and the whole school, without my prior knowledge at the first public assembly in the gym. I recall how devastated and humiliated I felt as my name was read out. It was a horrendous moment that I have never forgotten. In my heart I felt ashamed and really stupid, at least that's what I believed about myself. My self-image and identity hit rock bottom, something that remained with me for many more years to come.

Words can Break your Heart.

I remember the childhood chant we used to shout at one another when we were arguing; "*Sticks and stones may break my bones but words will never hurt me*". That statement is just so untrue. Something I have understood more profoundly as I have grown up: words can destroy you. Don Henley of 'The Eagles' expressed it a little differently in one of his songs, that it is only takes a word to break your world apart; words do break your heart.[23]

It's not only the pen but indeed also the tongue which is mightier than the sword and it can devastate in a moment. The Apostle James understood this and wrote about the power of the tongue and equated it to a fire that can set a forest ablaze.[24] The fire of those words that were spoken in public about me in the gym were like an inferno of destruction in my young life. Education had become a place of insecurity and humiliation for me and I reacted by becoming very rebellious. Looking back I believe this was a catalyst to the fire that was smouldering within me and ignited my vagabond lifestyle.

---

[23] Don Henley, CD. Cass County. Track 9. Words Can Break Your Heart, Capitol Records.

[24] James 3:5,6.

After that excruciating experience I often played truant, missing classes or even complete days at school. I became a part time vagabond and found it exciting and adventurous as I escaped my source of disapproval and pain, wandering around the streets and alleyways exploring Banbridge town, but also discreetly keeping out of the public eye.

On one occasion, an older school friend who knew of my escapades wanted to play truant and spoke to me about heading off to another town for the day. I agreed and as soon as we got off our school bus in Banbridge, we headed up the street to hitch a lift to Newry, a town about ten miles away and incidentally where his girlfriend lived. Unfortunately for us, one of our school teachers was travelling into Banbridge by car as we left and he saw us hitching out of town. The next day we were called up to see the headmaster who was quite an intimidating character. I stood nervously before him as he berated me, but also said he thought I was influenced by the older boy. If only he knew!

He wrote to my parents to inform them of my truancy and I was grounded for quite a while for my irresponsible ways. My truancy was part of my reaction to the negative and hurtful experience I now had of my school. It triggered my increased lack of interest in learning, and inspired my desire to escape and do something more interesting and adventurous. School had become a shame-filled negative place and learning in the classroom felt like a prison. It took a long time before a hunger to learn reignited. From that time on I began to take a walk on the wild side.

Is this a private fight?

I remember hearing the somewhat tragic yet comical story of the Irish drunk standing outside the pub watching a brawl going on and shouting: *"is this a private fight or can anybody join in?"*

It reminds me of how my early teen years got off to a bad start. At 14 years of age I had my first taste of alcohol; in fact I drank quite a few bottles of Guinness, then along with my other merry friends off I went to the local dance hall. We were eventually thrown out for fighting with other lads from out of town: we were very territorial. My insecurities which fuelled my aggression were very much alive and well during this time.

This kind of behaviour became quite normal for my friends and me. It was exciting and somewhat dangerous, but it gave us the adrenaline rush we wanted. It was probably the only way we could get something like it in our small town and we wanted all of it. The Irish do have a dubious reputation for jumping in the deep end of anything adventurous or even dangerous.

What was needed in my life was for all of that energy and attitude to be turned into something constructive. It's amazing how God can take all that seems negative about us and turn it around into something positive and beautiful if we give it all to Him to shape and fashion. It is certainly true that; *"in all things God works together for good for those that love Him and are called according to His purpose"*.[25] He will work out even the most negative circumstances for good as we walk in a love relationship with Him. I have since discovered that in my own life. He never gives up on us even though we may give up on ourselves. In fact let me say to you, if it's not good yet then it's not over yet for you. It would however be quite a number of years of alcohol, drugs, fights and other unhelpful experiences before I fully discovered that truth.

---

[25] Romans 8:28.

Chapter 2. Travelling Man

The only time you should look back, is to see how far you've come.

Short back and sides!

After several years of struggling at school, coupled with a strong recommendation from the headmaster, I finally left Banbridge Academy at the first opportunity and got myself a job. My Father was a well-trained gents hairdresser, having learned his trade at "Stewarts" of Princes Street in Edinburgh, Scotland, a very prestigious salon in it's day. Dad was often specifically requested to visit Edinburgh Castle to cut some member of the Royal family's hair when they were in residence.

When we moved to Rathfriland, my dad opened his own hairdressing salon. As I grew up, he trained me to cut hair and I followed somewhat in his footsteps. After leaving school, I trained to be a ladies hairdresser which I presumed was a more stylish profession.

After training, I worked in a number of hairdressing salons in different towns. It was okay but I soon got fed up with the monotonous routine of 9 to 5 and my interest in travel and adventure kept reemerging.

After some consideration I decided with a friend, Reg, to leave home and head to the island of Guernsey, for a summer working holiday. Guernsey is part of the Channel Islands just off the west coast of France. We had heard it was a great place to hang out. Lots of summer jobs were available packing tomatoes and the big plus was that the weather was good. Another new adventurous time in my life was about to begin.

Down on the Island.

Guernsey is famous for tomatoes and became a leading exporter of the fruit from the 1860s' through to the 1970s', when oil prices increased and production costs went up causing the demand for tomatoes to decline. Back in the late '60s it was fascinating to fly into Guernsey and see the whole island littered with greenhouses shimmering in the summer sun.

Upon our arrival in Guernsey, we couldn't find work to begin with. So when our money ran out we had to leave the guesthouse we had been staying in. Along with some new hippie friends we met who were living rough, we went to sleep in the old, second world war Nazi Germany tunnels up on the Guernsey cliffs near Saint Peter Port.

The Channel Islands were the only part of the British Isles to be invaded and occupied by German forces from June 1940 to May 1945. It was quite exciting for us to sleep in a place where German soldiers had billeted during World War II.

Eventually, after a few weeks living rough in the tunnels, we got jobs packing tomatoes. A short time later we were able to rent an old top floor flat and move in. We packed tomatoes by day and had fun at night. On the floor below our flat, some other hippie friends also moved in and we were introduced to marijuana for the first time. We tried it but to begin with it didn't seem to make much difference, nevertheless we smoked it every now and again. I had no idea where that novelty would eventually lead me.

Late one Saturday night after an evening of drinking and clubbing, I returned to our flat to discover the police were all around the place. As I walked up to our top floor flat, the police were already inside where Reg was fast asleep, after a hard night partying. The police were carefully removing some substance which was lying on the dining table and very carefully bagging it. I tried to point out to them that it was only burnt toast scrapings from breakfast but undeterred they took it away for testing. Reg never woke up throughout the search, but when he did the next morning we laughed about the toast scrapings being taken for analysis. We never heard any more about it and thought the whole thing was great fun! We were very naive back then... but not for long.

After six months of packing tomatoes I decided it was time to head back to Northern Ireland. However Guernsey was going to be an important location in my life as I would later discover. Once home I got a job at a top ladies salon, Fredericks in Belfast. It was enjoyable as well as prestigious, working in a fashionable salon in the big city and I had fun as I worked. I really enjoyed the atmosphere in the large salon working with about twenty other hairdressers.

However after a couple of years I became unsettled working for an employer and decided to start my own hairdressing business. I set up in my home town and did this successfully for a couple of years. You will be familiar with the outcome by now. After two years successfully running my own business I was bored and began looking for a new adventure. Nowadays my wife Linda frequently reminds me that I was born restless. I have finally come to the conclusion that she is right!

Rock n' roll Days: The rocky road to Dublin.

There's a great old traditional Irish song written by The Dubliners entitled: 'The Rocky Road to Dublin'. It's the story of a young man heading out from his country home walking to Dublin and then setting sail across the Irish sea in his quest for adventure. It comes to my mind on occasions when I remember my time in Dublin's fair city. The song speaks of this man carrying a 'stout blackthorn', an Irish war club, otherwise known as a 'Shillelagh', cut from a thorn bush and used by the fighting Irish! Of course I didn't carry one of those. but as the Dubliners song continued, the young man's heart was positive, and so was mine for the next step in my adventure.

Upon my return from Guernsey to my hometown, I started attending a new youth club at the local secondary school. It was at the youth club that the idea to start a pop group emerged. My friends and I bought guitars and equipment and started practising and rehearsing.

We named the group "The Crypt" and we soon got booked to play some gigs in and around our home location as well as in

Belfast. One night after playing at the Marquee club in central Belfast we headed home, but as we drove up the Ormeau Road we saw a lot of people on the street and a vehicle burning. As we approached somewhat cautiously we were quickly stopped by a police officer who yelled at us to turn around and get out of the street as quickly as possible. It turned out there were paramilitary demonstrators setting fire to large vehicles, like ours, and blocking the street. The police were keen to get us out of the way quickly and we were also very glad to oblige them. Life in Northern Ireland back then could be dangerous.

We had another moment of tension traveling through Newry late one night after a gig in Dublin and discovered that other paramilitaries had closed the city down and were checking all the vehicles driving through. We were halted by a masked man carrying a machine gun. Once he had spoken to us he let us pass, telling us to drive the wrong way along a one way street. When I naively mentioned that I didn't want to get caught by the police for that, he quietly replied with a wry smile on his face, *"no one will stop you tonight"*. We drove on nervously in total darkness but could see soldiers crouching in side streets preparing to deal with the situation, but no one stopped us! We were relieved to eventually get home safely. Fortunately, we never had another of those moments.

I do unfortunately have some sad memories of the troubled times we lived in back then. On a different night in a different location near the border between the North and South, a band was stopped en route home after playing in a Northern venue. They were taken out of their van and murdered by terrorists.

I also had a childhood friend who became a reserve police officer. He lived two doors away from my parents home. One day, two men came into the store where his family business was. They asked to speak to him and were told he was in the yard behind the store. My friend was walking towards them as they came into the yard. They pulled out a gun and shot him three times, he died almost instantly. He was only 34 years old. I was very shocked when I heard the news. These tragedies made no sense at all but evil things were happening in Northern Ireland in those days and it could be a very dangerous place to live.

First big break.

On a more positive note, one night in Banbridge we played the first set in a dance hall for a well-known Irish showband 'Joe Dolan & The Drifters' who were the main attraction. At the end of the evening the drummer, Maurice told us that he enjoyed our music and style. He continued to say that his brother in Dublin was looking for a band to manage. If we were interested he wanted to invite us down to Dublin for a weekend to play at a club and meet his brother. We jumped at the opportunity and soon we were off to the bright lights of Dublin's fair city.

We had a great time playing in the Dublin clubs that weekend and Maurice's brother, Sean, enjoyed us so much that he became our manager. So began a successful time playing all over the South of Ireland. We became quite famous on the circuit, becoming minor celebrities, recording our songs and playing on the Irish television pop programme "Like Now".

However, after a couple of years my restlessness started to reappear once again. I began looking for even more adventure than I was experiencing. It wasn't long before I was reintroduced to the drug scene and I jumped in with both feet.

An old friend, Malc returned from Guernsey where he had been staying and brought with him a quantity of marijuana, alongside some other "unnamed" tablets. He travelled with the band to Dublin for a Christmas Eve gig we were playing. Just before we started he gave me one of the "unnamed" tablets and said, *"just pop it in your mouth and swallow"*. I asked him what it was and all he said was, *"It'll get you high"*. So I took the tablet and waited. After a short time my perception of reality transformed into an explosion of incredible hallucinations and colour, along with heightened sensations and sound awareness, It was amazing. I discovered later that what I had taken was the hallucinogenic drug, LSD.

One of the side effects of LSD is unpredictability. I couldn't focus on what I was doing and my coordination was impaired. My condition, coupled with the other guys in the band who had consumed a lot of alcohol made us totally unable to play properly. The crowd was not impressed so we came off stage and spent some time in our 'green room' splashing our faces with water and consuming lots of water and orange juice. Eventually we straightened up somewhat and were able to return to the stage and do a great set. It was a crazy night for all of us but especially for me as I entered a completely new world.

From that time I began to regularly smoke marijuana and take a lot of LSD. I should have realised at the time how powerful and dangerous LSD was. I do not recommend that anyone reading this tries to experiment with drugs at all. But back then I was living a crazy, adventure-filled, vagabond lifestyle and I didn't think much about the consequences. I would discover those consequences in a frightening way some time later.

During the '60s, LSD had been made famous by Dr Timothy Leary: a writer, psychologist and campaigner for psychedelic drug research and use. He coined and popularised the famous phrase: *"turn on, tune in, and drop out"*.

Many of the pop groups and singers of the time, including, Bob Dylan, The Beatles, The Rolling Stones, The Byrds and The Doors, to mention a few, started experimenting with this drug also and producing psychedelic rock music. The most famous of all for me was the Album, 'Sgt: Pepper's Lonely Hearts Club Band' by the Beatles. One of the songs *Lucy in the Sky with Diamonds* was allegedly a subliminal theme for LSD with the first letters from Lucy, Sky and Diamonds being the operative words. Whether true or not I don't know, but the album proved a huge success and still is to this day selling around 30 million copies by 2014.[26]

The height of this psychedelic experience came around 1967 with 'the summer of love', when as many as 100,000 hippies converged on the Haight-Ashbury district of San Francisco, inaugurating the beginning of what came to be known as 'The

---

[26] http://en.wikipedia.org/wiki/Sgt._Pepper%27s_Lonely_Hearts_Club_Band accessed 7/2/19

Counterculture'. It more or less peaked in 1969 with the Woodstock Festival on Max Yasgur's dairy farm in the Catskills, near Bethel, New York.

Interestingly, around that time another revolution was taking place on the west coast of California, when thousands of hippies started giving their lives to Jesus. The term coined for them was 'The Jesus Movement'. Some churches like Calvary Chapel were able to adjust to this large influx of hippies but eventually new churches like the Vineyard movement also emerged with more informal meetings to cope with these weird and colourful 'Jesus People' hippies. Many of them were great musicians and produced excellent contemporary music, which would have a positive impact on the church worldwide. Artists and bands such as Keith Green, Barry McGuire, Larry Norman, Love Song and Second Chapter of Acts are a few that I remember. The impact of the Jesus movement and their musicians went around the globe and in time their influence affected me as well.

In the early days of 'The Crypt', we travelled to Dublin every weekend to play in clubs. We often stayed with friends in other groups. We met Eric Bell, a great blues guitar player on one occasion up north when he was playing with the band we opened for. Later Eric teamed up with Phil Lynott and Brian Downey to form Thin Lizzy. They were signed by Decca Records and had their first hit record with a rock version of the traditional Irish Song, 'Whisky in the Jar'. They went on to become a world-famous rock band playing mostly Phil's own compositions.

Back in those early days they were trying to succeed like us, and had an apartment in Dublin where they invited us to stay at weekends when we were in town. I became good friends with Phil who was the lead singer and bass player. He would often sing his newly penned songs to me in the wee small hours of the morning when our bands had returned from gigging. He always invited my comments on his songs. He was a terrific songwriter. I counted it a privilege to know the inside story behind the lyrics in a number of his songs.

Sadly, the success that Thin Lizzy went on to achieve also brought with it tragedy for Phil. The rocky road to fame can unfortunately bring with it a darker side for many. At the height of his music career Phil died of heart-failure and pneumonia. The rock star lifestyle he enjoyed was also accompanied by alcohol and drugs and brought his life to a tragic and untimely end.[27]

Know the Author, know the meaning behind the words.

I mentioned Thin Lizzy's song 'Vagabond of the Western World' earlier.[28] Thousands of people have listened to and enjoyed their music over the years. Not so many have had the privilege of sitting up late at night with Phil and learned the truth behind the lyrics of songs like 'Look What the Wind Blew in'. Was it about a gale force wind blowing through his life? No, it was about a girl from the north of Ireland who was called Gail who breezed into his life for a season.[29] I only knew that because I had met Gail and spent time with Phil as he unfolded the meaning behind his lyrics. It was a lesson of immense value when I began reading the Bible some time later. I began to understand the importance of knowing the author of the book and not just read the words. Just as I knew Phil as a friend and gleaned personal insight into the meaning behind his lyrics, I also gained insight into the real meaning of the truths of the Bible as I became a friend of God, but that took a while to come about.

The rocky road to Hell.

As I continued my crazy reckless life in the pop/rock band culture, my use of LSD became more frequent and almost always with an amazing transcendental experience. I was doing

---

[27] http://news.bbc.co.uk/onthisday/hi/dates/stories/january/4/newsid_4041000/4041511.stm accessed 7/2/19

[28] Chapter 1. See under, Vagabond of the western World.

[29] Track 5, Look What the Wind Blew in. Thin Lizzy, Debut Album, Deram Records.

far more drugs than my fellow band members and subsequently began to move in different circles. A short time later, I left 'The Crypt' and tripped off back to Guernsey to *'turn on, tune in, and drop out'* as Timothy Leary propagated. The reality was that I needed to sort myself out and try to clear my head. I spent a few mellow months in Guernsey but the pull of the rock band drug lifestyle quickly brought me back to Dublin. I met up with my former manager Larry Mooney and together we set about forming a new band. Larry had managed another Northern band called 'Taxi'. They had just split up so some of us got together and formed a new band called Ironhorse. Our musical focus was heavy rock in the style of Led Zeppelin or Black Sabbath. By today's health and safety standards we wouldn't have been allowed to play in many places because of the volume, but back then no one cared.

My life was spiraling downwards but I wasn't aware of it. The move from singing in a pop rock band to a heavy rock band had a darker emphasis. It was all in line with my lifestyle which was degenerating very quickly.

The new group lived together in an apartment block in the Rathmines area of Dublin. Doing drugs was an everyday event, we were all stoned most of the time on a variety of drugs. When we were getting plenty of gigs we lived well, but when we ran out of money we'd busk on the streets or sometimes just simply beg to get money for food and drugs.

At other times we'd score some marijuana to resell and make a profit. Of course we'd always use some, so our profit margin wasn't very good. There was a fish and chip shop across the road from us so we'd take a large pot over and get them to fill it with chips for a discount price, then back to the apartment loaded up with the chips and bread and butter and have a feast. We'd live on those pots of chips with bread and butter for days on end as it was about the cheapest way to eat and feel full. No matter how degenerate it sounds, to me it was all a great adventure; I had no idea how vagrant my life had become. In the midst of this drug haze, the band fared well for a while, even getting an opportunity to be heard by a well known London based record company. We had an audition with a manager from the company but unfortunately we were all too stoned on the day to play well and we missed a big opportunity. A drug induced lifestyle has a lot of downsides and this was one of them.

The windmills of my mind.

It all came to an end when I went on a 'trip' one day in a park in Dublin. The experience was anything but enjoyable. After an hour or so as the drug kicked in I began to feel very anxious, paranoid and troubled. I had no idea what was happening but it was terrifying. The windmills of my mind were spiralling, somewhat like the ones in the song sung by Noel Harrison;[30] endlessly out of control as I began to see weird and grotesque images in the trees and grass at the park where I was hanging out at the time. The trees would turn into demonic monsters and the grass would begin to resemble snakes slithering around. All of it was horrific and I was deeply distressed. The thing about taking acid (LSD) is once you have consumed it, there is no turning back for up to eight hours or more. It seemed like an eternity to me. Eventually one of my friends took me back to our apartment where he got me to drink lots of orange juice heavily laced with sugar. One thing we had learned was that orange juice and sugar helps to 'bring you down' to normal again. However it occurred, the concoction worked and I eventually came round. That experience had life changing effects on me that I was not aware of immediately. I never took LSD again.

From my bad LSD experience, I emerged with what felt like scrambled eggs for brains and lots of questions, but in particular two simple ones dominated the windmills of my mind.

"Who am I"? and *"What is the meaning of life?"* These questions stimulated my journey towards a spiritual awakening. I was a very mixed up individual. A poverty mindset, school humiliation, eastern mysticism, crazy drug-fuelled rock band lifestyle and my Sunday school Christian background led to a confusion of

---

[30]The Windmills of your Mind. Alan & Marilyn Bergman, Michel Legrand. Sung by Noel Harrison, 1968.

thoughts, emotions and ideas. I was still smoking marijuana which of course did not help but I didn't know that at the time.

Light begins to shine, but slowly.

One day not long after my 'bad trip' I decided to head back from Dublin to my hometown Rathfriland to see my parents and also spend some time in the nearby seaside resort of Newcastle, one of my favourite laid back locations. As I wandered down the main sea front street of Newcastle lost in my muddled thoughts, I noticed a couple of older ladies walking toward me and I knew instantly that they were 'Christians' by their hairstyle and plain dress code. The typical hairstyle for older religious ladies back then was known as the 'Plymouth roll," often used, I believe, by ladies in the Brethren church, a conservative evangelical movement. To me it was an unattractive style with the hair rolled up tightly around the back of the head, and epitomised religion to me. They approached me and before I could get out of the way, they handed me a leaflet about Jesus. This, as I later realised was to my knowledge step one of the 'God coincidences' in my life. To my own surprise I was quite curious and endeavoured to read it but I couldn't make much sense of it. My messed-up brain may have had a lot to do with that at the time.

I continued walking along the seafront musing over the content and thinking of my friend Ernie with whom I had gone to those gospel meetings a number of years ago. I considered that he might be able to help me decipher the leaflet. I hadn't seen him for a long time but had heard he'd become a 'born again' Christian. No sooner had that thought entered my head when I heard a voice calling my name. I looked up across the street and lo and behold there was Ernie and another friend Eddie beckoning me. Totally surprised at the coincidence, (another one yes, I know better now!), I wandered over and began to chat with them.

I found out later that these two men sat down one day to pray together and considered who was the most 'lost person' they knew in Rathfriland. It didn't take them long to come up with my name. For six months before I 'bumped' into them on the seafront they had been praying regularly for me. Looking back, I am so thankful for their persistent faithfulness to believe for my salvation. God was apparently working behind the scenes to bring answers to my questions. There are no coincidences in the economy of God, He was setting me up for His purposes as I later discovered.

But back to the seafront encounter, I told them about the leaflet and asked some questions. Ernie along with Eddie responded to my questions and then invited me to hear an open-air preacher down on the promenade. Quite happily I decided to accept their invitation as I realised I was hungry to learn more. All I recall of that open-air meeting was that the preacher was very passionate but in the middle of his preach his false teeth popped out of his mouth onto the ground, much to the amusement of the gathered crowd. He carried on regardless, only stooping down to pick up his dentures and replace them while pressing home his message. I found the whole thing fascinating but didn't understand very much of it at the time apart from the funny incident with the dentures. I had a long way to go before the good news would become good news to me!

I spent numerous evenings and weekends with my new friends, going to special church services and afterwards back home discussing relevant Bible topics. The meetings were better than my early gospel encounters. However I was still very mixed up, my recent background was centred around experiences with drugs and I was looking for some mystical high with Jesus now. As well as that, I lived in a completely different cultural world with my hippie values, dress code and lifestyle. This was a world that none of the Christians I met had ever encountered. It must have been hard for them to comprehend me, just as much as it was for me to connect with them. My two friends nevertheless were never condemnatory with me and accepted me with my strange attire, ideas and notions. On one evening with them I stated that I was trying to work out if Jesus was better than drugs, (that's how far away I was from the truth). They were very patient with me and never got annoyed with my weird questions or odd behaviour but I sensed that they struggled to understand where my thinking was coming from. I would travel on a long spiritual journey before the lights turned on in my understanding.

There were, however, some legalistically religious people around Northern Ireland who looked at me with an unimpressed attitude. On one occasion a few years after I had truly given my life to Jesus, I went back with my new family to visit my parents in Rathfriland. I was talking to Eddie in the town square one day when a lady from a local church came up to us and looked directly at me, before saying: "So *this is the young man who is supposed to have become a Christian"*? Her statement was filled with an air of disbelief and even derision. I lived totally outside her world view of what a Christian should look like. Her problem was that she could not see beyond the long hair, beard, jeans and beads, to a heart that was beginning to be transformed by Jesus. Yes, my journey had only started but Jesus had already begun a work in me that He would keep on refining.

Fortunately, Eddie fended her off but I realised then how hard it would be for me to stay and grow as a Christian in that very religious atmosphere. God however had other plans for me which would take me far away from that culture in order to teach and prepare me for my calling.

As I've grown in God, I've learned that our times are truly in His hands and He has marked out the journey He wants us to take. We set off thinking we know what is going on but God leads us on paths we have no idea about to bring us into a place where we can be most fruitful in serving Him. He knows the end from the beginning[31], and works all things out according to the wisdom of His own will and foreknowledge. As I look back, I am glad that God was leading and directing my way. This is true for all of us, so even if right now you are not sure where your journey is taking you, just remember He knows what is going on. Even if you have made huge errors in the decisions of your life, (as I have), He will take them and turn them into something fruitful and beautiful. I would learn that many times as I followed Jesus on my rocky road.

---

[31] Isaiah 46:10.

The wild rover returns.

Eventually I returned from Newcastle to Dublin to see my musician friends in Ironhorse. We all agreed we had run our course with the music and it was time to pack it up. In fact, we were all in bad shape from too many drugs and needed to get away to try to find some kind of rehabilitation.

Shortly after leaving Dublin, I flew back to Guernsey again to unwind and restore some sense into my life. Living in Guernsey suited me very well, I got a job as a kitchen porter in a seafront hotel which meant three good meals a day and a non-stressful working environment.

Reg was still living in Guernsey and along with another Rathfriland friend, Errol, had opened a Hippie shop, designing and selling Eastern clothes, bags and jewellery. One day I wandered into the shop and began idly browsing through the shelves filled with Indian shirts. As I was looking around, I discovered a card tucked under some garments. A Christian undercover agent had been at work! It was another of God's little 'coincidences' on my journey. I began to read it, and discovered it was an invitation to a Christian youth club.

It rekindled my spiritual quest, so along with Reg, who was open to all things spiritual, we went to the group the following Saturday night. I was expecting to find some very straight people there but to my surprise the leader of the group was wearing blue jeans, had long sideburns and was very laid back. We hung out at the coffee bar area and at the end of the evening this leader, Steve, invited us back to his home to chat and listen to music. After some hesitation, we decided to go. The music Steve played was not what I was expecting. Instead of some religious stuff, he started playing jazz. I was blown away that a Christian listened to this kind of music. My limited experience with other Christians led me to believe that all secular music was frowned upon.

From this encounter, Steve and I became friends, meeting up regularly to chat. He would talk about anything and everything and only spoke of Christian things if the conversation headed that way. Steve had become another God ordained 'coincidence' on my journey.

Eventually I decided to go along to the church that Steve attended. It was a small independent church led by his parents. The meetings were traditional by my limited understanding of church but the people were very friendly and welcoming. One thing I noticed was the lack of hell fire type preaching. On the contrary, these people were very loving and kind. I got to know some of them and enjoyed their company but I still did not understand the Christian message. I was still smoking marijuana while reading an old King James Bible I had been given years ago, as well as listening to Hare Krishna music in my Saint Peter Port apartment. That's how confused I was. However, after some time I decided to stop smoking weed and worked on cleaning myself up. Although I was not a believer I was on the journey towards sorting myself out, or so I thought!!

At that time, I also met the girl who was to become my wife. She worked in the same hotel as me as a chambermaid. Linda had given up a secure job working for the British government in the civil service in order to travel. I like to tell people that we met and fell in love over the hot plate cabinet in the kitchen. Though it isn't strictly true, it was where we met. Linda had an Anglican church background and considered herself to be a Christian. We dated for some months, fell in love and decided to get married. It was a bit of a whirlwind romance! Our youngest daughter Amber tells us jokingly that we were very irresponsible, and she is probably right!

We used the Vale Mission hall, Steve's parents' church as the location for our marriage and Steve's father officiated the wedding ceremony. Our parents and families came to the island for the wedding and all my hippie friends showed up for the day also. Errol, the co-owner of the hippie shop was my best man.[32] The two of us were quite a colourful sight with both of us having elbow length red hair and wearing eastern kaftans as our wedding outfits. I bought my wedding trousers the day before

---

[32] Sadly my friend and best man, Errol, passed away just as I finished this book.

the wedding and sold them again the day after. I had no use for them as I usually wore Levi jeans every day. Three nurses from the church provided a wonderful reception for our families and hippie friends, It was quite a festive and vibrant occasion altogether.

Gotta get back to the garden.

Some time after our wedding day, we joined together with two other couples and rented a large country farm house in the centre of the island. Errol, along with his wife was one of the couples. He was into organic gardening and cultivated his own marijuana plants, though for obvious reasons he grew those up on the Guernsey cliffs well away from the farmhouse. It was a great house and we had a very relaxed hippie lifestyle to begin with. We were trying to get back to the garden and liberate our souls as Joni Mitchell sang about in her song 'Woodstock'.[33]

Steve would call round regularly to chat and it was always great to see him but unfortunately I slowly drifted back into smoking weed. Steve never gave up on me though and always remained a friend. His loving influence on my life cannot be understated and Steve and his family remain good friends of ours to this day. However, I had much to discover before I would get back to the real garden Steve knew about and I was still looking for!

Our Princess arrives.

Shortly after moving into our hippie house, Linda became pregnant with our first daughter, Zara. In Hebrew the name derives from Sarah and means Princess, though we didn't know that at the time. In the midst of my spiritual confusion, this little bundle lit up my life.

On the day she was born, I returned to our home 'Le Friquet farm house' and climbed onto the roof to sit and reflect about this little princess who had become part of our lives. I didn't know how to really pray back then so sitting on the roof and

---

[33] Joni Mitchell, CD, Ladies of the Canyon, 1970 Reprise records.

smiling at the heavens was my best attempt to say thank you to the God I didn't know for my adorable daughter. All three of us subsequently settled into our commune lifestyle.

Divine directional detour.

I had been offered a job as a cook by a Christian businessman I had met through Steve's church connection. He owned and ran a delicatessen in Saint Sampson which was just a two mile drive from our home. One morning as I drove to my workplace, I passed a tall young man walking along the road. For some reason I took particular notice of him. Fifty metres down the road I pulled in to get petrol (gas) for my car and this same guy walked past the station. As I pulled out I had a strong urge to stop and ask him if he needed a lift anywhere. I didn't know it at the time but this was another of God's directional coincidences for later. He jumped in the car and as we drove, he told me he had arrived that morning from Holland and was walking to his new job. It didn't take long for Oscar and I to realise we shared a similar hippie lifestyle outlook. From that encounter we became good friends and met up regularly to smoke weed and talk about life in the Netherlands. This friendship was going to have huge consequences for my future but back then we just liked hanging out together.

Back in the early seventies, Amsterdam, Holland was the starting point for any serious hippie who intended to travel east. Along with that, marijuana was very easily bought in most Dutch cities without much police scrutiny. To me, at the time, it seemed like the ideal place to go and find fresh adventure. Oscar encouraged me to go to Holland, offering his home there as a place to stay. I made the decision and talked to Linda about making plans to move there. She had never ever taken drugs and was not all that excited about the adventure but decided with me that we should go. We started making plans and shortly before we were due to go Steve called in to say hello. When I told him we were going to Holland to live he mentioned he had met a Dutch businessman briefly the year before on the island. Steve also told me this man was a Christian and offered to give me his address as a point of contact and possible practical help.

Oscar mentioned Haarlem as the city where he lived so when I told Steve about our new location he said he thought that the businessman lived in another town. However when he phoned me the next day to give me the address it turned out to be the same village, Bloemendaal, on the outskirts of Haarlem where Oscar actually lived. Another divine coincidence! What are the odds of that happening? I also found out later that this was the village where Corrie Ten Boom lived. I'll tell you more about this amazing lady in another chapter. A year or so later I would realise how God directs our steps even when we are not asking Him.[34] My journey was unfolding in amazing ways that I had no understanding of, but then God does that when He is on your case!

---

[34] *"A man's heart plans his way but the Lord directs his steps"*, Proverbs 16:9.

Part II. New Adventures.

Chapter 3. Going Dutch.

Off on a journey, don't know where,
Headin' off without a care,
Life is for livin', no misgivins',
The journey is only for those who dare

A new beginning.

A short time later, we left Guernsey and flew to Linda's sister and brother-in-law's home on the southeast coast of England. Bill and Judith had graciously invited Linda and Zara to remain until I got settled into a new job and found a place to live in Holland. Within a few weeks I was on my way to the Netherlands and a new adventure.

What I was not aware of upon arrival at Haarlem train station was that some days earlier Oscar had moved from his family home to the north of Holland. Fortunately, his mother Mrs Licht met me at the station and along with her daughters Renée and Lydia, welcomed me into their home. I quickly got settled in and went to the unemployment office the next day where I was given a number of jobs to apply for. The first two or three didn't materialise and I became concerned about getting work.

One day I was sent to an Oil refining plant and as I walked into the building, I threw up a prayer asking God to help me get the job. Even though I was not a believer in the proper sense, I was desperate enough to cry out to the God of my childhood when I needed help. I suppose we are all a little like that at times. We want God's help when we are in difficulties but we don't want Him around after we have the help we need.

The job was well paid with good benefits and to my surprise I was offered the position. At this time I began to feel agitated about the truth of Jesus but tried to push it to the back of my mind. I had decided I was not going to get in touch with Frans Vellama, the Christian Dutchman whom Steve had told me about. I was feeling more and more uncomfortable about my lifestyle, so I wanted to keep away from Christians altogether. I had become a little like Adam and Eve in the garden when they disobeyed God, and, becoming aware of their nakedness, hid from God.[35] I was also becoming aware of my spiritual nakedness. I didn't like it and wanted to hide.

Desperation, and more divine appointments.

After a number of weeks living at Mrs Licht's home in Holland and searching for an apartment, I was still unsuccessful. I was getting discouraged and more so without Linda and little Zara being with me.

Linda phoned me one Friday evening and when I told her that I had had no luck finding a place to live, she suggested I contact Mr. Vellema. I was reluctant but the desperation to have our own place pushed me to call him later that evening. It turned out he had just received a letter the day before from Steve in Guernsey telling him all about me so it was no surprise to him that I called. He told me he lived only a ten-minute walk from the Licht's house and arranged to pick me up the following day to take me into Haarlem city centre.

He arrived the following morning in a red open top Fiat sports car looking very much like the Virgin empire boss Richard Branson. I walked out to meet him with my elbow length red hair, beads and Levi jeans. We were an unlikely couple, a hippie and a very wealthy businessman in the advertising industry, but we soon hit it off and became good friends. He and his lovely wife Martha were not like some of the religious folk I had

---
[35] Genesis chapter 3.

encountered in Ireland. They were always gracious towards me and not at all phased by my hippie appearance.

Most Saturdays, Frans would take me into Haarlem centre and drop me off at the Christian coffee shop he had established in one of the buildings he owned. I met a number of young Dutch Christians there who became good friends and have remained so to this day. The Dutch are a very direct people, they say what they think but once you have a Dutch friend you have a friend for life.

During this time, the more I hung out with these lovely young Christian people, the more I became increasingly under conviction of the truth of who Jesus really was, along with my awful bankrupt life and spiritual condition. The great thing was that these new friends never made me feel guilty; just like Steve in Guernsey they just loved me. It was God who was at work in my heart making me realise the futility and emptiness of my life and need for Him.

One Saturday morning, Frans as usual picked me up and took me into the city centre. Over the course of the previous few weeks I had been thinking a lot about Jesus. The intercessory prayers and initial gracious input from Ernie and Eddie, the loving witness and prayers of Steve and his beautiful family plus the kindness of Frans and Martha, and the other Dutch Christians spoke volumes to me and showed me so much of God's love. That love had been terribly missing in my early encounters in those Gospel halls in Northern Ireland. Underpinning all of that was my Mother's prayers for her prodigal son. Never underestimate the power of a praying mother.

The day my Life changed forever.

That day as I walked around the centre of Haarlem I was stopped by a member of the Hare Krishna cult who wanted to convince me of his beliefs. I told him before I realised it that I was a follower of Jesus. He left me alone quite quickly and there and then I knew I had to surrender my life to Jesus Christ.

I waited until we were returning to Bloemendaal before telling Frans that I did believe in this good news of Jesus and that I wanted to pray. He looked surprised but we stopped at a lay-by where he instructed me how to pray. He said he would pray in Dutch and I could pray in English. After he prayed, I prayed the best I knew how and handed my life over to Jesus. I literally felt the heaviness in my heart roll away, and a weight lifting off my shoulders. It was replaced immediately with a joy I had never known. What a wonderful moment I shall never forget, I was overwhelmed with love and peace and the mystery of what had just taken place in that lay-by. When I arrived back at Mrs Licht's house, I went straight to my room and picked up all the drugs I had stashed, then walked into the bathroom and flushed them down the toilet. That was the last time I ever held drugs in my hand, it was the beginning of my new life.

God steps in again and again.

Later that day, when I phoned Linda back in England and told her what had happened, she was not really impressed. She had seen me dabble in eastern religions over the last couple of years and thought that it was just another phase I was going through. Of course, she was right about my past dabbling but to me this was totally different, yet it remained to be tested.

During this time, Mrs Licht graciously told me to fetch Linda and Zara from England as it wasn't good for us to be apart. Frans had tried his hardest to get me a place to live but had been unsuccessful. That's when Mrs Licht offered me a room in her home for us to stay together until we found a place of our own. This was God's blessing to us at this time. A short while later, I had a wonderful reunion with Linda and Zara at Schiphol airport. We were a family once again.

Oscar's sister, Renée, took up the challenge to find an apartment for us. She found some adverts in the local paper and followed up on them on our behalf. We received a response from one advert she had written to and Renée took us into the city to speak with the landlord.

When we arrived there, we discovered the whole family were waiting to interview us. Mr Timmers, the head of the family showed us the pile of applications they had received about the apartment. It made my heart sink to think there were so many people looking to rent this place. What chance would we have as foreigners in Holland? It appeared, however, that they were interested in us as they had read in our application that I was from Northern Ireland. They knew of the difficulties there with the terrorist activities and, because of that they wanted to interview us.

As we left the house I silently prayed my naive desperation prayer and gave the apartment to God without really understanding what I was doing. By the time we had made the short journey back to the Licht's house the phone was ringing. Renée answered to hear Mr Timmers say that the whole family were in agreement and wanted us to have the apartment. This was now God's second intervention in our desire to be together as a family in Holland and my first answer to prayer as a true believer.

Looking back on those days, I realise God answered prayers that were mostly a cry into the unknown at the time. He is listening even when we don't realise it or understand. He hears the cry of desperate searching hearts.[36] I was learning lessons early on about trusting God. Believing for something yet letting God take charge, it was a deep lesson I would see repeated many times over in the years to come.

Coffee bar hang out.

I quickly discovered that our new home was literally just around the corner from the local Youth for Christ (YFC) coffee bar. The friends I had made at Frans' coffee shop spent time at YFC as well so I was able to regularly hang out and enjoy time with them there.

---

[36] Psalm 34:1:8.

Every Saturday evening, the YFC coffee bar held a youth event with a guest singer or speaker heading up the evening. On one occasion, Corrie Ten Boom, whom I mentioned earlier, was the special guest. I knew a little about her having just read her book 'The Hiding Place'.[37] It is the famous story of her family hiding Jews in their home above their clock shop during the Second World War. The clock shop was only a few hundred metres away from our new apartment in the centre of Haarlem. An American friend was the curator and we had visited the place on a couple of occasions. Corrie's family saved many Jewish lives by courageously hiding them in a secret compartment in their home. Tragically they were eventually betrayed and all sent to concentration camps for the remainder of the war. Corrie's family perished and only she survived.

Her life story is an amazing testimony of God's faithfulness to her in the midst of horror. A film was made of the book and some of it was shot in Haarlem while we lived there. I remember riding my motor scooter through the backstreets of Haarlem to work and passing by the street that was used to film the clock shop scenes. Of course they couldn't use the real shop as it was still open for business in the city centre, so a back street area was used for filming. That area was in the red-light district[38] at the time and I found it fascinating. Isn't it just like Jesus to have such a wonderful film of God's grace shot in a district with a shady reputation?

That Saturday evening, I listened intently as Corrie told her story at the YFC coffee bar. It was incredible. One thing that stood out was her illustration of life using a simple small tapestry. It is a picture of God's working in our lives during the good times but especially the hard times. *"God is weaving a beautiful tapestry together of light and dark colours"* was something she said which I have never forgotten. As Corrie spoke I was completely absorbed in her story. She held up a piece of cloth and on one side was a lot of knotted loose threads

---

[37] The Hiding Place by Corrie Ten Boom, Hodder & Stoughton, Nov. 2004. ISBN 9780340863534

[38] An area of a town or city containing many brothels, strip clubs, and other sex businesses.

and frayed edges. She explained that on this side of Heaven there are many situations in our lives that seem knotted and frayed. Sometimes we don't understand what is going on but then she turned the tapestry over to reveal a beautifully woven richly coloured crown. That, she told us, is what God is working in us for our life and for eternity. As Jesus said to His disciples when He washed their feet, *"What I am doing you do not understand now but afterward you will understand"*.[39] Jesus was serving them to illustrate their future ministry. So often we don't understand what Jesus is doing in our lives until a lot later in life.

I began to realise that God was also working on things in my life which up to that point I had no understanding of. Looking back on my life, I now have a better awareness of how He was leading me in those days.

There may be a lot happening in your life right now that is confusing or painful and you don't understand what is going on. Be assured God will take you through these times and bring you to the place of peace and purpose that He has destined for you. Have you ever seen the cartoon photo of the large Heron with a frog halfway into it's mouth? While halfway into the bird's mouth, the frog still has it's 'hands' gripped tightly around the bird's throat preventing itself from becoming dinner. The caption underneath reads "DON'T EVER GIVE UP".

There is someone greater than you working to throttle whatever is trying to swallow you up right now, His name is Jesus. Many times in my life it looked like I was being swallowed by my circumstances and history (which I'll tell you more of later), but God has always brought me through to a broad and spacious place.[40] He is our defender and provider, He won't let us become prey for the devourer. Keep holding on to Him, look to Him and trust Him and He will make a way through. I have gone through a lot of unknown and sometimes difficult, even desperate seasons in my life. Although I may not have been aware, God was directing and redirecting my steps. There would

---

[39] John 13:7.

[40] Psalm 18:19.

be many more steps to take which I had no great understanding of, but He was leading me every step of the way.

In our lives we make lots of plans but when God puts His hand on our life we need to realise that He will direct our steps. I was finding out how true Proverbs 16:9[41] was. My life wasn't a bunch of tangled loose ends, God was making a beautiful tapestry of my life, I just didn't realise it then.

Here is the poem which highlights the tapestry story Corrie ten Boom told at the coffee bar.

"My Life is but a Weaving",[42] the Tapestry poem.

> *"My life is but a weaving, between my God and me*
> *I cannot choose the colours He weaveth steadily,*
>
> *Oft' times He weaveth sorrow, And I in foolish pride,*
> *Forget he sees the upper, And I the underside.*
>
> *Not 'til the loom is silent and the shuttles cease to fly,*
> *Will God unroll the canvas, and reveal the reasons why.*
>
> *The dark threads are as needful, in the weaver's skilful hand*
> *As the threads of gold and silver, in the pattern He has planned*
>
> *He knows He loves He cares, nothing this truth can dim,*
> *He gives the very best to those who leave the choice to Him".*[43]

Sixteen years after I first heard Corrie tell her tapestry story, the last line in the poem would be used by God to enable me to trust Him for a house we were trying to buy in Sheffield, UK. I'll share more about that episode later.

---

[41] In his heart a man plans his course, but the Lord determines his steps.

[42] My Life is but a Weaving. Author unknown. See https://www.goodreads.com/quotes/741391-life-is-but-a-weaving-the-tapestry-poem-my-life. Used in Ten Boom's book; The Hiding Place, Chapter 3. See under, Coffee bar hang out.

[43] Chapter 7. See under, Sheffield Steel.

Chapter 4. Down on the Farm

*Some of the best memories are made on the farm,
Into the field I go to lose my mind and find my soul.*

From the Ark to the Farm.

Back in Haarlem, we settled into life in our new flat at 13, Kleine Houtstraat. We lived above a bakery, 'La Boulangerie', owned by our landlord. Walking through that bakery was always a tempting experience because of the delicious aroma of bread and cakes that filled the shop.

I was able to spend some of my free time chatting with my new friends around the corner at YFC and learning more about Jesus. I also began playing guitar and singing in a few of the Dutch YFC coffee bars. During this time we discovered 'The Ark' in Amsterdam through friends of Frans Vellema. 'The Ark' was a houseboat ministry situated behind the Grand Central Station in the city centre.

Floyd McClung headed up the work there. He and his wife Sally had travelled to Asia with 'Youth with a Mission' (YWAM) to minister, and while in India Floyd was confronted by a hippie begging in the centre of New Delhi. Upon their return to America, that memory stayed with him and eventually he felt the Lord was directing him to go east again to minister to the many hippies there. In a short time, they established the first 'Dilaram House' ministry in Kabul, Afghanistan. I've been told the word, 'Dilaram' means 'peaceful heart' in either Farsi or Dari and so began the 'House of the Peaceful Heart ministry'.

After spending a few years setting up 'Dilaram' ministry in Kabul, as well as sending out leaders to establish houses in New Delhi, India, and Kathmandu, Nepal, Floyd and Sally came to Amsterdam. They realised through many interactions with hippies that this famous city was the starting point for many of the travellers. Their plan was to establish a house ministry here to reach out to the hippies and hopefully save them from many of the pitfalls that awaited them in Asia.

Houseboat church.

At that time, two large, barge houseboats became available from YWAM who had used them for a summer outreach in Amsterdam, and so 'The Ark' was established. One boat was a sleeping and dining space and the other had a large meeting area where open meetings were held every Sunday night. This was the beginning of a great time of learning and discipleship for me. Floyd was excellent at teaching and discipling people. I was greatly challenged by his teaching and began to grow spiritually.

According to Linda, it was from this point that I began to change quite dramatically. She was still skeptical at this time about my conversion but when I began to change so much in a positive way, Linda declared that there had to be a God as only He could have changed me. That statement gives a glimpse into the kind of person I had been before I met Jesus. He began to turn me around and I began to grow spiritually as well as in practical ways.

Linda was still quite suspicious to begin with because of all the Christian 'hippies' on 'The Ark'. She had shared life with me in a hippie environment for a few years and it didn't make sense that these people were believers. She had grown up going to an Anglican church with its traditional services which had shaped her thinking about religious matters. Even though she did not have a real connection with Jesus, nevertheless she did have a belief of some kind. Her traditional background in religion had no comparisons with 'The Ark' community. It was strange to her and she was wary, both by nature and observation.

She persevered and came to meetings with me. She got to know some of 'The Ark' community, especially Floyd and Sally. Slowly her suspicions were allayed over a period of nine months. She finally opened up to Jesus herself one day after a long conversation with Floyd and gave her life to the Lord.

A fresh vision

We enjoyed our days in Haarlem. Linda enjoyed getting to know our Dutch friends and exploring the town during the day with little Zara. We spent lots of our free time visiting 'The Ark' and strolling around Amsterdam. I was now singing in YFC coffee bars all over Holland at the weekends, and I was invited to become a listed regular singer on the YFC circuit in the Netherlands.

One day as I considered this opportunity during my prayer time, I had an interesting vision. I saw a road ahead of me that divided into two. As I contemplated this I had a realisation that one road was leading to a more ongoing participation with YFC and the other was leading to a full time involvement with Floyd and 'Dilaram' ministry. I knew immediately in my heart that I was inclined to go along the road leading to 'Dilaram'. After talking it through with Linda and then Floyd we began to consider how to take this forward.

Floyd had just moved to the north of Holland as they had acquired a property which was officially called 'Heidebeek' but unofficially known as 'The Farm'. Formerly it had been a recuperation place for people who had contracted leprosy while in one of the Netherlands far flung colonies. There was a large central building with lots of small-personal dwelling properties around it. It sounded ideal for a community-based ministry. The place was going to become a training base for everyone joining 'Dilaram'. It was a great pioneering opportunity and my adventurous spirit was excited about the whole project, but Linda was not so sure. With her more conservative and wary nature, even more heightened as a mum with all her motherly instincts, she was not easily convinced. I would be giving up my well-paid job; how would we live? We decided to visit the area to check it all out. The locality was beautiful. It was right out in the countryside but also near to the city of Zwolle.

When we arrived at the base, we saw this delightful row of small stone bungalows, one of which we would have the opportunity to live in. That was a deciding factor. When we returned to

Haarlem, we shared our thoughts with our Dutch friends. They were positive and some quickly committed to supporting us financially. This was the first of many occasions in our lives where we would see God work through faithful believers to look after us financially. Eventually we made the decision, said our farewells to our Haarlem friends and moved to 'The Farm'. The next adventure had begun.

DIY = Destroy it yourself!

We arrived with all our worldly goods which meant really our clothes, my Sony recording stereo system and my little motor scooter.

Altogether about 50 people had come to live on the base. A number of young families arrived around the same time so Zara had lots of friends to play with. We quickly got busy with the work required in establishing the base as it was quite run down.

One day as I prayed, I felt the Lord tell me He was calling me into leadership. I was very excited about this and naively went to speak to one of the leaders. After patiently listening to me, he agreed and said, *"I have just the job for you"*. He wisely put me on toilet cleaning duty! Though initially I was very surprised at his response, I worked very hard at my new 'leadership' position. Before long I was promoted to overseeing the work of public toilet duties, floor cleaning and laundry responsibilities. Later on, along with my existing responsibilities, I was promoted to overseeing all general maintenance on the base as well. I believe this was God's sense of humour as I was not very good at DIY.[44] My friend Dave Mansfield who is also a non-expert often reminds me that our idea of DIY is 'Destroy It Yourself'.

As I look back now, it was good training for leadership though I did not understand it at the time. The Bible says, *"Whatever your hand finds to do, do it with all of your might"*.[45] I really took a lot of pride in keeping the toilets, laundry room, public

---

[44] DIY. Do It Yourself.

[45] Ecclesiastes 9:10.

walkways, and buildings in shape. It was also good for my humility. If Jesus could wash His disciples feet then I should have no problem cleaning toilets! The lessons were not really about DIY, they were about having a servant heart and learning to lead people, getting them motivated to do what was required, and also doing it with a happy heart.

Bell ringing for beginners.

On one occasion it was my task to appoint someone as the early morning bell ringer. Apart from single dorm housing in the main building, we also had a number of small bungalows for couples and families scattered about the property. The bell ringing task entailed someone rising very early at around 5:30 am before anyone else. The job was to walk round the property at 6am ringing the old school master's bell to wake up everyone on the base. Breakfast was being prepared in the main kitchen and everyone had to get there promptly to either eat or pick up breakfast for the family. This of course was not the most popular job on base as I was to find out.

I happened to choose a former US army ranger, though I didn't know that at the time. He was not very pleased about this and let me know the very first morning by opening our bungalow door and ringing the bell as loudly as he could. A few minutes later as I walked across the main courtyard to the kitchen I saw him and smiled as he finished his 'tour of duty'. He marched over to me and quite aggressively pushed the bell in my face as he remonstrated with me about being chosen to do this menial task.

After a few intimidating moments of this, I quietly asked the Lord for wisdom and then replied, *"If you are not prepared to perform this task how could the Lord use you for something really meaningful?"*. Suddenly the light came on in his mind as he understood the implications of what I had said. He apologised quickly and from that time we became good friends. Looking back, if I'd known he had been a former member of the United States Army Rangers special forces unit, an elite military unit that trained and empowered men with special fighting skills for dangerous tasks, I might have been more nervous about our encounter that morning. As it was, God gave me the words I needed and Jesus won the day.

God was teaching me valuable lessons in servant leadership. Today I still apply the same principle in my ministry. When I see someone who is prepared to do a menial task joyfully, I see someone who is capable of great things. Those were foundational lessons for me at that time, and I have endeavoured to continue to walk in them all my life.

Leading with humility.

Later I read in John chapter 13 how Jesus taught us this lesson very clearly when He was with His disciples. After supper, He took off His outer garment, and got down on His hands and knees to wash the disciples feet. We have to remember this was no mere symbolic act. In those days when a traveler arrived at a house, their sandal-shod feet would be very filthy from the dirt of the road. Not just dust but animal droppings and every other kind of dirt was left on the road as they didn't have a road cleaning service like we have today. A servant would greet the guest as he arrived and proceed to wash his feet and clean them. It was a very menial task given to the least of the servants.

In later years as a church leader, I've been disappointed to observe an unwillingness amongst believers to take on small jobs around the church. Simple things like making the tea, vacuuming the floor, greeting people at the door, and so on. Granted, some are not called or gifted in certain areas but how much gifting does one need to wash dishes or clean floors!

I believe the problem arises out of a lack of understanding about who we truly are in Christ. Jesus Christ the Son of God, the Alpha and Omega, was completely free to take off His outer garment and serve His disciples by washing their dirty feet. What was it that enabled Him to do this without losing His self-worth?

As I read, I began to understand it was firstly because He walked continually in an intimate relationship with His Father. He always heard His Father's voice.[46] It speaks of such intimacy in His relationship with God. His security came from that personal relationship with God as His Father. The good news is that we can all walk in this personal, intimate, loving relationship with God our Father. We can hear Him and receive affirmation, instruction and encouragement. The more we discern His voice, the more we will become secure in who we are in Him.

Emanating from this intimacy came authority. Jesus knew all things had been given into His hands.[47] Authority comes from knowing what has been given to us. We hear this as we walk in intimacy with Father God. Authority is knowing in our heart that Father God has empowered us to serve His purposes. A menial task like washing feet will not change that.

Furthermore, He understood His identity, He knew He had come from God.[48] The scripture informs us that Jesus knew. This one would take me a while to learn. My orphan spirit kept getting in the way for a long time. It is such a key issue for many today. We have no idea who we really are. There is such an orphan spirit not only in the world today but in the church as well.

We have no idea where we have come from, therefore we have no idea who we are. It can cause us to strive for recognition in unhelpful ways. The truth is that Jesus told us He wouldn't leave us as orphans.[49] He has come to dwell in us by His Spirit, adopting us as sons and enabling us to know the security of who we are in Him. It is so liberating to carry this revelation in our heart. I would truly discover it some years later.

Finally, Jesus was secure in His destiny.[50] He knew where He was going. When you are driving in the fog you have to drive

---

[46] John 12:49,50.

[47] John 13:3a.

[48] John 13:3b.

[49] John 13:14:8.

[50] John 13:3c.

slowly with no clarity about where the road is. Likewise, if we do not know our destiny, we will wander in a spiritual darkness and foggy confusion most of the time, which leads to insecurity. But if like Jesus, we know we are children of destiny with divine purpose stored up inside us, we will walk with clarity and courage without any of the side effects which insecurity produces.

Jesus knew where He was going because He was in a personal relationship with His Father. He knew He was a son that was loved[51] and lived in this intimacy all the time. In fact, He said one time "I and the Father are one".[52] That's very close!!!

He heard His father's voice clearly directing Him, He had authority to fulfil His ordained purpose, He was secure in His identity as Son of God and was therefore free to fulfil His divine destiny in any way required. All of this freed Him to wash feet without any sense of insecurity at all.

If we can absorb revelation of these truths in our hearts, we will also be free to wash dishes, make tea, vacuum floors and whatever other apparently menial task without it affecting our sense of value and personhood in Christ. As I discovered much later, it really is liberating to walk as a son of God and no matter how menial the task that you have to do, there will be no negative effect on who you are.

If only we could realise how much we are loved, that our identity is as sons who are loved, and that we have a great destiny in store, not only in eternity but right here right now. We're designed to walk in intimacy with Father God and enjoy fellowship with Him, being able to do anything required for the sake of His Kingdom. His grace has enabled all of this. It is futile to try to earn His favour, because we already have it through Jesus. We are now free to love the one who loved us first.[53] This is where passion and vision arise from, and this is grace in action bringing freedom and heart motivation, where sons are

---

[51] Luke 3:22.

[52] John 10:30.

[53] 1.John 4:19.

liberated to serve and still remain sons. My former Ranger friend and I learned a little of this through our encounter that morning but I needed much more heart healing to really live in these truths.

Life lessons through bell ringing was another of God's unusual ways of training this ragamuffin. I had many more to learn, as beneath the positive exterior of leadership, the nagging memories of stupidity, humiliation, failure and poverty spirit of my early years still haunted me and taunted my mind often. I felt at times like the junkies I had known, who, when weighed down in desperation for a fix said, *"The monkey is on my back"*. I felt that the monkey of accusing insecurity was on my back at times, driving me. It will take you over the precipice if you don't get it dealt with as I later found out.

A heritage from the Lord.

During our time at 'Heidebeek', our son Kyrie was born. When Linda became pregnant God gave me a verse in my RSV Bible which stated, *"Sons are a heritage from the Lord"*.[54] We had been praying about having another child and as I read that verse, it seemed to jump out and hit me between the eyes. I believed that God was telling me we were going to have a boy. Excitedly and naively, I mentioned my revelation to some people who replied that in their Bible it didn't say sons, it said children. I struggled with that for a day or so but then realised that God knew the version I was reading. If He knew the number of hairs on my head[55] then surely He knew which Bible version I was reading. It was another lesson in believing that God knows the details of our lives. Nine months later and with the help of our friend Meike, (a midwife who was living at Heidebeek), we had a home birth and our handsome boy was born on Easter Sunday evening. We named him Kyrie, which is Greek for Lord, as a reminder that he was born on resurrection Sunday.

As soon as I possibly could, I lifted my son and took him to our front window where a large number of people from the base

---

[54] Psalm 127:3.

[55] Matthew 10:30.

were waiting to hear the news. As I opened the curtain and showed them our boy, they all cheered jubilantly. My promised son had arrived. Another lesson in hearing and believing His still small voice was established. Today, those lessons remain as we continually step into the unknown, knowing that He leads us every step of the way.

India calling.

Sometime later when we had settled in well at 'Heidebeek', a family arrived from the ministry house in India. Dave and Ange Andrews had established and led the 'Dilaram House' there for a few years, but had now come to 'Heidebeek' to help develop the overall ministry of 'Dilaram'.

They settled in next door to us and we quickly became good friends. They often shared stories about India and my imagination was fired up with the infectious adventures they experienced. On one occasion, Dave and Ange hosted a video evening about the ministry in New Delhi, and afterwards I had a strong desire in my heart to go and work there.

There was only one problem. Linda was absolutely not interested in travelling to India with two small children. On top of that, she suffered with severe eczema, which is a very painful and irritating skin condition. We had enjoyed a very hot summer in Holland that year but it adversely affected Linda's eczema especially on her hands and arms. To consider going to India where the heat became almost unbearable in summer was unthinkable for her. I was discouraged but continued to pray into my heart's desire for India. One morning during my daily Bible reading, I was impacted by the story of Peter walking on water.[56] The verses that grabbed my attention were when Peter began looking at the wind and waves and began to sink. At that moment, I felt the Spirit of God impress upon me not to be distracted by the circumstances surrounding India but to keep my focus on Him. I was greatly encouraged by this and decided to do what I felt compelled by the Holy Spirit to do. For some

---

[56] Matthew 14:22-23.

time I just kept looking to Jesus, believing it would all work out regarding India.

A short time later, we had the opportunity to visit Linda's Mum in the northeast of England for a much needed holiday. After an enjoyable rest in England, we returned to our base in Holland. A few days later Linda spoke to me and said she had been praying about India and now felt God was saying we should go. I was so excited we went straight away to see Floyd and share our news. His immediate reply was *"if Linda says it is right, it must be God"*. How often that lesson would come back to me over the years. Linda and I walk with God to the beat of different drummers. I am always the adventurous one, getting vision and direction quickly. Linda however takes things more slowly. Some years earlier as we were getting married, our Guernsey friend Steve said to us that we were good for each other. Linda was the string and I was the balloon. I would take her on great adventures, but she would keep me from getting carried away on every whim. How true that has been. Her drummer beats slower than mine but by the time she reaches her decision I have usually changed my mind a few times! Ultimately though we usually discover His will brings us to the same conclusion and we go forward together. It's called teamwork!

He supplies all our needs.

With affirmation from Floyd, we began praying seriously about the means to get to India. We had no extra money at all, as I had felt that the Lord wanted me to give all my savings to help get 'Heidebeek' established, (much to Linda's concern!). However, we did have some financial support and always saw our needs met.

On one occasion we had run out of money and we needed to buy essential items like toothpaste and soap. As I prayed one morning there was a rattle in our letter box in the front door. When I went to check, an envelope with a small amount of money was lying on the floor. It was a wonderful answer to prayer.

My only problem was that I began to worship the letter box. Let me explain. Any time after that when we needed money, I would look expectantly at the floor in front of the letter box to see if any envelopes with money had arrived. It never happened that way again. God taught me another valuable lesson I would need to recall time and time again. He was our provider, not the letter box. Our problem begins when we put our trust in a method or a former means of His supply. When we do this rather than trustfully look to Jesus, we will usually run into difficulties.

When God supplies our needs, it is so important to keep looking to Him as our source and allow Him to change the supply as He sees fit. If things change it's because He has something better lined up.

As we continued to pray and prepared to go to India, we received sporadic anonymous gifts of money over a period of time until we had enough for our airfares. We naively bought one-way tickets to India. I declared, *"God has told us to go, He has not said anything about coming back"*. I had much to learn.

God knows your phone number

One final lesson in trusting God before leaving for India happened while trying to phone my parents the night before our departure. International phone calls were not as easy as they are today. I tried to use the main base, office phone to connect with my parents in Northern Ireland. However I could not get through as the line was continually engaged. I desperately wanted to speak to them and knew it would be very important for them to hear my voice before we travelled to the *"far ends of the earth"* as they put it.

As much as I tried, I could not get a connection. So I sat down and prayed. As I did so I remembered there was a public phone box across the street from my home. I thought I would try to call it and if someone answered I would ask them to go over to my parents and get them to hang up from whatever call they were making so I could speak to them. Remember my hometown was a village so that was not as strange as it may sound, nearly everybody knew everybody else! The problem was that I could not remember the number. So I simply prayed and asked God for the phone number. Quickly I had an impression of a phone number in my head. I wrote it down then dialled the number. To my surprise the call was answered quickly so I asked to whom was I speaking? To my utter amazement the man replied, *"Pastor George"*.

Pastor George was a very well-known and respected local Pentecostal Pastor in Rathfriland. Amazingly, the number I called, thinking it was a public phone box, was in fact the home phone number for this Pastor. I quickly shared my predicament with him. No one else in the whole town would have understood my story like him. He took it as if it was the most normal thing in the world for me to get his number from God, which as a matter of spiritual fact, it was. He quickly drove over to my parents' house and explained the situation. My parents' had been on the phone line but quickly hung up so I could call and talk to them before our departure to India.

There is no price I can put on the immense value of these spiritual lessons in trusting God for every detail of our lives. Pastor George became a prayer supporter of ours during our time in India and wrote to me with his prayer strategy covering the world as well as us, and also gave us many words of encouragement.

One issue persisted in preparing to leave for India which was very important. Linda still had eczema. She shared with a fellowship group at the 'Heidebeek' base about her concern. They prayed for her and someone said they believed that God wanted to heal her but she needed to claim it for herself. She took the advice but didn't really know what to do with it. However, we were to discover God's wonderful answer when we arrived in India.

Chapter 5. The Far Pavilions

*India and its peoples; a place of sensory overload,
with every possible form of contrast,
a clash of colour and a cacophony of sound,
both wealthy and poor, educated and illiterate,
cultured and wretched, a land of gold and gods,
decaying, yet beautiful beyond imagination.*

Incredible, mysterious India.

The Far Pavilions is the title of a book by M. M. Kaye. It was first published in 1978 and is an epic novel of British-Indian history. It tells the story of an English officer during the British rule in India. The book later became a TV mini series. It is a sweeping saga of India during the time of the Raj.[57] I watched every episode on TV. The title alone captivated me regarding the mystery of India and it reminded my wife and I of our amazing adventures there. We loved it so much we bought the DVD series and watched it again and again.

The mystique of India was very apparent straight away, as we flew into New Delhi and took a very early morning taxi ride from the airport to our new home in the suburbs. The sights, sounds and smells during that drive to our new home were overwhelming as I tried to digest the wonder that is India.

India is a land of extremes, from the searing heat of the plains, to the pleasant warmth of an English style summer in the foothills of the former Raj hill stations.[58] From the beauty of magical buildings like the Taj Mahal to the squalor of the slums of Mumbai (Bombay), the wealth and the poverty live beside one another. There are many religions, yet there is a lack of hope in people's faces and lives. The poverty is overwhelming, and the bureaucracy is frustrating. Hot, overcrowded, noisy,

---

[57] British Sovereignty in India.

[58] Summer retreat locations in the mountains

smelly, despairing, adorable, majestic; this is India! Beautiful India! Oh how I love it!

New Delhi is the capital of India, established by the British in 1911 with the imperial visit of King George V and Queen Mary. The announcement was made while laying the foundation stone for the establishment of the Viceroy's residence that the capital had shifted from Calcutta to Delhi. Subsequently another foundation stone was laid by the King and Queen for the establishment of New Delhi.

British architects set about designing the new city and laid it out with wide boulevards and large roundabouts. Today there is still evidence of the grandness that once was in New Delhi. Some examples of this are, Rajpath, Janpath, Connaught Place and Connaught Circus.

New Delhi sits cheek by jowl with Old Delhi and the contrast is still striking, showing the albeit decaying grandeur of the new with the squalor of the old. This was our new home.

It ain't half hot here!

We already had friends in New Delhi. John and Sue from Australia had spent time next door to us at 'Heidebeek' before flying out to India to take over the running of the New Delhi house. We settled into life in the community quite quickly. It was a relaxed environment and a great place for our children Zara and Kyrie to enjoy.

The issue of Linda's eczema, remained unresolved, however. Shortly after arriving in India it began flaring up due to the intense heat. During the summer period in northern India from April to June, temperatures can rise during the day to 32-40°c, (90-104°f). The highest ever temperature recorded in New Delhi is 48.4°c, (119.2°f) in May 1998. Summer in the city can feel at times as if you are living in a very hot oven. One day in desperation after a lot of discomfort with her eczema, Linda called out to God praying, *"if you want me here you will need to do something about this"*. Within a week the eczema disappeared never to return. She still has some small scars on her arms where the eczema existed but never again has she been troubled by the condition. God is so faithful. He cares about the detail of our lives. We would learn many more lessons about His faithfulness during our stay in India.

Hope for Hippies.

Our ministry was focused on Western travellers. We visited the many cheap hotels on a regular basis to find out if any hippies needed help. This was a good way to reach this alternative group. Many of them got sick from drinking untreated water or were in bad shape due to drug abuse.

Others had difficulties with their passport. Usually the passports had been sold or stolen or their visas had expired. Whatever the reason we tried to help in whatever way we could. We had a good relationship with a number of the embassies in New Delhi. They quickly realised that we could help them with the problem of the travellers in a way that they were not equipped to do.

They often asked us to take care of sick travellers while they tried to sort out their passport problem. It was cheaper for us to take them in than to try and put them up in a hotel. As well as that, we understood their mindset and could connect with them and help prepare them for repatriation. It was heart rending to see the condition of some of the people that were brought to us.

Marco was a young Italian man who came east in search of enlightenment. Instead, he almost literally fried his brains on drugs and was brought to the Italian embassy in a vegetable like state. They hospitalised him in a psychiatric unit and asked us to keep a twenty-four hour watch over him as he was totally incapable of looking after himself. He didn't talk or communicate in any way. Instead, he just sat with a vacant stare on his face or wandered around with no road sense at all. He had clearly become a danger to himself.

We appointed two of the team, Tony and Dave, to watch over him constantly at the hospital, which they did in a wonderful way. After some days, we were able to bring him back to our community in agreement with the embassy, as we could better look after him there.

His hair was long, matted and full of lice. I sat him down one day and using my dormant hairdressing skills, began cutting his hair, but in the middle of it he just got up and walked away. He had no sense of anything going on with himself at all. At least that is what we thought. For days he just wandered around the house with a dull vacant expression on his face. No one knew what was going on inside his head and we began to think he was a lost cause.

One day however, Marco heard the children in our community playing in the back garden and walked over to observe what they were doing. They were jumping up and down on an old disused mattress in the garden and laughing as only children can. Marco approached them and without a moment's hesitation the children took him by the hand and invited him to join in with them.

What an amazing moment in time as we stood at a distance and observed how the innocence of children brought the light of life back into Marco's eyes. As he bounced on the mattress with them, he also began to smile and respond to the kids. It was a fantastic sight and for the first time we knew that there was hope for Marco.

A few weeks later, the embassy arranged for Marco to fly back to Italy. On his last Saturday night with us, he joined in our regular love feast. This was an occasion for all of us to dress in our best T-Shirts, jeans or Indian clothes and celebrate together. Our Indian cook, Punjam, always made a special meal for our Saturday evening celebration. Usually it was buffalo meat curry with rice and perhaps as a treat a fruit salad dessert. We always had a time of worship afterwards, and on this occasion we had decided to have a foot washing time, following Jesus' servant example,[59] to bless one another in the community. A bowl of

---

[59] John chapter 13.

water, soap and towels were placed in the middle of our circle as we always had our love feast meal seated on the floor, Indian style.

A few people took the bowl of water and washed the feet of someone they appreciated. To our amazement Marco got up and took the bowl of water to Tony and Dave and began to wash their feet. We were all overjoyed as we observed the miracle of Marco thanking these two guys for looking after him at the hospital. His mind was beginning to work again; he was aware of the love and care he had received from Tony and Dave and the rest of the community at 'Dilaram'.

We can never underestimate the power of childlike acceptance and servant heart caring to bring healing to the most damaged people. We saw this many times over at 'Dilaram'. So many lives were transformed by the loving, serving atmosphere of the community. All we did was live together in a world that was falling apart. We continued to love one another and love those who came across our path. We did it without a great strategy, just a heart full of gratitude for God's goodness. Ragamuffins, ruffians and, vagabonds, who were all discovering that they were loved unconditionally by God and wanted to pass it on.

When the cupboard is bare.

We ran the New Delhi ministry on a financial faith basis. Everyone in the house contributed whatever money they could to help keep things going.

One humorous story to illustrate our frugal lifestyle happened when our friend Geoff Walvin came to stay with us. Geoff had been a hippie traveller who got sick in Kabul, Afghanistan a few years earlier. He was helped by the Kabul, 'Dilaram' house and became a believer before returning home to England. He later went to Amsterdam where we met him and became good friends during our time living in Haarlem.

Geoff travelled from Amsterdam to Nepal before our departure to India and was doing a wonderful work with Nepali nationals. Up to this day as a result of Geoff's foundation laying ministry in

Nepal all those years ago, thousands of indigenous churches have begun in Nepal and Northern India.

While staying with us on one occasion in Delhi, Geoff joined us for breakfast one morning in our room. We had porridge, toast, butter and jam laid out on the table. Linda asked Geoff what he would like for breakfast and he replied toast. Linda asked if he would like butter or jam. He replied *"both"*. Linda responded in astonishment *"Both?, You can't have both"*. This was because both were luxuries so we savoured them individually. Geoff laughed but still had both!

In later years, he has jokingly repeated that story very dramatically as only he can. We laugh every time he tells it as it really is so funny. In a humorous way, we are always reminded of our poverty spirit back then. We had so many lessons to learn from God. He was beginning to teach us more thoroughly about trusting Him for abundance in every area of our lives.

From time to time we ran out of funds at the house which left the cupboard bare and the rent due. At these times we began to learn the lesson of taking every need to God in prayer.

On one occasion, we were completely broke. Linda and I sat on the side of the bed in our room talking about our desperate plight. She was crying and, I was fretting but in the middle of all this need we cried out to God for an answer.

I finally said, *"Well God has just got to show up"*. I don't know how much faith we generated, all I know is we were desperate.

A few minutes later, there was a knock on our door and I got up and went to open it. Immediately I recognised the man at the door, he was from the American Embassy. We had met a few times at the Delhi Bible Fellowship Church. He greeted me and went on to tell me that he and his wife received a regular amount of money from an inheritance and they always prayed about what they should do with it. He then told me that God had directed them to give it to our ministry that month. He handed me an envelope, I thanked him and he quickly walked away as he was late for work. I stood in the doorway and slowly opened the envelope to find that it was stuffed with Rupees, more than enough to take care of rent, food, and extras for all the needs of the house. I walked back into the bedroom and with a look of bewilderment on my face. I told Linda what had just happened. We just started laughing, thanking God for such a wonderful and supernaturally instant answer to our prayerful cry.

We began to learn many lessons like this during our time in India. God was laying foundations in our lives for the future. My problem sometimes was that even though I knew verses like, *"Trust in the Lord with all of your heart and lean not on your own understanding"*,[60] they were in my head, but not yet properly instilled in my heart. I had a long way to go to fully comprehend the extent of His love and faithfulness to me. He would show up in awesome ways and yet I still had issues in my heart that at times left me feeling insecure, cultivating that reactive vagabond attitude.

Overland to Afghanistan.

Occasionally we had to leave India to visit our other ministry bases in Asia. On one occasion, we went to the city of Kabul in Afghanistan to spend time catching up on the work there. We left our two children back in New Delhi with Lynne, one of our key workers. The journey itself was quite an adventure. We took the train for the long journey from Delhi to the border town of Amritsar where the, 'Harmandir Sahib', (better known as, 'The Golden Temple') is located. It is the holiest Gurdwara (worship place) and the most important pilgrimage site of Sikhism.

Built by Guru Ram Das in 1577, the Gurdwara is constructed of white marble overlaid with genuine gold leaf. It stands in the centre of a pool of fresh, clear, reflective water which is fed by the River Ravi. Some say the Ravi river originates from the Ganges River. It truly is an amazing sight.

From Amritsar we had to cross the border into Pakistan. We caught another train from Lahore and travelled right across

---

[60] Proverbs 3:5-6.

Pakistan to the border city of Peshawar before crossing over into Afghanistan. We were fortunate enough to sit with some Pakistani men who were returning from the Middle East where they had been working. They were a friendly bunch, sharing food and jokes as we travelled. They say travel broadens the mind. It certainly did for us as we appreciated afresh the Eastern tradition of hospitality to strangers.

Finally, we reached Peshawar on the western border of Pakistan, only to find that the tour bus we planned to take on the next leg of our journey had been cancelled. We were stuck thousands of miles from our New Delhi base and didn't know what to do. However we quickly prayed and asked God for direction.

Alongside us was another bunch of westerners with the same predicament. Fortunately, amongst us was a young French hippie who had travelled this route before and knew where we could get public transport up to the border. So we grouped together and off we went to the bus station.

A bus was ready to depart complete with sheep and goats loaded onto the top of the bus. It was a sight I will never forget! We bundled in and off we went, with six of us squashed tightly onto a seat built for three. Driving up through the Khyber Pass, a mountain road connecting Pakistan and Afghanistan, we eventually arrived at the mountain border crossing which was the home of the Pathan people. They are often characterised as a warrior and martial race.

One modern Pathan is Malala Yousafzai. At the age of 17, she became the youngest Nobel peace prize recipient in 2014. She became known worldwide after being shot in the head by the Taliban for speaking out boldly about education rights for females in her country. Malala survived the assassination attempt and continues to speak out on issues regarding education. She is one very courageous Pathan, and a warrior hearted, young lady.

In this mountain border area, most of the Pathans walked around with rifles and bullet belts over their shoulders. It was a slightly unnerving sight for us as we went through the numerous border control checkpoints. At the Pakistani frontier post, travellers were advised not to wander away from the road, as the location was a barely controlled, federally administered, tribal area. Along the Khyber Pass, monuments left by British Army units and hillside forts could be viewed from the highway. It's an amazing place, but one which cannot be accessed these days due to the Taliban conflict.

We are so grateful that we had the opportunity to travel along these amazing, history filled routes. Major historical invasions of the area have occurred predominantly through the Khyber Pass, such as the invasions by Darius 1, Alexander the Great and also Genghis Khan. During the Second World War, the British also erected tank obstacles on the valley floor known as 'Dragons teeth' due to fears of a German tank invasion of India.

Finally after going through a maze of checkpoints we were through the border and caught a coach from Jalalabad to Kabul, travelling along the national highway. This two-lane highway runs for 64 kilometres along 600 metre high cliffs on one side. On the other side lies the Kabul River Gorge, which is now Taliban territory.

The Pass became widely known to thousands of Westerners who travelled it in the days of the hippie trail. Many of those hippies ended up at our 'Dilaram' houses ministry either in Kabul, New Delhi or Kathmandu.

Fatal traffic accidents often occur in this area, mainly due to reckless driving. Back then we had no idea how dangerous the road was and just enjoyed the austere scenery around us, including the jaw dropping sheer cliffs at the side of the highway. At last, after thirty six hours of travelling by train, bus and taxi, we arrived at our ministry base in Kabul.

God so wonderfully looked after us every step of the way, even providing a French hippie to help get us across the border when we had absolutely no knowledge of how to do so. He makes a way when there seems to be no way. We had more lessons to add to the amazing ways God looks after His children. He is no respecter of persons; if He would do this for us He will do it for you. Trust Him to look after you every step of your journey.

Even where there are road blocks, closures or detours, God will bring you through. I would learn deep lessons about that later on in my life journey.

Learning to love in Kabul.

We spent a few days in Kabul. The city itself was a mixture of old and new. The schools and hospital were very modern, and were mostly manned by Christian missionaries. There were lots of markets selling everything under the sun. It was noisy and very dusty. On one occasion, we entered a jeweller's shop to look at some bracelets. The man behind the counter engaged me in conversation and we chatted about the various items in his display cabinet. As he talked to me, I noticed that he did not once speak to or acknowledge Linda, although he had been looking at her from time to time.

At last he said to me, pointing toward Linda's forearm, *"Where did your 'friend' get her bracelet"?* He was referring to an unusual piece of jewellery she was wearing. I immediately replied, *"My 'wife' bought it in Amritsar, in India"*. As soon as he heard me say, *"My wife"* his attitude changed immediately, and he began discoursing with Linda about the jewellery in the store.

We encountered the same attitude at border cross points until the officers concerned looked at our passports and saw we were married. They became even more friendly when they saw that our children's names were included in our passports.

In general, of course, it was partly cultural but also the hippie lifestyle of casual free love had led to a disdain for Westerners. The lesson I learned in Kabul was not to make judgements on whole people groups, based on the behaviour of some, whatever their culture, race, or religion. Our job is to learn to love those we encounter and let God's love be seen in us and through us.

As Paul said, we need to be rooted and grounded in love[61] and abound in love for all.[62]

Learning to Love is the greatest aspiration for any believer. It is at the very core of God's heart for this planet. The verse, *"For God so loved the world..."*,[63] is probably the most famous verse in the Bible. Love is His foremost attribute and was fully demonstrated in Jesus Christ on earth.

Bob Jones was recognised by many as a prophet of the Lord and according to 'MorningStar Ministries',[64] he was a prophet with a great love for the Lord Jesus and His truth. His prophecies have spanned over three decades, as the Lord enabled him to foretell earthquakes, tidal waves, comets, and weather patterns. He moved with a clear revelatory gifting, accompanied by gifts of healing and miracles.[65]

On one occasion in August 1975, he had a near death experience and received a revelation from God. He saw people coming before God in Heaven and there was one question God asked them, *"Did you learn to love"?* When they answered, *"yes Lord"*, He would welcome them into heaven.[66] I am not implying by this that if they had answered "no" they would have been excluded, I am simply relaying the encounter Bob Jones had.

Bob finally went to be with the Lord on February 14th 2014, Saint Valentine's Day. I don't think that it is a coincidence that he went to heaven on the day that most people consider to be

---

[61] Ephesians 3:17

[62] 1.Thessalonians 3:12.

[63] John 3:16.

[64] MorningStar Ministries is a diverse and expanding international ministry founded by Rick and Julie Joyner in 1985. www.morningstarministries.org

[65] https://www.morningstarministries.org/biographies/bob-jones#.W-sLcpP7SS4 accessed 7/2/19.

[66] http://www.elijahlist.com/words/display_word.html?ID=13128 accessed 7/2/19.

the day of love. His widow Bonnie Jones said this was Bob Jones's greatest message since his near death experience in 1975.

"*Did you learn to love?*" was the message God gave him to share with the Church. Without love you have nothing because "*God is love*",[67] and as Paul said,"*The greatest is love*".[68] Bob believed he was sent back from death with that message to reach the leaders of the church for the end time harvest.

When you boil it all down, love, sacrificial love, as demonstrated by Jesus Christ is what counts. Without this love you have nothing because God is Love and we cannot exist without Him.

Blocked at the Border.

After our visit to Kabul, it was time to return to India. On the way into Afghanistan, as we had walked through the maze of passport controls in the Khyber Pass cross border checkpoint, we missed a check area where our passport should have been stamped. As we were leaving, an official checked our passports and to our horror he told us we had to return to Kabul, to sort out the missing stamp. This was not what we wanted to hear as we were keen to get back to our children. It meant adding an extra three or four days to our trip.

We went and sat on a bench and quietly began praying and praising God, asking Him to hear the cry of our heart and intervene on our behalf. Of course we did this like Hannah of old, with our lips moving but without a sound being heard.[69] We didn't want to be arrested for our Christian activity in a strong Muslim location; that could have been disastrous.

A short time later, the same officer beckoned us back to his desk. It turned out a friend of his sister, who was also leaving Afghanistan on the same coach as us had had the same

---

[67] 1.John 4:8.

[68] 1. Corinthians 13:13.

[69] 1.Samuel 1:12,13.

problem. He had restamped her passport and decided to also be merciful to us. If only he had known it was the gracious hand of God who knew beforehand our forthcoming predicament and had a plan in place to intervene on our behalf. Our prayers just activated His favour toward us. We thanked him of course and walked through into Pakistan, giving thanks to our Heavenly Father for His continuing care for us and looking forward to a wonderful reunion with our children.

Medieval Kathmandu trip.

During our time in India, we had the opportunity to travel to the mountain Kingdom of Nepal. Lynne, our resident babysitter and one of the staff workers at the Delhi house, was relocating to work at the 'Dilaram house' in Kathmandu and needed travelling company for the journey. Linda, myself and Lynne, along with our two young children, headed off on the overnight train to the border between India and Nepal.

Travelling by train in India is an amazing experience. It was a ten-hour overnight adventure as we piled in together with a host of Indian families also on the move. When a family travels in India, they carry everything except the kitchen sink, or so it seems.

Not long into the journey, most of the families pulled out small stoves and having lit them proceeded to cook chapatis and curry for their respective group. Can you imagine lighting an oil stove on a western train? Back then, there were no health and safety regulations on Indian trains and perhaps not even today. However, we were invited to participate and thoroughly enjoyed the friendly atmosphere.

Our small son Kyrie was very popular due to his very blonde hair. We discovered him toddling along the carriage with his new found Indian friends, carrying a chapati in each hand, much to the delight of everyone on board.

On one occasion he was lifted onto the knee of an Indian gentleman who proceeded to teach him the Indian art of spitting out of the carriage window. Something he did with great relish. Once again we learned to appreciate people from a diverse background to ours. The communal spirit was very heartwarming and once more we discovered that love has no borders.

We finally arrived at our destination where two towns, Raxaul and Birganj straddled the border between India and Nepal. We disembarked with the hope of finding a small plane to fly us the final leg of the trip into the ancient city of Kathmandu. Unfortunately the plane wasn't operating so we had no choice but to take the bus. The trip to Kathmandu was an exciting and frightening twelve hour ride as we drove over two mountain ranges and finally arrived at our destination.

Kathmandu was for us and for most travellers, an unmatched experience. It's a fusion of sights, sounds and smells, akin to India but with much more dust. The experience can make you stand with your mouth open in amazement and wonder. It reminded me of a medieval city, at least my perception of one. I felt like I had gone back in time to this ramshackle place of temples, street sellers and old rickshaws travelling along very narrow streets. I was captivated by the noise, the dust, the heat, the animals, and the smell. It was a distinct aroma of incense, dust and dung. The place was thoroughly intoxicating.

Nepal was designated as the end of the hippie trail which led all the way from Amsterdam across Western and Eastern Europe through Turkey into Afghanistan, Pakistan then India and at last to the Shangri-La of Nepal. Shangri-La is a fictitious place of course, first described by British author James Hilton, in his novel, 'Lost Horizon'.[70] It conjures up dreams of a mythical and mystical earthly paradise, a sacred place of refuge. To the hippie travellers, it was to be found in the mountainous Kingdom of Nepal, or so they thought.

Once again, many who made the long passage overland from Europe to Nepal ended up sick or in trouble with no real help available. Our ministry was very aware of this and established a house in Kathmandu (similar to the ones in New Delhi and

---

[70] Lost Horizon, James Hilton, Macmillan 1933, ISBN 1840243538.

Kabul) to reach out and care for these people. Most of the workers in the houses were former hippies themselves and knew only too well that this elusive Shangri-La was not to be found, but instead the outcome for many was sickness, diarrhoea, dysentery and other nasty diseases.

Many overdosed on badly cut drugs which were usually mixed with dangerous chemicals. They were the ones we looked for and found in the cheap doss (Guest) houses they ended up in. Those who responded to our invitation to stay at the house found a haven of rest and healing. Many fell in love with Jesus and to this day continue to serve Him both in the West as well as in other far-flung places around the world.

Sharing the wonderful, healing love of Jesus with hurting people has no equal. As I reflect on those days in India, Afghanistan and Nepal and the fruit of the radically changed lives we encountered, it still fills my heart with love and gratitude to Jesus who does all things well.

After some time in Kathmandu, it was time to say goodbye to Lynne and the Kathmandu 'Dilaram' House. It was time to head back 'home' to New Delhi. We endured another wild ride on the bus back over the same two mountain ranges down to the border. Only this time we had a guest driver. Our son Kyrie who was now two years old caught the attention of our Nepali driver and he invited him to sit beside him to blast the bus horn as we negotiated sharp bends in the road with a 400-foot sheer drop on every corner. Kyrie thought this was wonderful while his mum was petrified. After another twelve hours of this hair-raising and twisting turning journey, we finally made it to the border and caught our train back to the relative civilisation of New Delhi.

Destiny unfolds. Summer in Mussoorie, India.

Mussoorie is situated in the foothills of the Himalayas and is known as 'the Queen of the Hills'. It is about 1,880 metres . 6,170ft), above sea level. There are commanding snow ranges to the northeast of the town and with it's green hills and varied flowers, plants and animal life, it is a fascinating mountain resort.

It was established as a British hill station by Lt. Frederick Young of the East India Company during the days of British occupation, where, later, the families of British soldiers as well as civil servants established themselves to get away from the summer heat.

During the British Raj, signs on the Mall expressly stated: "*Indians and Dogs Not Allowed*". Racist signs of this type were commonplace in hill stations, which were founded 'by and for' the British. Motilal Nehru, the father of Jawaharlal Nehru,(the first independent prime Minister of India), deliberately broke this rule every day whenever he was in Mussoorie and would pay the fine. The Nehru family, including Nehru's daughter Indira (later to become Prime Minister, Indira Gandhi) were frequent visitors to Mussoorie from the 1920s to the 1940s, and stayed at the Savoy Hotel.[71]

Mussoorie was once said to present a 'fairyland' atmosphere to tourists. In our day, even though it appeared a bit run down, it was nevertheless a good place to get away from the searing summer heat of the plains.

Long-term missionary families would spend time here in the summer and it was here that we had another divine encounter in meeting up with Geoff and Pauline Williams. We didn't know it at the time but a couple of years later our paths would cross once again in England, in the great planning of God who sets things up way ahead of time, as He knows the end from the beginning. Little did we realise that our summer escape from the Delhi heat would lead to a major destiny relocation in our lives a few years down the road.

In Genesis, another God orchestrated, divine encounter occurred when Abraham told his servant to go and find a wife from his kinfolk for his son Isaac. It was not an easy task and one that his servant was concerned about with regard to the

---

[71] https://en.wikipedia.org/wiki/Mussoorie accessed 7/2/19

success of his venture. The servant, however, went in obedience and arrived at the city of Nahor where he stopped by a well to water his camels. He prayed and asked God for guidance. No sooner had he done so, the answer to his prayers came in the form of Rebekah, who was standing at the well.

Overcome with gratitude to God, the servant began to pray saying, *"As for me going on in the way(of obedience and faith) the Lord led me to the house of my master's kinsmen".*[72]

Sometimes just getting on with our lives within the general will of God can produce some amazing God encounters. We don't always realise, but God has been behind the scenes, bringing things together for His plans in our lives. God will always lead us in His purposes, sometimes clearly and sometimes with only minimal understanding. He was certainly setting up some wonderful, 'accidental' encounters for us as we discovered within a couple of years.

---

[72] Genesis 24:27, AMP.

Chapter 6. Culture Shock in Reverse.

*The restless heart will never be completely at home in one place.
It's what happens when one has lived and breathed in other lands; but it's worth it.*

We're going home.

We had been ministering in India for over a year and enjoying it immensely, however our daughter Zara had just turned five years old and was ready to start school. Linda began to feel it was time to return to the UK for this purpose. I was not keen on the idea as I loved living and working in India, being fulfilled in helping travellers get back on track. The lifestyle was also relaxed and I felt a great sense of freedom there. The weather was also bearably hot most of the year which I loved. The thought of going back to cold, damp England did not fill me with any great joy.

In the land of smiles.

In the midst of this dilemma, I had to fly to Thailand. It is often called the, 'Land of Smiles', not only because visitors love its natural beauty and historical riches, but also because of the country's friendly people and fascinating culture.

I went to help retrieve the Thai wife of a hippie who was staying with us and had just been delivered from demons before giving his life to Christ. Once he 'normalised', he told us about the wife he had abandoned in Thailand. Whilst in Bangkok waiting for a visa for this lady, I had more time to pray regarding Linda's suggestion about returning to the UK. I complained to God about my situation and told Him that I didn't have any leading to return to England. Quite quickly I had the impression that the problem was that I was not listening! Humbly I submitted my will to His and immediately began to know, albeit reluctantly, that it was the right decision to go home to England.

In the meantime, Dao, the Thai wife of our demon-delivered hippie, returned to New Delhi with us to become part of our community. She didn't speak much English and we wondered how we would communicate the good news of Jesus to her. We shouldn't have been concerned. One night in her room she had a divine encounter with Jesus. She later told us Jesus appeared to her and in her words He said, *"Dao bad bad, but Jesus good good, He make Dao good"*. It sounds simplistic but that encounter changed her life forever, she was a transformed person. Years later I met her in England and she was still following Jesus.

Out of the mouth of babes.

Once the decision had been made to return to England we all began to pray about the details. Of course, we had travelled to India on one-way tickets so now we needed four tickets to get home. We had considered travelling overland as it was cheaper but Zara shared with us that she believed we should fly, so we began to pray about that. It wasn't long until someone in our community approached us and surprised us by saying they wanted to cover our airfares back home. Zara was right! We were once again totally blown away by God's faithfulness through His people, and before long it was time to say goodbye and head back to the West, not knowing how we would fare but trusting that God would open doors for us. My heart was heavy as we flew away from our 'Far Pavilions', but I didn't know then that God would bring me back again.

Re-entry.

Upon arrival at Heathrow airport, London, and in transit to fly on to Northern Ireland we had a humorous experience as we moved through the large terminal. We had brought Kyrie's three wheeled, plastic tricycle with us, one of the toys he enjoyed riding on back at the Delhi house. He saw it on the baggage carousel and quickly pulled it off and began to ride it looking cute in his Indian clothes and sandals. Many passers-by smiled and spoke to him as he trundled through Heathrow.

As we got to our new departure lounge, we discovered that one of his sandals had broken and fallen off his foot. He now looked like a beggar boy from the slums of Delhi, but he was blissfully unaware and kept cycling much to the amusement of passers-by. We thought it was funny as well although I knew my mother would not be impressed when she saw her small grandson looking like a pauper upon arrival at Belfast International airport.

We arrived in Northern Ireland at the end of May so the weather was getting warmer but I felt as if I had arrived in the winter. It was so cold after the heat of India. It took me a while to adjust to the cooler temperature but more than that I struggled to adjust to life back in Northern Ireland. My parents welcomed us warmly (apart from the sandal incident) and looked after us wonderfully but I struggled with a sense of displacement. I hadn't lived in Ireland for a few years and adjusting was difficult, even though all of the folk we met were friendly.

Our time there went by quickly, and after a month it was time to say goodbye and fly over to the Northeast of England and stay with Linda's Mum. The welcome was great from her also but all the time I was wondering what had happened to my life. I thought I had come to a dead end with nothing to look forward to after the last five years of community life in one form or another, and India being the highlight for me. Adjusting was hard; I felt like a rocket on re-entry to the earth's atmosphere and I was burning up and exploding. It was culture shock in reverse. We had lots of memories, wonderful experiences, and life-changing encounters and I had started to enjoy some freedom within myself. Since returning back in the UK, I started to feel like it was all over.

The Amber glow.

After a month of enjoying Linda's Mum's hospitality, we moved south to stay with my friend Reg and his wife, who had relocated and recently rented a church manse near the city of Leicester.

Another very important reason for returning to England was that Linda was pregnant with our third child. During our time at the Manse, our second daughter was born. Her name was given to her after Linda read, Ezekiel.1:27 in the KJV version of the Bible. The passage talks about the amber glow surrounding the Lord.

As Amber has grown up, she has carried that glowing radiance in her life. Amber filled our lives with fresh joy and for me, her arrival helped brush aside my UK re-entry blues.

Finding a home.

After Amber's birth, we realised we needed a house of our own but we didn't qualify for council housing and there didn't seem to be any private housing available. We had learned some valuable lessons about seeking God for everything, so we took the matter to Him in prayer. A lady from church discovered this small terraced house that was empty nearby and enquired about it on our behalf. She discovered that the owners were not keen to rent out the property even though it had been empty for a long time. We kept praying and one morning as I prayed I just knew in my heart that the house was ours. Later that week we heard that the owners were prepared to let us rent the house. Faith lessons we had learned abroad were still working, and God moved another small mountain in our lives.

We moved in and with the help of our friends, we got some beds, couches and various pieces of furniture to make the house a home. There was no heating apart from a coal fire, and the place needed redecorating throughout, but we were thrilled to have our own home at last.

New wine, old wine!

We got involved in the life of the Baptist church, which was next door to the Manse we had been living in with Reg. We didn't have much understanding of traditional church apart from the early upbringing we both had with Sunday school and the Anglican church, but we were enthusiastic.

However, it was hard to adjust to a traditional service with an older congregation. There were a few younger people attending who were trying to bring something contemporary to the church, but it wasn't easy. Eventually we began to see renewal, but it was met with resistance from the older, more traditional members.

They felt overwhelmed by the fresh influx of new, younger people. We threatened their established values and we felt stifled by their traditionalism. Looking back, perhaps, more wisdom and grace may have helped on both sides, but as I have discovered, it's easy to have 20/20 vision after the event.

On one occasion during a small mid-week church gathering, Linda shared how, during our time in India, we had trusted God for all our needs. She was met with comments such as, "*it is selfish to pray for yourself*" and "*prayer is only for others*". Linda asked, "*what would you do if you had no money?*". The reply was,"*we would sell something*". Linda told them that we had nothing to sell, but there was no response to this. It was quite a negative experience which affected Linda a lot. It left us wondering how God felt about us praying in this way. Our faith had taken a blow, but we continued with the church.

Faith, lost and found.

A couple of years later, I had been made redundant from my job. It was Christmas time and we were still hoping to give our three children a special Christmas, but with little money we thought it was going to be difficult. Our faith to ask God was still lacking from the knock we had taken about trusting Him in prayer. We asked our children what they would like for Christmas. Our two eldest asked for bicycles and our youngest asked for roller skates. We couldn't afford new bicycles, so we considered buying second hand ones. We thought we could afford the skates and proceeded to buy a pair of cheap plastic ones.

During that time, Linda and I had just read Yonggi Cho's book The Fourth Dimension.[73] We were inspired to articulate the faith emphasis Cho taught. After the previously mentioned negativity we had encountered about trusting God, Cho's story ignited our hearts once again to reach out in faith.

We decided to believe God for new bikes rather than second hand ones. In order to identify specifically the kind of bikes our two eldest children desired, we took them to a bicycle shop where they chose the type and colour bicycles that they wanted. Once we had a clear vision of the bikes, we returned home with a clear objective of what to believe for.

Very soon an anonymous financial gift was sent to us, and it was enough to buy the desired bicycles. Beyond that we were delightfully surprised a day or so later when our friend John Cass, who worked in a haulage company, came to visit. A truck driver at John's depot had unloaded a box which he didn't want to take back to Europe. Inside were three pairs of top quality metal roller skates. John had two daughters who each took a pair, but the third pair he offered to us. They were superior to the cheap plastic ones we had bought, and we gratefully accepted them for our daughter. We were delighted that God had given us exceedingly abundantly more than we could ask or even believe for.[74]

We learned a very valuable faith lesson through all of this. Always build an altar of remembrance in your heart of what God has done for you. Abraham built altars to remind himself of God's faithfulness.[75] Don't allow unbelieving words to move you from those faith lessons in your life.

---

[73] The Fourth Dimension, David Yonngi Cho, Logos International. 1979. ISBN0-88270-380-3

[74] Ephesians 3:20. NKJV

[75] Genesis 12:1-7; 8-13; ch. 13:14-18; ch. 22:9-14.

Over time, it became more and more difficult for us to be involved within the confines of a traditional church structure. We had very different views on almost everything about church life. Along with quite a few of the newer members, we tried to resolve our differences, but it wasn't working.

God gave me a Church to train me.

After a series of fruitless 'Church membership meetings', a number of us decided the best course of action was to resign our membership. It didn't take long before a new house church fellowship was formed. I eventually took on the leadership of this group and we flourished into a young family church.

During that time, I had found a job working for a Christian book company and had to attend the Christian Booksellers Convention which was held in Blackpool, a seaside town in the north west of England. As I stood in the aisle of the book stalls one day, lo and behold I saw Geoff Williams walking towards me. The last time I had seen him was when we were staying in Mussoorie, India, but we had lost touch. Now we were laughing and rejoicing at our reunion. Geoff and his family had returned to the UK shortly after we had met them, having spent sixteen years in India as missionaries with 'Christian Literature Crusade' (CLC). They were now living in Sheffield, South Yorkshire and helping to lead a large, charismatic house church.

I told him of our venture with the new Christian fellowship and he offered to introduce me to Peter Fenwick, the senior leader of Sheffield House Church, as he rightly believed that Peter would be able to help us in our new adventure of leading a church.

I didn't understand it all then, but looking back to our short holiday away from the heat of New Delhi up in Mussoorie, the previous year, I can see that the hand of God was directing our steps in his unique way to orchestrate an encounter with Geoff and Pauline. It all dovetailed so that we could be introduced to Peter who would become my friend and spiritual father.

We spent five years establishing the fellowship under Peter's watchful, overseeing eye. I was very inexperienced and all the nagging hang ups and drivenness still haunted me. I needed Peter's help and he was always there when I needed him. If I had a problem I could always get to see him no matter how busy he was. He always made time for me. We'd talk about the issue and no matter the outcome, I always left feeling inspired and loved. His input was always healing to me. He had a wonderful shepherd's heart coupled with profound wisdom.

Better caught than taught.

I had grown up spiritually in an environment which was open to the things of the Holy Spirit, albeit somewhat cautiously. This was possibly due to my leaders having had a negative experience in their Pentecostal background. I did exercise some gifts of the Spirit[76] in a measure but apart from that, I had not really encountered the Holy Spirit in a powerful way. That was about to change dramatically.

Everything changed in 1985 when I went to a day conference in Nuneaton, UK, entitled: 'Living in the Supernatural'. Ken McGreavy was the keynote speaker. He was a quietly spoken Yorkshireman with an outstanding teaching, healing and prophetic ministry. During an interval, I was introduced to him by my friend Dave. Ken then prayed for me very powerfully. Later in the day, Ken approached me and said that he believed God had spoken to him about visiting me in Leicester. He told me that only once before, in his fourteen years of ministry, God had directed him that way. I was so surprised and grateful for this opportunity and eagerly agreed to meet him.

In due course, he came to our small house in Leicestershire and spent time ministering to Linda and myself. During that time, I encountered the Holy Spirit in the most powerful way ever. As Ken gently prayed, I began to feel physical waves rippling over my abdomen, over and over with increasing intensity and along with that a strange pulling on my face especially, around my

---

[76] 1. Corinthians 12:1-11, & 14: 1-5

mouth as if I was impersonating a fish face! This continued for quite some time and then began to subside. Linda also experienced the Spirit's touch but in a more gentle manner.

Ken then explained how the Holy Spirit was ministering to me. He told me that the abdominal rippling sensation was indicative of the Spirit bringing some inner healing to me. He also pointed out that the strange fish face manifestations on my mouth were a sign of the prophetic anointing that was coming on me for ministry.

I had no grid for the experience, as it was way before 'The Toronto Blessing'[77] manifestations happened. Some things are better caught than taught, however, the understanding came later. I was invigorated and energised as he quietly prayed over me. The anointing was powerful and set in place the calling on my life to preach and exercise a prophetic ministry with words of knowledge. This continued and increased over the years, as Ken befriended me and invited me to travel with him to a number of nations to learn and experience how to minister. Because Ken's life was so full of integrity, and he was relaxed and without hype, we knew for certain this was a God moment and to be taken very seriously. From that time, I have ministered significantly in this anointing. Back then I still had so much to learn, but God already had that learning curve in place.

From that point on, Ken and I along with Linda and Ken's wife Hazel, grew in friendship. As Ken and I travelled together, he would usually teach a session then later he would debrief with me, helping me understand how the Holy Spirit moved in the meeting. I thoroughly enjoyed these times with Ken and looked forward to them immensely.

Sometime later and, after a number of trips together we were ministering at a church in the northwest of England. At the end of this teaching session, Ken said, *"We are going to have a time of ministry now and I will bring the first word of knowledge and Barry will bring the second"*. I suddenly felt terror begin to grip

---

[77]The Toronto Blessing, describes the Christian revival and associated phenomena that began in January 1994 at the Toronto Airport Vineyard church,(Catch the Fire) Canada. Chapter 7. See under, Toronto Comes to Town.

me. It had been fine observing Ken for the last couple of years or so, but now suddenly it had all changed. He hadn't warned me and now I had to do something, I was no longer just an observer.

However, I had been exposed to this ministry for some time now and Ken obviously felt I was ready to get out of the boat. After he ministered, I hesitantly began to share a word that was forming in my thinking. As I shared, more revelation came, and to my joyous amazement, someone responded to my word and received ministry. It was such a wonderful moment. This was my first experience of really *"doing the stuff"* as John Wimber put it.

Ken had patiently taught me over a period of time, and now he launched me into the deep. No words can describe how elated I was that God had actually worked through me, but it was only the first of many occasions when God would do that.

From those early days, Ken became a very close friend in life and my mentor in ministry. His ongoing input and impartation of the Holy Spirit and gifts to me laid the foundation of how I minister today. I am eternally grateful to God for choosing such an anointed, Godly, and humble man to be my mentor.

Sadly, he went to be with Jesus quite suddenly one morning in December 2010, and four months later my wise spiritual father, Peter Fenwick also went to heaven. Within a few months I lost the two men who had watched over me. It was a difficult time in my life but the foundations had been laid by both of them for which I am so thankful. I think of them nearly every day and carry them in my heart with great affection and gratitude for all they did to prepare me for my calling. I still, however, had some deep and painful lessons to learn. The 'Simon Peter' inside me would have to experience some breaking in order for His grace to truly shine through.

The valuable lessons from Peter and Ken about ministry and leading a church helped me enormously, as I stumbled through my baptism into church leadership. I still had so much to learn, and it was very hard at times. I made many mistakes and failed hugely in many ways, but God kept working in me. There was a lot of unhealed junk inside me from my upbringing that needed the touch of God.

With Peter's and Ken's wise counsel and oversight, the church flourished. I realised later on that God had given me a church, not so much for me to lead as for me to learn. The people were by and large gracious and forgiving of my many mistakes, and even in spite of me, the Church grew. I was zealous, driven by insecurity, and lacking in grace, keen to take the next mountain to prove something to myself but I often forgot that others were needing a more pastoral approach, and not a zealot. I wish I had the wisdom back then I have learned to some extent over the years, but I think that may be true for many of us in life. The good news I have discovered is that God never gives up on us; He has invested too much in us to do that. Don't lose heart, there is more.

Elastic walls.

We had been working with the church in Leicestershire for five years. It was growing and doing well. We still rented our little 'two up two down' terraced house in the area, but desperately needed somewhere larger for our growing family. Linda and I had one bedroom and our three children all shared the other bedroom. We were squashed, but as Linda always said, *"a house filled with love has elastic walls"*.

On one occasion a young teenage girl had been kicked out of her home and came to us looking for help. Even in our tiny house Linda found room to house her on the upstairs landing. That's when our 'elastic house' really got stretched. We knew we needed somewhere bigger, but the problem was that we had no money to put down a deposit to buy our own place. I'd given away all of our savings to support the ministry we were involved with while in Holland. We prayed and looked for a larger house to rent, but found little success.

Unknown to us, folk in the church started a savings account to help us get a deposit on a house. After some time they came to us and presented us with the savings account which had quite a large amount of money in it, £6,000 to be precise. At that time, it was more than enough for us to put down a deposit on our very first 'bought' home. We were completely overwhelmed at the generosity of our church. Very quickly we began house hunting. We looked and looked, and made offers on a couple of houses but they all fell through. We didn't know what to do, but God did!

Chapter 7. Called to God's Own Country.

Doesn't tha know I'm from God's Own Country?
Stop Gawpin' n' faffin' when I 'appen t'say a word
not t'taste of thissen.[78]

Which more or less means....

Don't you know I am from God's own country?
Stop staring and messing about when I happen to say a word, that's not to your taste.

God's agenda.

After much fruitless searching, we finally prayed and asked God what was going on. We then began to realise God was speaking to us about moving. I had been speaking to one of Peter Fenwick's leaders on the phone, and, while sharing my frustrations about not being able to secure a property, he casually said, *"Why don't you come to Sheffield and help with the church here"*. Eventually after dismissing the question I realised it was a serious proposition and we needed to follow it through.

After much prayer and many conversations with Peter, and the other leaders of Sheffield House Church, along with confirming prophetic words, we realised God was moving us. No wonder we couldn't find a house in Leicestershire! We eventually shared this with our church and they agreed it was God's will. They had given so sacrificially for us to buy a house and now we would be leaving, but they saw the hand of God in it all and, blessed us by confirming our sense of direction. So we began to look for a house in Sheffield and prepared ourselves for the next step in our adventure.

---

[78] God's Own Country. Sophie Chekruga. Posted in Lifestyle Articles, My Poetry.

Sheffield steel.

Within the borders of the historic county of Yorkshire are areas which are considered to be amongst the greenest in England. There are vast stretches of unspoilt countryside in the Yorkshire Dales and North York Moors. No wonder Yorkshire folk call it God's own country.

Sheffield, situated in South Yorkshire, is the largest city in the county of Yorkshire and the fourth largest in England. It is allegedly the greenest city in Europe which surprises many people. Historically it was well known as a great steel-making city and was therefore expected to be filled with dust and grime. It was almost destroyed by Nazi bombs during the Second World War because of the many steel factories producing armaments for the war effort.

The steel industry remains today, but not like it was during the early twentieth century. The city has been largely regenerated into a modern attractive place. Along with the existing steel industry, Sheffield cutlery has a worldwide reputation. This city, built on seven hills, was to be our new home.

We began checking out a number of properties in Sheffield and finally found one with four bedrooms, one for each of the kids as well as one for Linda and myself. What luxury! But just when we thought the deal was done, our agent called to say someone else had put in a higher offer. I was very disappointed as I believed that this house had been earmarked for us by God.

As I mentioned in a previous chapter, later that day I visited the Christian book shop in Sheffield and as I browsed absentmindedly, I came across a poster on a wall in the basement which struck me right between the eyes. It was that last line of Corrie Ten Boom's poem which she had used in YFC Haarlem some years previously, *"He [God] gives the very best to those who leave the choice with him".*[79] I knew in my heart God was speaking, telling me to relax as He had it all under

---

[79] Chapter 3. See under, Life is but a Weaving, The Tapestry Poem.

control. The next day my agent rang again and told me the higher offer had fallen through and the house was definitely ours. A short time later, we moved into our house and began our new adventure in Sheffield. God indeed does *"give His very best to those who leave the choice with Him"*. God was certainly weaving some good things for us in the tapestry of our lives.

Rebuilding what has been broken.

Before I arrived in Sheffield, God had given me two verses as I was praying about the move. One was from Judges ch.5:2. *"when the leaders took the lead in Israel, the people offered themselves willingly"*. The second verse was also from Judges, ch.21:25. *"In those days there was no leader, everyone did what was right in his own eyes"*. Once I arrived I understood the importance of the verses.

I soon discovered my new church venture was more difficult than I had originally thought. The church was going through difficulties with division in the camp. One of the reasons I had been invited to come to this particular congregation, one of the six that made up Sheffield House Church, was because the very gracious leader of the congregation had become ill and was finding it more difficult to lead the church. Sadly, because of this, some schisms emerged in the church with divisive voices which gave rise to a negative atmosphere. I quickly realised the importance of the two verses God had shown me.

When God is building, you can be sure the enemy is retaliating. His attacks are subtle, sly, and seductive.[80] Sometimes though, Satan sets up a siege attack which goes on for a long time and is particularly debilitating. However he attacks, his objective is always to wear down the church and it's leaders.[81] We need to be very aware of his designs to destroy what God is building. We are not called to fight people, we are called to fight the devil who is the destroyer of all that is good. Sadly however, sometimes people get caught up in the middle of the warfare.

---

[80] Genesis 3:1.RSV.

[81] Daniel 7:25.

I remember a few years prior to this, I heard Bryn Jones, an established apostolic leader in England say that one of his early church plants grew to twenty before growing to twelve! We all laughed at the time but there was an important truth in the tale.

His point became a very present reality to me in those early days, when some folk left as I refocused the church and sought to restore fresh direction. I took seriously the two verses God had given to instruct me to take a clear step of directing the church into the new, and as I did, the church would respond positively. It took some time but eventually we began to move forward with fresh expectation and joy. It was busy and exciting but at the same time demanding. We began to grow again with lots of students attending, adding an enthusiastic dynamic to the church. Eventually due to growth in numbers, three services were needed on a Sunday. It was a stretching time for many of us.

God's healing presence.

We began to see wonderful things happen in our midst. I only heard recently about one lady who visited the church in my early days there. She had skin cancer. I spoke to her a short time ago and she told me she had been healed of the condition after a time of prayer at the church.

Another marvellous healing happened to Richard, who was a regular member of the church. He had fallen off a ladder while working and not only broke his ankle but also separated his heel from the bottom of his foot. He went to hospital and had it fixed and set in a plaster cast. He was told it would be months before he could walk on it again. He came for prayer the following Sunday and was touched mightily by God. The next week he went back to the hospital and told them to take the cast off as he had been healed. They were skeptical but to their amazement when the cast came off his ankle was perfect and his heel was realigned to his ankle again. However, not all of the healing stories had an ending we hoped for.

Limping junkie.

One Sunday at the end of our meeting, someone brought a young man to me for prayer. He was limping badly. It turned out he was a heroin addict and had inadvertently injected heroin into an artery in his leg instead of a vein. This was the cause of his limp. His leg had become badly infected and his doctor told him he would probably lose it. I talked to him for a few minutes then prayed for his leg to be healed. Off he went and I thought no more about it.

During our mid-week service, he turned up and wasn't limping. Of course I was very curious to find out what had happened. He told me he went to see his doctor the following morning after being prayed for. As he walked into the office, the doctor exclaimed *"you aren't limping"*. He looked down and to his own amazement he realised that he had been completely healed. After celebrating with him privately over his healing, I asked him if he would share a testimony of this healing with the church. Well, he certainly did. He started talking about his damaged leg and how I'd prayed for him. Then suddenly he exclaimed *"Now I am f***ing healed."* I didn't know whether to laugh, cry or just disappear. Fortunately, my congregation were smart enough to appreciate his lack of protocol at church and just rejoiced with him.

What a wonderful story! But the sad part was he never gave his life to Christ. There was, however, a positive twist to the tale. When his mother found out what had happened, she came to church and became a follower of Jesus. So we rejoiced over his healing and his mother's conversion, but we were saddened by his lack of response to the amazing grace of God in his life. Still we reminded ourselves that we were in good company, as, the same thing also happened to Jesus at times.

The church continued to grow and it was exhilarating, but I was beginning to feel the effects of an increasing and unending demand on my time. I am sure you have seen the plate spinning trick before. The entertainer starts spinning one plate on top of a long stick. He keeps increasing the amount of plates on sticks he is spinning till he is running back and forth like a sprinter to keep all the plates in the air. I also began to feel like I was spinning plates but there seemed to be no end to the number of plates that I was running after.

It was as if I was a performer on stage, constantly needing to keep things going and if I didn't, I had this underlying thought that God wouldn't be pleased with me and things would fall apart. It was just under the surface, but lying there waiting to pounce.

I discovered some years later that during my early Christian days, I had inadvertently absorbed a performance-based walk with God. If I kept all the 'spiritual (legalistic) rules' God would be pleased but if I didn't then God would be unhappy with me. Looking back, I know now that my understanding of grace was lacking, hence my drivenness and performance-based approach. It was also touching on my insecurities from my younger years. It was like a time bomb waiting to blow up, but that was later. In the meantime, something else happened which would shake the church worldwide.

Toronto comes to town.

The first we knew of it was when someone who was a church member went over to experience this phenomena which was happening at the Airport Christian Fellowship in Toronto, Canada. Very quickly it spread like fire into my church. I didn't know what to think at first, even though I had had a similar experience from that very first power encounter years earlier in our living room as Ken McGreavy prayed for us and again when he prayed for me the year before we became aware of the Toronto blessing.[82] Looking back, it was about the same time in 1994 as the Toronto outpouring began that I had received my second power encounter via Ken.

However, I wasn't prepared for it to overtake the church. Linda and I decided we needed to go to Toronto to find out for ourselves about this 'thing' that was happening. We spent a

---

[82] Chapter 6. See under, Better caught than taught.

week there and had powerful encounters with the Holy Spirit and returned convinced this was from God. We began weekly meetings having our own 'Toronto blessing' meetings.

Our Sunday night meetings were packed every week. At first it was an amazing and powerful time of manifest blessing, but after some time, instead of it being a blessing it became more of a battle for me as I tried to pastor the extreme manifestations and mixed responses to the 'blessing'.

I was burning out and stressing out with it all. There were genuine times of the Holy Spirit's anointing and manifestation but there were also times of fleshly and even demonic manifestation. It was such a demanding time, trying to lead the church in the midst of all this 'upheaval'. Some loved it, some were distressed by it, some joined and others left because of it. Nevertheless, the church attracted more and more visitors every week. Some became part of the church but others just came for the experience.

After two years of this I finally decided it was time to stop. There were too many plates spinning and I had run out of steam. With hindsight there could have been a better way to handle things but I had never been involved in anything like that before and I was unprepared, wrung out and needed a break. There were negative as well as positive reactions to that decision, but we brought things to a close and sought to keep moving forward. I didn't take time to recover from that period and continued leading, but with a weariness in my heart and a lack of enthusiasm for the way ahead.

How the mighty have fallen.

Back in the 60s, Jackson Browne wrote and sang a song entitled 'Running on Empty'. It highlighted his own life trying to keep up with all that was happening, the road was his but somehow it turned and he found himself trying to keep his love alive but he was way behind and running on empty, running blind. It sounded just like me; I was overstretched, worn out, carrying my own love deficit, running blind and running on empty.

When I took over the church in Sheffield, I worked hard cleaning up some of the underlying problems. After some time, I saw the church begin to flourish and grow significantly. It was well respected in the city with a thriving, young congregation and multiple services. With all the positive press I was receiving I am sure I became impressed with my own ability in leadership though I didn't recognise that at the time. However, underneath it all I was overly busy, worn out, increasingly isolated and stressed most of the time, trying to keep all the spiritual and practical plates spinning.

My underlying insecurities, low self-image and poverty spirit took advantage of my weariness, and started gnawing away at me again, driving me to an unrealised, self-destruct strategy. Those lurking 'demons' reared their ugly heads easily when the pressure cooker of my life hit overload point. It was almost inevitable that I'd blow up somewhere along the way.

Some time after those very demanding and stressful years trying to steer through 'the Toronto Blessing', it finally culminated in my total crash and burn. I won't go into the detail of my descent into the abyss of failure and despair, but my time leading the church came to an end. It was a devastating time. The weariness, depression, and desolation I felt was immense. I was broken in every way.

Failure was not a word I had allowed into my thinking for years, ever since my traumatic experiences as a boy. I had pushed those thoughts and feelings way down but I was not able to get rid of them. *"Pride comes before a fall"* was a phrase my mother had taught me as I grew up. I had striven to be successful but the foundations had become faulty; I got sidetracked chasing the god of success, which was fuelled by my performance mentality. That was not the same as my call from God.

Now I was living that failure in reality, as I retreated into a world of darkness, depression and fear. A sense of rejection, and both natural and spiritual negative voices were clamouring to drive me further down into despair and defeat. I had become a victim of my own success, like an insecure actor I believed my own publicity and then came the premature curtain drop. It had become impossible for me to continue as leader of the church.

In the devastation of my depressed state, I told myself there was no way out. There was no hope anymore; I was finished. Like Samson of old, my hair had been shorn and my eyes gouged out. Not literally of course, but in my heart I felt the same humiliation which I assume Second World war enemy collaborators must have felt when they were exposed and put on public display with their hair shorn. I had collaborated, compromised even with my own enemy, the god of success and he had won. I felt as Samson must have felt, empty, bereft of my anointing and blind concerning the vision of God in my heart. I gave up hope of ever serving God again.

For a long time it was nearly impossible to have any positive thoughts. 'BUT GOD'.... Have you ever noticed those two words in scripture? Joseph's brothers sold him into slavery *"BUT GOD was with him"*.[83] Epaphroditus *"was ill, near to death, BUT GOD had mercy on him"*.[84] Asaph cried out *"my flesh and my heart may fail BUT GOD is the strength of my heart"*.[85]

No matter how low you may have gone, God will come find you and bring you out again into His sunlight. People may drop you, reject you, and forget you, but God never will. He is the God of reconciliation and restoration; the God of many chances and new beginnings. I was about to discover that God is the restorer of the unrestorable.

"God, your God, will restore everything you lost; He'll have compassion on you; He'll come back and pick up the pieces from all the places where you were scattered. No matter how far away you end up, God, your God, will get you out of there and bring you back to the land your ancestors once possessed. It

---

[83] Acts 7:9.

[84] Philippians 2:27.

[85] Psalm 73:26.

will be yours again. He will give you a good life and make you more numerous than your ancestors".[86]

I was going to discover that He would restore everything. He would put the broken pieces of my life back together again. There was a light shining in my darkness.

It was and is the light of the everlasting love of God, displayed in Jesus for people like me who have gone over the edge. I was about to discover, that when we turn to Him, He is always there.

---

[86] Deuteronomy 31:3-5, MSG.

Part III. Light Shines in the Darkness.

Chapter 8. The End is Just the Beginning.

*Ye fearful saints, fresh courage take,
The clouds ye so much dread
Are big with mercy, and shall break
In blessings on your head.*[87]

The darkest hour is just before the dawn.

I lived in a dark, hidden world for some time fearing the outside world. We only went out at night to the supermarket, as condemnation, depression, paranoia filled my being. I couldn't face seeing people I knew. I still had friends who visited me but some stepped back from me. It was painful in many ways. The anti-depression tablets my doctor had prescribed were of no help to me. To add to my wretched state, we were also in very real practical difficulties, as my income had stopped. Within a couple of months we had run out of money and there were still bills to pay. My greatest fear was that we were going to lose our home if we couldn't keep up the mortgage payments.

One day, a friend from the church visited and asked how we were doing. In the ensuing conversation she enquired about our financial plight. She returned the next day with a large cheque to cover our needs for some time. She was an angel in disguise. Other friends continued to call in every day to encourage and try to lift me out of my depression. Those faithful friends kept my

---

[87] http://www.public-domain-poetry.com/william-cowper/light-shining-out-of-darkness-13298 Accessed 23/4/19

head above water, but I still couldn't see the way forward. Most of the time everything was just dark and hopeless. I needed a job but didn't think I had much chance of getting anything because I felt so unworthy and useless.

Linda was my rock during those dark days. She loved me, encouraged me, challenged me when I needed it. Together with our children, she stood with me through the darkness and never gave up on me. Thank God for a strong, Godly woman, and I do every day!

His light shines in my darkness.

When things appeared to be at rock bottom, God came through in a wonderful and very unexpected way. It's amazing to me how He weaves things into our lives, often years prior to their apparent relevance. Slowly my dawn was beginning to appear.

Some years earlier, a student had turned up at my church. He had been going through some personal issues at his own local church. I offered him some help and told him he was welcome to come along with no strings attached. He came for a season, received some input from a church pastoral leader and when he was doing better returned to his own church.

I had forgotten about him but when he heard of my difficult circumstances he called in to see me. He worked as a Director in his family's business now, and they had a job vacancy which he offered to me. It was a blessing as it got me out of the house, but I had to overcome my depressed state and knuckle down to a routine that was completely out of my experience. I worked hard but every day was difficult for me. My bosses were very patient and understanding, and gave me room to get used to my new environment. The job kept me busy and distracted me from my depression most of the time.

The discipline of getting up and going to work, and doing something very unfamiliar, was in a strange way an aide to my recovery. Too much inner speculation only leads to more self-condemnation, a never-ending spiral always ending up with the same destructive conclusion. A self-loathing, which paralyses and neutralises completely.

Even though the job offered some good practical therapy, I wasn't earning enough money to be able to pay the mortgage on our new home. Reluctantly we decided to put it up for sale. That was a big blow to me as it was my dream house and now it was going to have to go.

Once again God showed up to rescue me. After a number of months in my new found employment, I heard there was a vacancy being advertised for a sales representative with Kingsway Communications, a prestigious UK Christian book company. I had prior experience working in the Christian sales industry and I was keen to apply. Peter, my spiritual father was Chairman of Kingsway at the time, as well as maintaining his position as a church pastor. He told me of the vacancy and encouraged me to apply. I prepared a rather hurried resume[88] and sent it off with my application, having a sense in my heart that this was a job from God for me. However, to my dismay I received a letter some time later stating that my application was unsuccessful. I was devastated and retreated back into my depressed hole. I was somewhat confused and greatly disheartened as I had started to believe again that God was opening this door for me.

A few weeks later I received another letter from the company stating that the interviews for the sales position had been unsuccessful and they were interviewing again. If I wished, I could re-apply. I spoke to a business friend who helped me rewrite my resume in a more professional way and sent it in.

To cut a long story short, I was interviewed and was offered the position. I was elated and began to feel encouragement rise in my heart again. I got busy straight away, travelling up and down the country to represent Kingsway selling books and music. I began to feel alive again, as I was back in an environment where I was dealing with the Christian community.

---

[88] Statement of employment history.

God handles Real Estate.

There was still one problem. Someone had offered the asking price for our house before I got my new job, and we reluctantly agreed to the sale. I gave my word to the buyer that I would not go back on my agreement to sell the house to him, but he had to wait until we found another house to buy. Now I had this new job and our income was sufficient to remain in the house, I did not want go through with the sale. But I had given my word, and I could not go back on it. Legally it meant nothing but in my heart I knew I could not change my decision.

One weekend we had a storm and the sold sign outside our house fell down. I had been praying for God to do something about the house sale and as I looked at the fallen 'board' I called out to Linda that the board had fallen down and it was a sign from God. She laughed and said, *"Yes it's a sign alright, a sold sign"*. I laughed as well, but I held on to the impression that God was doing something on our behalf.

A couple of weeks later while on the road working, I received a call from Linda to tell me our house sales agent had called to tell us that the couple who had bought our house had pulled out of the sale. The house was ours again. I was ecstatic and began singing praise to God in the car as I drove down the motorway. Other drivers must have thought I was crazy, but I didn't care. God had shown up for us miraculously once again just as He had with our previous home. He's very good at negotiating real estate! I realised He had not walked away from me and was still looking after me even though I had failed Him. What an amazing lesson I had just learned.

When your Brook dries up.

I continued to enjoy working with Kingsway for three years, until they went through a difficult financial time and had to make redundancies. I was laid off and was confused by the loss of the job God had so clearly given to me. I got on my knees and questioned why God had set this job up for me if He knew this would happen? As I murmured in my heart I was distinctly made aware of the story of Elijah and the Brook Cherith.[89] God had directed him there when there was a drought. He had running water to drink every day. Then the brook dried up. As I mused on this in prayer I spontaneously spoke out to God and asked, "*why did you lead Elijah there and then allow the brook to dry up?*" I distinctly had this impression where God totally bypassed my question and went to the heart of the matter saying, *"Barry, like Elijah's brook, the job is not your source, I am"*. I was immediately chastened in my heart as God showed me from this story that He was my provider, and if one source dried up, He would open up another, just as He did for Elijah. I apologised to God and stood up with a renewed trust that the God who had shown up for us in India when we had no money, and, who gave me all my needs when there was no other opportunity, would show up again with something better.

Bringing light to persecuted believers.

That is exactly what He did. A few days later one of my former work colleagues contacted me to say he had read about a vacancy with a Christian organisation which seemed very suited to me. I took the information and saw that it was a Development Manager's position with Release International[90] (RI), an organisation that helped persecuted Christians around the world. I applied for the job and got an interview. Once again God helped set things up for me. The C.E.O.[91] of the organisation was a former disciple of my other spiritual father, Ken. He recommended me for the job just as Peter had recommended me for the Kingsway job. God has a way of orchestrating things to our advantage and granting us favour. Just like the previous job, recommendations were not a guarantee, I still had to pass the test of the interview. The interview went well and I was offered the post as Development Manager for the north of England. My responsibilities included

---

[89] 1. Kings Chapter 17.

[90] Also known as "The Voice of the Martyrs" in other countries.

[91] Chief Executive Officer

representing the plight of persecuted Christians to the church in the UK as well as having the privilege of travelling to places like Egypt, Sri Lanka and of course, India. My responsibilities in these countries were to find out first hand about the difficulties believers faced there, in order to assess and provide help. During this time my eyes were opened to the horrific persecution of Christians in many countries around the world, making my problems seem quite insignificant in light of theirs.

Return to the 'Far Pavilions'

I first met Pastor Samson Paul from Bengaluru, India, at an RI conference in Luton, England. Bengaluru (formerly called Bangalore) is the capital of India's southern Karnataka state. I didn't know then that God would use that divine encounter with Samson, to fulfil one of my dreams.[92]

The following year, I visited Pastor Samson in Bengaluru on behalf of RI. The day before my arrival a young man from his church had been witnessing for Jesus and was attacked and murdered by Hindu radicals. I had the sad privilege of attending his funeral on my first day in Bengaluru. My Far Pavilions[93] had taken on a more sinister turn.

I also traveled to Hyderabad, the capital of southern India's Telangana state. Albert Lael, formerly of Operation Mobilisation, introduced me to Hephzibah, the widow of Pastor Daniel. Together they had started a Christian church in the Hyderabad area by distributing Christian leaflets. She told me her husband Daniel was opposed and beaten several times as he ministered. One morning after saying goodbye to his wife, he rode off to visit some church members. He never came home and was found murdered a few days later. When Hephzibah went to identify Daniel's body, she could only recognise him by the socks he'd been wearing when she last saw him. Acid had been poured all over him. When I spoke to Hephzibah, she told me *"the future is blank but God has called me and He will show me how*

---

[92] Chapter 12. See under, Bengaluru, Dreams Realised.

[93] Chapter 5.

He will accomplish His plans through me". I was humbled and challenged by this young widow's attitude.

I met many other believers in India who suffered for their belief in Jesus. When I thought about their very real life-and-death struggles for their faith, I realised I had much to be thankful for and nothing to complain about.

At the same time as working for RI. I began studying for a Masters Degree in Theology as I wanted to develop confidence in my abilities and overcome that destructive, shame-filled and humiliating feeling of being stupid when I was at high school. I worked hard on my essays for two years tapping away on my computer keyboard late into the night. It was very difficult adjusting to the academic world of thinking, and at times I thought I wouldn't make it. Fortunately, my friend Dave Mansfield was studying for the same degree and he constantly told me I could do it. His encouragement helped me enormously and I kept going. Thank God for faithful friends.

My final dissertation was entitled: *"Does Church Growth Cause Persecution or Does Persecution cause Church Growth?"*. I gained a distinction for that and also for my overall degree. I was totally surprised and elated that I had done so well. I used to say jokingly *"if I had a brain I'd be dangerous"*. Now I could say I did have a brain after all! My experience in studying for my masters degree was of much more value than the graduation certificate hanging on my study wall today. I had put to rest, finally, the lie I had digested at school that I was stupid. I was being healed from the inside out. When I told my Mum, all she said was *"I'm glad you've made something of yourself at last, it's a shame you hadn't done it sooner"*, but of course she was very proud of me.

Grace upon Grace.

God had supernaturally opened doors for me with three successive jobs becoming available at exactly the right time. Now, after three years with RI, I felt God was pushing me out of the nest. A Bible study had begun in our home during my time with Kingsway Communications. It began when a friend who felt displaced from his local church asked if he and his family could have a Bible study with us one Sunday evening. We agreed and it had gone so well that they asked to have another and also if a mutual friend could come along. We were reluctant at first because of the pain we had experienced with church, but we agreed to try it.

Soon more people asked to join and before we realised it, we had a church in our front room. The numbers soon outgrew our living room space as more people kept turning up, so we began to meet in a rented location. I didn't start the church, it just seemed to evolve, but at the same time my dormant leadership and Pastoral gifts began to function again as the needs arose. Before I knew it, we were pastoring a church again without realising it.

In the midst of this I was still representing RI and doing my masters degree. It was quite a workload but one I was beginning to thoroughly enjoy once more. However, I had a lot of week-end commitments with RI which took me away from Sunday services with 'Charis', the name we had given to our new fellowship. Grace summed up everything I had been discovering about God, so it was only appropriate that we named it the Greek word meaning GRACE!

Eventually the fellowship asked me to give up my job to concentrate on the church, which interestingly coincided with my sense that God was pushing me out. Linda and I prayed about it a lot as we didn't want to fall into the previous destructive patterns of church ministry. After some deliberation, we decided to say yes, and I said farewell to RI. The dawn of my journey began once more in my calling from God.

Radicalised by Grace

Charis began to grow even more, with many broken people coming along to find grace and a place to be healed and restored. What I had gone through was a catalyst for the grace healing balm that became Charis church.

This grace became the foundation stone of the church. So many broken people who came to Charis were healed by this message. This grace had such a profound impact upon my own life, it was a discovery of something that I had never been taught or perhaps fully grasped before as I was growing up spiritually. The apostle Paul was a terrorist before he was radicalised by grace. The change in him was so profound, so powerful, and so dramatic. It so revolutionised him, that apart from the dangerous missionary journeys he embarked upon, he also became the most prolific author in the New Testament writing 13 of the 27 books.

His message was at its simplest, yet at its most profound, all about grace. I believe Romans 5:17 sums up his message: *"Those who receive the abundance of grace and the free gift of righteousness shall reign in life through the one man Christ Jesus"*. We are called to reign in life, not by doing but by believing. It is something we receive not achieve. It is not just grace, it is the *abundance* of grace. It is not just the gift of righteousness, it is the *free* gift of righteousness. It is as if Paul is straining to emphasise that this offer is totally, totally free, and as we believe and receive this incredible gift, we begin to reign in life. Reigning in life begins when we get out from under the treadmill of forever trying to earn our place in Heaven. Something which many of us subconsciously do. When we fail, we perform even harder without success, before falling into a treadmill of destruction.

Grace is not a licence to sin, as some may infer, but a gift which enables and empowers us to live victoriously for Jesus. Titus 2:11-12 tells us, *"The grace of God appeared, bringing salvation and training us to renounce ungodliness"*.

I was learning that this grace message is so radical that if properly preached, as Paul did, it will possibly be misunderstood, and yet we are called to preach this radically dangerous message.

Dr Martyn Lloyd Jones, the former Pastor of Westminster Chapel in London, in defence of the Biblical Gospel of grace, was of the opinion that; if we are not giving rise to a misunderstanding of the Gospel when we preach it, we are not truly preaching the radical, New Testament Gospel, as Paul did. It may be necessary for us to check out what we are preaching, as the Biblical Gospel has a dangerous aspect to it.[94]

It is indeed dangerous: it's truly radical. It's this amazing grace that empowers us. Because He loved me first, my response is to love Him back.[95] This love is the greatest motivation in the universe. It's no longer a matter of living under law but living under love. That, dear friends, is the revelation that radicalised me.

It seemed to me like a long time coming, but only long enough in God's economy to bring healing for my many damaging hang-ups and to rebuild, restore, and reinstate me. His glorious grace light shone through the cracks in my life and made a massive transformation on this broken vessel, because now more of Him could be seen.

Goin' back in time. Lost and found.

As our lives began to move forward once more, there was still something in the back of my mind which kept resurfacing. Years before when I was living in Dublin, I was in a relationship which wasn't working out. This was, in part due to the scrambled and confused state of mind I was in as a result of drug use. As the relationship deteriorated and splintered, I discovered that the lady in question was pregnant. My psychological state wasn't good and I wasn't functioning very well. I don't excuse the action I took, but I felt the need to get away from the situation. I left Dublin and went back to Guernsey.

I found out later that she had given birth to a boy and subsequently had him adopted. The information was always in the back of my mind as I began to 'normalise' from my drug haze. I thought quite a lot about this boy. I told Linda about it all in the very early days of our relationship so she always knew.

---

[94] Martyn Lloyd-Jones Romans: Exposition of Chapter 6 (Carlisle, PA: The Banner of Truth Trust, 1989). Paraphrased

[95] 1. John 4:19.

I wondered at times whether it would be helpful or not to him, if I tried to find out about him, and get in touch. I procrastinated for some years. By then as a believer, I often prayed about the matter and finally a number of years ago I took the plunge to enquire about him.

I was able to contact Social Services in Belfast, and even though my information was sketchy, the social worker was able to inform me that she had the files about my son in front of her. Unfortunately, she could not give me any information as he had not enquired about his birth parents. That's how things worked in Northern Ireland. All I could do was leave my details and if he ever checked things out, I could be contacted if he so wished.

Fast forward from 2009 to 2013 and one day I received a letter from Social Services in Northern Ireland informing me that a relative of mine had made some enquiries about me. The letter continued by inviting me to phone their office to find out more. I was a bit shell-shocked as I knew immediately what it was all about. I phoned and spoke to the Social worker handling the situation. I was informed that my 'lost' son had been in touch and would like to make contact.

Delighted, frightened and elated are just some of the words to describe my emotions at that moment.

Following my phone call with Social Services I wrote a letter to my son apologising for not being there for him as he grew up and also told him a little about my life as it turned out from those crazy Dublin days.

I got a reply from him almost by return of post with gracious and accepting words, which touched me deeply. He put his phone number at the top of the letter, so after talking to Linda about it we decided he must have been open for me to call him. I took the plunge and called the number. We talked for a long time; it just seemed very comfortable, and yes, he had hoped that I might call him. A few months later, Linda and I were able to visit Gus and his family in Belfast. We got on so well that it seemed as if we had known each other for a long time.

We continue to keep in touch regularly and we have spent time together both in Belfast and Sheffield. His brother and sisters as well as Linda have welcomed him with open arms. They all get on well together and Gus's two lovely daughters have also teamed up well with their two Sheffield cousins. They have enjoyed becoming family.

Gus now calls me 'Dad' and I call him 'Son', it was a natural progression that just happened as if it was the most normal thing in the world, which it was, because when God does things, He always does them well. My son who was lost to me has been found and I am so grateful for this miracle of restoration in my life. Restoration is a major word in God's vocabulary.

In order to conclude this story I have included below a Facebook post from Gus as he spoke in third person about our first Christmas Eve conversation via Facetime.

A lovely Christmas tale: by Gus Moore.

"23 years ago at 20 years of age, in Belfast, a boy found out he was adopted when he discovered his adoption certificate in the attic of his parents house. Angry and confused, he decided not to do anything with this new found information and instead built a life full of fun, laughter, friends and love. At the age of 43 he decided to search for his parents to see what he could find. What he found was a father who had not forgotten or stopped thinking about what had happened in his son's life. What he found was a brother and two sisters. What he found was a wonderful family so accepting of this new brother. What he did on Christmas Eve was to share a drink (via FaceTime) with his dad and wish him happy Christmas for the first time ever. That boy would go to bed happy on Christmas Eve knowing that he needed no presents and that no gift could make him happier than he already was".

I can't begin to explain my gratitude to God who turned this painful part of our history into a wonderful redemptive story. A son coming home, families reunited, and hearts made whole again, God does all things well.

Chapter 9. Learning to Love Again: Who Loves ya Baby.

Telly Savalas can make slang sound like poetry. He talks in such a way that you listen.

Code word 'Kokolat'.

We remember catchphrases quite easily, don't we? This chapter's title is taken From the TV series, 'Kojak'. Theo Kojak was a NYPD police detective Lieutenant played by none other than Telly Savalas. He often used the sentence, *"who loves ya baby?"*, as a throw-away line in the series. There didn't appear to be any real context or meaning to the phrase, but people remember it to this day. It has become part of the American vernacular.

Savalas's question raises a real question for many people today who have a huge love deficit in their heart. I was one of those people and I discovered that this void can only be filled by God's love. There really is only one love that satisfies and that is the love of the Father.

My own story has been one of living in need of approval. I had such a huge love vacuum in my life that was never satisfied. I believe partly because of that deficit, I became a wild rebellious young man getting into trouble, causing trouble and always living as close to the edge as possible.

By the time Charis church had begun, I had been learning many lessons about *"who loves ya baby?"*. I was being set free from a performance-driven lifestyle of trying to please God and I was truly living in His unconditional love and amazing grace.

A big lesson in learning about love came one day as I talked to my eldest granddaughter. When she was just two and a half years old she had one word which I will never forget. That word was 'kokolat'.

She and her younger sister often come to stay with us overnight. Upon arrival at our house one day, she looked up at me, smiled and said, *"Have you got kokolat for me Bampa?"*, (her baby name for Grandpa). It wasn't so much a question as a statement of total expectation. By the way '*kokolat'* is code for chocolate in case you hadn't guessed! Of course, I had already set aside a secret supply for the occasion. So out came the *kokolat.* It was a wonderful lesson about unconditional love! My granddaughter knew how much Grandpa loved her and had no insecurities at all about asking. There was no need to perform to receive anything. That kind of love does good things to you. I thought about that encounter with my granddaughter for a long time afterwards.

Unlike Grandpa's imperfect love, God loves us perfectly, beautifully, tenderly and abundantly. He has such an unending bounty of Father heart love for us.

Unfortunately, we have been sold the lie that we are not loved: we're unacceptable, rejected, and useless. I believed those lies for many years. Those negative thoughts cause us to do anything necessary to get some attention, even if it is the wrong kind.

Loved forever.

The truth is we are children that are loved forever. He loves us so much that He has made us the righteousness of God in Christ Jesus.[96] I had been looking for that love everywhere else without realising that I could only find it in Jesus. So many people I have met are in that same position.

Why do we scrape the bottom of the barrel looking for any form of affection. Why do we beg for crumbs when we can come to His banqueting table[97] with confidence and total expectation to receive God's bountiful love?

---

[96] 2. Corinthians 5:21.

[97] Hebrews 4:16.

My granddaughter had a total childlike trust in Grandpa's imperfect love. She knew she was loved, and it gave her great confidence. Like her, we all need that deep understanding of being loved unconditionally. I was beginning to learn a wonderful lesson.

From rebellious and rejected school boys, to burnt out rock singers in Dublin, spaced out hippies in Kathmandu, bone-weary office and factory workers in Sheffield, stressed out business executives in New York, streetwise cynics in London, adventurers and romantics in remote corners of the globe, apostles and evangelists, and everyday Christians, the need of the heart is universal. We need to become like little children again, children who know they are loved. It's His unconditional love that changes us from the inside out. Didn't Jesus say *"Let the little children come to me for to such belongs the Kingdom of God"?*[98]

The answer to Kojak's question.

We all need to know the answer to Kojak's question, *"who loves ya baby?".* The answer is only found in Jesus. We all need His love and nothing else will satisfy that emptiness. I began to realise that the big hole in my heart was being filled with His gracious, wondrous, forgiving, reconciling love.

In reality it is so easy, but we make it so difficult. For some of us the performance mentality makes us believe we have to add our own pieces of righteousness to be accepted. As I stated earlier,[99] others, I believe, are frightened by the very radical nature of God's grace as taught in the New Testament. They say it sounds like a licence to sin and that is why a little bit of law is mixed in, just to keep the saints on the straight and narrow!

The law is good though. It shows sinners their need of a Saviour because no one can keep the whole law, and we all fall short somewhere along the way. In total there are 613 laws in the Old

---

[98] Luke 18:16.

[99] Chapter 8. See under, Radicalised by Grace.

Testament. The apostle James says, if we keep the whole law but fail in one point we become guilty of all of it.[100] The law shows all of us God's moral standards but it doesn't enable us to keep that standard. The law is the standard we aspire to, but it is grace that declares us already righteous, while at the same time, empowering and motivating us to live that way. In this respect, we are no longer under law.

If only we could learn that it is that very lavish grace of God which trains us to say no to ungodliness and worldly passions.[101] It's not a mixture of law and grace, it's grace all the way. I am no longer motivated by fear to keep the law, I'm motivated by a higher law, the royal law of love,[102] and Paul tells us, that love is the fulfilling of the law.[103]

It all comes from that love which was demonstrated for me at the cross. I just had to learn to rest in His finished work.[104] There is nothing more to do because He paid for it all. The more I fall in love with Jesus because He paid for all my sins, and doesn't count or remember them anymore,[105] the more I want to, and choose to please Him. I don't want to disappoint Him.

The law can't motivate me to do that, only grace can. That unconditional everlasting love of the Father makes me confident to run to Him without fear. Any time I am in need, I know I can ask Him for *Kokolat*!

---

[100] James 2:10.

[101] Titus 2:11-12.

[102] James 2:8.

[103] Romans 13:8-10.

[104] John 19:30.

[105] 2.Corinthians 5:19, Hebrews 8:12.

How long does everlasting last?

God is the ultimate romancer. Just read Song of Solomon. John Arnott, the leader of Catch the Fire, in Toronto has rightly said: *"we need to get out of analysis and into romance"*, and I totally agree with that sentiment. God is love. He loves us with a passionate jealousy and we are moved to love Him in return.

I remember watching the film 'Romancing the Stone' with Michael Douglas and Kathleen Turner as the main players. It was an action adventure with the oddly matched couple chasing after a large diamond around South America. They stopped at nothing to win back the stone from unscrupulous criminals and dumb bad guys. Danny Devito played one of the dumb bad guys to great effect.

In a much more profound way, God chased me around the world to shower me in His love and forgiveness. He picked me up when I fell in the dirt and romanced the stone that was my hard heart, making it tender. He gave me a brand new, and very undeserving start in life, as well as many 'second chances'. Rita Springer sang it so hauntingly in her song 'I Have to Believe'.[106] She sang of the darkness she lived in, but God understood and empowered her to worship Him.

He knew all about my darkness and pain, yet still followed me into that dungeon of self-inflicted hurt and failure. He reminded me of His forever faithfulness to pay the price for my ransom, heal my damaged heart and empower me to praise His name.

In the film 'The Last Jedi', the First Order's supreme leader Snoke said: *"darkness rises and light to meet it"*, but even better, Jesus said: *"The light shines in the darkness and the darkness has not overcome it"*.[107] No matter how much

---

[106] I Have to Believe. Rita Springer. Track 2. CD. Worth it All. 2007. Entertainment One Music.

[107] John 1:15.

darkness we may have lived in, Jesus is working out His strategy to bring us back into His marvellous light. He destroys the darkness and shines the light of His love brightly into our lives again.

Springer just about encapsulated the story of my life in her song. He saw my wounded and destitute state. He found me, moved my mountains of pain and shame and has been forever faithful.

I remembered again His word to me years previously, that He loved me with an everlasting love and continued His faithfulness to me.[108] Those words went directly into my heart, reassuring me of God's love and faithfulness to me even in my failure.

I have pondered many times from that moment when 'everlasting' might run out! I still had to learn that 'love' lesson at a deeper level. My drivenness and approval needs kept me from discovering the depth of that verse for a number of years. It was my crash and burn experience that finally brought me to my knees again, and this time I discovered that endless ocean of love saturating my heart. It may be necessary for some of us to go right to the edge of devastation in order to discover His love really is as vast as the ocean.

> *"Here is love vast as the ocean*
> *Loving kindness as the flood*
> *When the prince of peace, our ransom*
> *shed for us his precious blood".*[109]

This great hymn which was the anthem of the Welsh revival, 1904-1905, became known as 'The love-song of the Welsh Revival', and was used mightily by God at that time. I knew the hymn, but when those truths were illuminated in my heart it was completely overwhelming. I was changed forever by His everlasting love shining in me. He loved me, saw past my flaws, called me His son and brought me back to His house again.

---

[108] Jeremiah 31:3.

[109] Here is Love Vast as the Ocean. William Rees, Robert Lowry. Public Domain.

Recently we were at the wonderful wedding ceremony of a dear friend, John, (from our days on the farm in Holland[110]) and his beautiful bride, Helen. The service took place on the border of England and Wales. The first verse of this hymn was sung passionately in Welsh by the worship team. Even though I don't understand the Welsh language, I was deeply moved again by the timeless truth of the lyrics.

God's love is as vast as the ocean and, He keeps loving us all the time. He is forever faithful, and that's why I love Him so much today. When Jesus hung on the cross and cried out *"It is finished"*,[111] He was declaring, *"I have completed the work you sent me to do, Father. I have fully paid for every past, present, and future sin of all mankind"*, which (by the way) includes you and me. All of our sins are future to the cross, in case you were wondering how Jesus could pay for sins that are not yet committed. All of your sins and mine have taken place at least 2,000 years after the event of the crucifixion! So we need to get used to that thought.

Michael Douglas aka Jack in that film 'Romancing the Stone', finally brought the diamond back to USA. He sold it and bought himself a large yacht. That sounds extravagant, but God is much more extravagant than that. He takes rough stones out of the dirt and gutter of life and polishes them beyond recognition. In His loving hands, we are being turned into the most exquisite diamonds that reflect His glorious presence. As a lover and a craftsman, God is in the business of tenderly removing our desperately ragged edges and flaws making us beautiful in His presence through Jesus, and He'll never sell us off for a yacht. He's committed to loving us forever as we are very precious to Him.

---

[110] Chapter 4, See under, From the Ark to the Farm.

[111] John 19:30.

Passion leads to vision. 'The greatest is love'.

When we experience everlasting, unconditional love, something springs forth from our heart. It is called passion! Over the last few years, I have continued to grasp more and more how much God loves me. He loved me when He found me in my desolation. He loved me and looked after me when I failed Him miserably, and I was in difficult circumstances. He still continues to love me even though I may fail Him today. It has taken a while, but I have begun to realise God is very persistent in His love for people like me.

That light of His went on inside me and I received this amazing love into my heart.[112] It ignited such new joy and purpose within me, giving me a fresh sense of destiny. It's true that without a vision people perish.[113] However, that dying vision can be reignited by a passion that comes as a result of God's love being poured into our hearts. No matter your background, whether a hippie, a rogue, a superstar, a business executive, a prostitute, a housewife, a mother, a father, or even a Pastor or anything else, only Jesus can fill the emptiness in your heart. Neither drugs nor alcohol nor any other 'fix' can do that; they only numb your heart and leave you desperate. His magnificent love is the most powerful motivator in the universe.

We need to know what our passion in life is, in order to become effective and fulfilled in who we are and what we do. Remember the postcard I found in Albuquerque`?[114] It can be summarised like this. Always pursue what catches your heart, that's where your passion lies.

Almost every day I bump into so many people who are filled with insecurity, and low self-esteem like I once was, wandering in a spiritual wilderness. But that's not what Jesus called us to.

---

[112] Romans 5:5.

[113] Proverbs. 29:18.

[114] Chapter 1. See under, Passion.

Passion has to do with what captures your heart. If Jesus' everlasting love has not enveloped your heart, then whatever has will be what directs your life. I spent years under this performance-oriented lifestyle, never ever feeling good enough for Jesus and just hoping I was pleasing him. My spiritual upbringing which had many good qualities, nevertheless, led me to believe that I had to please God in order to earn his favour. This was never intentional, but seemed to soak through everything that happened. Consequently, I lived with a lot of condemnation when I thought I wasn't living up to religion's standards. I worked hard at earning His favour, but was never sure from one day to the next how He felt about me.

Paul told the Ephesians that they were *"accepted in the beloved"*,[115] which literally means that they, and we, are highly favoured in Jesus, who is the beloved one of the Father. Paul used the same Greek word for 'accepted' as used in Luke's Gospel, (ch 1:28), when the angel spoke to Mary and called her *"highly favoured"*. Paul's words can be translated; *"We are highly favoured in Jesus"*.

You see, it's all about Jesus and what He accomplished on the cross for us. He does not remember or count our sins against us ANY MORE!!!!!!! God is love, and love keeps no record of wrong.[116]

The revelation that He loves me everlastingly stirs passion in my heart to love the one who loves me unconditionally. It empowers me with a desire to see His Kingdom come and His will be done on earth, right here right now. It took a long time but eventually I came to know the Father's unconditional love for a riotous ragamuffin.

---

[115] Ephesians 1:6.

[116] Hebrews 8:12, 2. Corinthians 5:19, John 4:8, 1. Corinthians 13:5.

From Ragamuffin to Royalty.

The world is full of ragamuffins. We all need to come with our messed up, screwed up lives, to sit at the feet of Jesus.

I unapologetically use the word ragamuffin, having read Brennan Manning's wonderful book,'The Ragamuffin Gospel'.[117]

As I look back it seems like my whole life (and not just the hippie part) was a ragamuffin one. Reflecting on this I realise I was not aware of how destitute I really was. It is amazing how one can adjust to living in some kind of squalor, perhaps for some, not so much physical, but for all, spiritual. I know from personal experience how the rejection and alienation of life can bring us to the level of surviving like rats living in the gutter. I've lived there like an orphan but thinking life was okay.

Living a life of alienation from God leaves a huge vacuum inside.[118] Every one of us carries in some measure an orphan spirit without realising it.[119] I had that emptiness inside, yet the hunger for more kept gnawing at my soul. It was into that squalor that Jesus came to show me a much better way.

When I first believed, I'd tell people I'd found Jesus but that was not true. I didn't find Jesus, He found me. He tracked me down to bring me to the place of surrender. Yes, I had a choice, (call it free will), but He cornered the rat that I had become, and made me aware of my spiritually bankrupt condition and hovered over me until I gave in. Eventually I realised He reconciled me to Himself by His death on the cross and made me royalty.[120] The pauper became a prince; He didn't find me to make me perform like a dancing bear in a circus in order to be fed. He found me to shower His love on me, bring me into an intimacy of relationship

---

[117] The Ragamuffin Gospel, Brennan Manning. Back cover. Multnomah Books.1990.ISBN 0-88070-631-7

[118] Ephesians 2:11-13.

[119] John 14:18.

[120] 1.Peter 2:9.

with Him, and direct me into my God ordained purpose on earth. It took some time though for me to discover that.

I've travelled to many countries of the world, especially those so-called third world countries. I have met thousands of people from all walks of life. As well as physical poverty, the common denominator is a poverty of the heart, perceived in most who haven't found the everlasting love of God. He is the only one who satisfies the deepest longings of our heart, and He is the only one who gives the true meaning of life, the identity and destiny we are all looking for.

Chapter 10. Come Away With Me.

Find a place where you can hide away,
where you can rest,
Until your heart is at peace.

Rest and recuperation.

The warm breeze wafted in through the windows of the library of the Juniper Tree Guest house in Hua Hin, Thailand.[121] Lazing on a large couch in the library, I drifted in and out of refreshing sleep, enjoying the sound of the waves crashing on the white sandy beach just a few metres away.

Prior to my burn out, I spent many relaxing times here. Hua Hin is a fishing village come holiday resort in Thailand, on the Gulf of Siam, and is still largely unspoiled by tourism. The guest house caters specifically for missionaries and pastors needing a well-deserved rest from ministry. It is a beautiful retreat resort and a place of healing for weary and burnt out children of God. I have had the privilege of ministering there a number of times over the years and have benefitted also from the restorative qualities inherent in the house. When I was travelling on a busy schedule of ministry in Asia, I knew that because of the heat and intensity of ministry whilst there, that it was vital to get a little rest and recuperation to recharge my batteries. The Juniper Tree was the best place to do that.

The name of my healing location guest house is taken from the story of Elijah and his encounter with Jezebel.[122] I had a 'ministry all the time' mentality, if I wasn't doing it I was thinking about it. I didn't know what it was like to take a day off to relax with my family and even when I did my mind was preoccupied with church matters. I only seemed to be able to

---

[121] The Juniper Tree has relocated since my visits there and is located at,
The Juniper Tree, Dolphin Bay, 240 Moo, 5, Samroi Yod District, Pranburi, 77120, Prachuab Kiri Khan, Thailand.

[122] 1.Kings Chapter 19.

take proper rest when the opportunity arose while on a mission trip but not at home and that was not a good way to live.

I had lunch very recently with my friend Dave Gilpin. He's a very busy Pastor of a large church in Sheffield and oversees 11 other growing churches that he has established in the UK and abroad. We talked about the pressures of ministry we've experienced and Dave commented on the relentless pressure as a Pastor to produce new sermons every week, plan Bible studies, provide pastoral care, and leadership oversight as well as trying to have a life. It reminded me of my plate spinning analogy. I'm glad Dave remained a true friend to me when I couldn't spin those plates anymore and everything came crashing down.

Driven people like myself find it hard to take time off and rest, but that's the very thing Jesus said to his disciples on one occasion. In fact He told them to go to a desolate place to rest. Ministry can be relentless as the disciples discovered, having no time to even eat.[123] I learnt that lesson the hard way.

Elijah had been very busy in ministry. After his victory against the 450 false prophets, Jezebel came and threatened him and he ran for his life, finally coming to lie under the Juniper tree. He was burnt out and fearful, and asked God to take his life. It happened to me. I was overwhelmed with fatigue, fear, doubt and a sense of failure, and I wanted to give up altogether.

After the two years I spent trying to pastor the Toronto blessing, I understood Elijah's situation and, I identified with him. He was hurting, but his cry was at one level a cry of self pity. That's how I felt, weary and vulnerable from the tiredness of ministry, given to self importance and self pity all rolled into one, and becoming preoccupied with the wrong things. I'm sorry to say that, like Elijah, I mistakenly thought on occasion that I was the only minister to do the work; an exaggerated position of negativity but one that also led me, and Elijah, to a place of desperation, depression and self-pity. From there, it was easy to fall for the deceptive overtures of the enemy, distracting my view of Jesus. From then on, falling over the precipice was just a matter of time.

---

[123] Mark 6.31

The good news is that God understands those of us with the Elijah syndrome. God first of all gave him rest before restoring him to ministry.

We need to make sure we are taking rest from our ministry and lifestyle as driven people. Elijah's problem wasn't initially failure but busyness doing God's will. I can track my own experience in this cameo picture from Elijah of success, weariness, depression, devastation and ultimate restoration.

Dealing with the performance Trap.

I was trying to earn God's favour by running on a performance treadmill. When we do that, we are heading for a crash. My own story was threaded with that performance mentality, always believing I needed to please God to avert His disapproval but never quite attaining it. After a while you just get worn down and become very vulnerable to attack and defeat.

Eventually out of the fire of my self-inflicted ordeals, I began to realise that Jesus had a rhythm of ministry. He ministered and then He took time off in the mountains or by the sea. If He did that (and He did, and also exhorted His disciples to do the same), then how much more do we need to follow His example?

We need to take time out without the guilt feelings we so often carry due to our performance-based approach to ministry. As someone once said, *"Do good, get good, do bad, get beat"*. That's how many Christians function in relationship to God.

As I tried to figure out what had happened in my life, I couldn't see that the barren place in my life was going to be the place that God would use to bring healing, restoration and a new dimension in ministry.

We misunderstand the work of God in our lives when we feel stuck in barren places. We feel abandoned or at the very least overlooked and maybe worst of all for some of us we believe we deserve it. However the God of Elijah is also our God who is 'no respecter of persons[124] and what He will do for one of His children, He will do for all.

There are times when He takes us into the desert to get us ready for the next phase of ministry and the very reason He created us. At other times, by our own folly, we end up in that place. However it occurs, He is the one who will use it for His divine purposes in restoring and preparing us.

Perhaps for many of us, we need solitude before we can be still enough to hear His voice. There, via His word and His Spirit, He restores to us our vineyards and makes our 'Valley of Achor(trouble) experience' a door of hope.[125] As I look back, I can see how He led me through my barren time from one oasis to another, refreshing my life, repainting hope on the canvass of my imagination and preparing me for ministry again.

I needed to remember that I was not on my own. I discovered there are others out there who are facing similar issues and hoping against hope to minister again. Maybe you are one of them? I want to encourage you to press on with the God who never gives up on you.

It happened to me and it can happen for you. Don't give up. As we stand together, we become an amazing grace army, connecting with other wounded but healed ones to further our heavenly Father's plans to see captives set free and the broken healed.

From the mountaintop to the valley of Achor.

It is easy to become too busy serving God to have time to spend with Him and that is a big mistake. When the trap door leading to your drop into the abyss of failure, depression, and hopelessness swings open it is horrendously painful. It may be self-inflicted or done so by others. It may be a set of

---

[124] Acts 10.34. KJV.

[125] Hosea 2.15, Achor in Hebrew means trouble.

circumstances that hits you or bad decisions you have made. Whatever the reason is, you will probably need time to get healed up.

If the child of your dreams has died because of something you have done, or had done to you, don't stay in mourning forever. There is a time to get up, get cleaned up spiritually,[126] receive His anointing again, put on the fresh garments of praise and begin to feast on God's amazing grace.

There are many Bible heroes who were also notable failures, just read Hebrews chapter 11. Noah got drunk, Abraham lied, Sarah laughed at God, Moses was a murderer, Gideon was a coward, and Samson was a womaniser. However Hebrews doesn't mention any of that. The great thing about the New Testament is that it views the people of the Old Testament through grace eyes and does not remember their failings. As these 'heroes of the faith' came humbly before God, they were restored and used in powerful ways. Don't allow what you did, or the hurt done to you, become a stinking, decaying grave you live in for the rest of your life.

Deal with it.

How you deal with what happens in your life determines what happens next. If you've had to step back from your God given dream and purpose because of things that have happened in your life, it's not over unless you believed the lie that it is. God says it's not over but you need to agree with God, not the negative voices in your head nor the negative talk from others and especially not from the voice of Satan.[127] Take time out to rediscover how much He loves you and allow Him to restore you. It's never too late, you've never been too bad, or gone too far for God to restore, establish and strengthen you for the destiny He has for you.

---

[126] 1.John 1.7.

[127] Revelation 12.11

I found out that God still loved me, believed in me and longed to bring me out of my darkness and my depression. He wanted to enable me to have hope, joy and purpose again. His desire was to reignite my childhood sense of passion and purpose.

He told us He would never leave us as orphans.[128] He is that kind of Father. If you listen, like Elijah, to the still small voice, you'll hear Him whispering to you, *"Come away with me"*. Trust Him once again, as I have done, to rescue you from the despair of your own mistakes and failure. Allow Him to restore you once again to your destiny.

Learning to get away.

After my crash and burn experience, God began to rebuild me. First of all He gave me favour to get good jobs which were of great practical help. He then enabled me to realise that there is life outside of ministry.

Linda and I began taking some breaks. Our first short holiday was to Edinburgh, Scotland, the place of my birth. Edinburgh is also known as 'Auld Reekie' which means 'Old Smokey'.

Princess Street gardens were once a sewage drainage site. The smells from this coupled with coal fire smoke trapped within the walls of the city gave rise to the name 'Auld Reekie'.

Today you would never know anything of its odorous past as the city is very pleasant to the eye and nose, with its splendid architecture and beautiful Princess Street Gardens which replaced the sewage swamp. It is renowned world-wide for its history, architecture, scenery and cultural attractions. It has become known as the 'Athens of the North'.

We spent a delightful few days enjoying the city, especially visiting the Royal Yacht Britannia which is located in Leith Docks. The Yacht became the Queen's favourite hideaway from all the

---

[128] John 14.18.

pressures of monarchy. She once described the Royal Yacht Britannia as the "*one place where I can truly relax*".[129]

Unexpectedly, in contrast to Buckingham Palace, the yacht was very simplistic in furnishings. In order to find rest and refreshment, the Queen, apparently, did not need grand surroundings.

On this break I gained an understanding of the importance of taking time out for myself. I began to discover the need for the rhythms of rest and ministry just as Jesus did by the sea or on a mountain. Sometimes, like Her Majesty the Queen, the simple things of life are enough. These 'break times' have become an important part of our lives now.

Be sure to wear some flowers in your hair.

As a teenager, I heard the haunting song, 'I Left my Heart in San Francisco.[130]'sung by Tony Bennett. Then as a young man, in the late 60s, with the hippie culture emerging, I heard of Haight-Ashbury in San Francisco, it was the birthplace of flower power which Scott McKenzie sang about in 'San Francisco, (be sure to wear some flowers in your hair)'.[131] We all loved the idea of flowers in our hair but not many of us did it.

I was living in Guernsey at that time and my friend Reg and I would chat during our tea breaks at the tomato packing factory and tell each other we were going to go to California one day, and in particular, San Francisco.

I longed to visit 'the city by the bay' and eventually, God made it possible for Linda and I to go. The highlights included standing on the running board of a cable car as it trundled down the hill towards the bay. What a sight, and what fun enjoying the short journey and gazing at the old prison of Alcatraz out in the bay.

---

[129] https://www.express.co.uk/travel/articles/880304/queen-elizabeth-relaxed-holiday-royal-yacht-britannia accessed 6/3/19.

[130] I Left My Heart in San Francisco, music by George Cory and lyrics by Douglass Cross

[131] San Francisco, CBS, written by John Phillips (The Mama and the Papas) June 1967

We then got on the ferry and sailed across to visit Alcatraz. What an eerie place it was. We were given headsets and a recorder so we could listen to the voices of former prisoners tell us stories about each part of the infamous prison. We could hear doors clanging and voices shouting. It was just like being 'inside' as a prisoner.

Visiting Haight-Ashbury was like going back in time. It is a district of San Francisco, named for the intersection of Haight and Ashbury streets. It is a mixture of vintage clothing boutiques, record shops, bookstores, bars and casual, eclectic restaurants. It still has that historic hippie vibe, I loved it.

From there we went to the Golden Gate Bridge which is an impressive, 2.7 kilometres long. It is painted orange vermilion, not gold as I imagined. The bridge is actually named for the Golden Gate Strait, the narrow entrance between the Pacific Ocean and the San Francisco Bay.

You can go across by car, bike, or on foot. I decided to walk as I had dreamed of doing that ever since my days in Guernsey. It was an amazing, emotional feeling walking across the bridge. There are sweeping panoramic views of the Pacific, the dazzling lights of the city, as well as Alcatraz prison.

A sense of freedom overwhelmed me, it was a mixture of dreams being fulfilled and walking over to a new day in my life. I didn't quite understand at the time, but later I realised that God was using the experience to speak to me about the old passing away and new horizons emerging. He was making a road in my wilderness and rivers in my desert.[132]

During the whole experience I saw myself free, then imprisoned but again liberated to walk over my bridge of grace into a new destiny. God was birthing something inside me again.

---

[132] Isaiah 43.19.

Rest for your soul.

As well as physical restoration, I have discovered some quiet places these days where my soul can be restored. *"He makes me lie down in green pastures, He leads me beside still waters. He restores my soul"*.[133] Some are nearby and others are far away across the oceans.

In New Mexico, there is a place called El Santuario de Chimayó. It is a Roman Catholic church in Chimayó, situated between Taos and Santa Fe, New Mexico, USA. I try to visit it every time I am in New Mexico.

According to folklore, on Good Friday, 1810, a group of men from a secret brotherhood were gathered together on a hill and saw a crucifix half buried in the ground nearby. They tried to move the crucifix, but mysteriously, it kept returning to its original location. Finally, a hermit who believed the site to be sacred, built a shelter around the crucifix which later became El Santuario de Chimayó.

Over time, the crucifix disappeared, but the dirt in the hole where the crucifix laid has been accredited with healing power. Thousands of people make a pilgrimage to Chimayó each year to worship, but many come for the healing properties allegedly inherent in the dirt in the hole. Displayed on the wall in the annex just outside of the holy dirt hole, there are many crutches and letters of testimony to healings which have occurred there.

This place has such an atmosphere of peace and I love to visit it to spend time reviving my soul. The peace is probably due to the many years of prayers offered in the chapel and surrounding garden area.[134]

---

[133] Psalm 23.2

[134] https://www.washingtonpost.com/lifestyle/travel/a-little-church-in-new-mexico-with-some-big-healing-power/2014/04/10/6989ca34-b9bf-11e3-9a05-c739f29ccb08_story.html?noredirect=on&utm_term=.7ebc188ef364. accessed 7/3/19

It reminds me of somewhere nearer to home in England, the Holy Island of Lindisfarne in Northumberland. It permeates the same spiritual atmosphere as Chimayó. It was established as a monastery around 635AD by Aidan who was an Irish Monk. After Aidan, another monk called Cuthbert looked after the monastery for a number of years. After his death, he was buried on Lindisfarne. When people came to pray at his grave, miracles of healing were claimed.

Today, if you visit Lindisfarne, you can discover the serenity established there by the many years of prayers offered by the monks. It is another wonderful place, like El Santuario de Chimayó, for the restoring of one's soul.

Sometimes you have just got to get away and find rest for your soul. You may not be able to go to these locations, but that is not important. A walk in the park, in your garden, a drive in the countryside perhaps, or a quiet corner in a cathedral or church building. The disciples spent forty days in an upper room.[135] Peter sat on top of the flat roof of a house beside the sea in Joppa.[136] I love my garden and often sit under the pergola and watch the variety of birds enjoying the fat-balls that Linda has hung on the tree for them to eat. I relax, I pray, and I enjoy God's creation and His presence. It has been said that we are closer to God's heart in the garden than anywhere else.

If you need a longer 'soul rest', perhaps you can take time to go on a spiritual retreat. There are numerous places available today and there will be somewhere that works for you, just find it.

He is still calling, *"Come to me all who labour and are heavy laden, and I will give you rest"*.[137] Find your own quiet place to step aside for a while and drink from the river of His presence. He has said, *"If anyone is thirsty let him come to me and drink.*

---

[135] Acts 1.12-14.

[136] Acts 10.5,9.

[137] Matthew 11.28

Whoever believes in me as the scripture has said, out of his heart will flow rivers of living water".[138]

Let the river of His healing love restore and strengthen you for your calling and destiny. Allow His love to be shed abroad in your heart by the Holy Spirit.[139] I've found out it is really worthwhile to get away for a while with Him, soaking in His presence and finding rest for my soul.

---

[138] John 7.37,38.

[139] Romans 5.5.

Chapter 11. Samson's Hair is Growing Again.

> "And some of them that are wise shall fall, to refine them, and purify, and to make them white, even to the time of the end; because it is yet for a time appointed".
> Daniel 11:35.

The roots are still there.

No matter how bad it has become, no matter how impossible it looks, and no matter how disqualified you feel, it's not over. God has promised to work out everything, including the missed opportunity things, the bad things, the messed up things, and the ugly things in your life until they are even better than before.

> "God, your God, will restore everything you lost; He'll have compassion on you; He'll come back and pick up the pieces from all the places where you were scattered. No matter how far away you end up, God, your God, will get you out of there and bring you back".
> Deuteronomy 30:3-5.MSG

He will give you double for your trouble:

> "Instead of your shame there shall be a double portion; instead of dishonour they shall rejoice in their lot".
> Isaiah 61:7.

Samson was called and set apart by God but he kept going off track until he was totally derailed and powerless.[140] Was that

---
[140] Judges chapters 13-16.

game over? NO NO NO. That's what the enemy wants you to think, but check this out...Samson's hair was growing again.[141]

God set Samson apart from birth,[142] but as he grew into a strong man, he became a wild, self-indulgent individual. When captured by the Philistines, his hair, which was the symbol of his power, was shorn off and his eyes gouged out leaving him powerless and defenceless. But the promise of God over his life still remained. As he lay in captivity, his hair began to grow again. Realising that God was empowering him once more, he was able to take down more of God's enemies in his last task than he had ever done before.[143] In his prayer he also asked God to let him die. That is the key for us also: we don't need to die physically, but we do need to die to our own desires and serve His. That's where true fulfilment lies. Samson accomplished his God-ordained destiny and then entered Heaven.

Even though Samson's hair had been shorn off, the roots of his hair were still intact. My friend Alan Hawkins wisely said, *"Samson never lost his faith, he just never had a very good grip on himself, but God had a mighty grip on Samson, and never let him go. God was not finished with him"*, and He has not finished with you either.

Believing your own publicity.

I think Samson began to believe his own publicity and I believe that I too walked down that dangerous road. Samson was renowned for his supernatural strength and power, but he forgot where that power came from. Usually in ministry our problems occur when we become flattered by the publicity about ourselves. We consequently take our eyes off Jesus and see ourselves as the one creating the success.

---

[141] Judges 16:22.

[142] Judges 13:3-5.

[143] Judges 16:30.

Many leaders; myself included, have found that success became a burden which plagued them. After experiencing much blessing in ministry, we continue to climb our destiny ladder, only to find that we have put it against the wall of success and recognition, instead of service to Jesus.

For many, that success affects us with a sense of entitlement, because we believe the deception regarding our own abilities and power. We have forgotten that God is the one who empowered us and opened doors for us. Paul said it well: *"what have you that you did not receive?"*.[144] Yet pride creeps in subtly and sets us up for a fall. Then comes the crash. Dreams lie shattered on the ground and a painful awareness of devastation pervades the heart.

'With you', Lessons from the rugby field.

Playing rugby was one of my great passions when I was younger. I enjoyed playing for my local team every Saturday. I was probably one of the lightest players on the team but I was quite fast on the break. On one occasion, I picked the ball up from a scrum down[145] and began to run for the goal line thinking I could make it on my own. However, as I ran, I saw a huge Goliath-like figure from the opposing team bearing down on me. He had a look on his face that suggested he was going to rip my arms off in order to get the ball.

I quickly realised I was in serious trouble, but just at that moment I heard the three words every lightweight rugby player wants to hear. To my left was the captain of our team running alongside me. He was even bigger and more muscular than my oncoming Goliath and he shouted to me, *"With you Barry"*. He was there to support and help me, and he wanted the ball (which I was only too happy to hand over!).

---

[144] 1. Corinthians 4:7.

[145] A scrum (short for scrummage) is a method of restarting play in rugby that involves players packing closely together with their heads down and attempting to gain possession of the ball. https://en.wikipedia.org/wiki/Scrum_(rugby)

He took the ball and steamrollered powerfully over my Goliath, leaving him in a heap on the ground. Immediately he passed the ball back to me and I ran for the line, scoring the winning try, much to the delight of my teammates who gathered around me, cheering and slapping my back.

In the midst of the adulation, I looked beyond the cheers and saw my captain standing nearby smiling and clapping my success. He was genuinely pleased for me. I realised in that moment that if not for his empowering presence, I could never have crossed the line and scored the try.

Just like my rugby experience, in my walk and ministry with God, I discovered in the most painful way that without my Captain, Jesus, I could do nothing; my spiritual Goliath was going to destroy me. I've realised that we can all become like Samson if we start to think that it's our ability that makes the difference.

Begin to reign.

No matter how far down you've gone, if you feel it's all over, your place of desolation is now God's place of preparation and restoration. Like Samson's hair roots, the roots of God's call are still embedded in your heart. Out of your devastating experiences you will be humbled. Yet you will become more powerful in Jesus to take down the enemy and see God's Kingdom advance. He is preparing and restoring you so that your latter years will be more fruitful than your former years.

If today, you are in your own prison of failure and shame, I totally understand, but don't give up. Realise and believe that, like Samson, God is growing your spiritual hair again. In a 'but God' moment, things will change and you'll walk out of captivity in the power of God. You will enter into the broad and spacious place He has prepared for you to serve Him significantly. You see, as I said in chapter 8, He still wants you to reign in life.[146] He has never given up on you, He's growing your hair again!

---

[146] Romans 5:17. Chapter 8, see under, Radicalised by Grace.

Restorer of Antiques.

After my friend Reg finally left Guernsey, he spent many years working as an antique restorer. He has a unique gift in this profession. I have watched him take an old damaged piece of furniture that is apparently beyond repair and restore it to an amazing piece of art again, retaining its' original beauty. Using some ordinary materials like sawdust oil and glue, he was able to blend them together so that the damage could not be seen anymore.

I have also read about another ancient form of restoration in Japan where the broken pieces of vessels are restored. It is called 'Kintsugi' Art. As a philosophy, it treats breakage and repair as part of the history of an object, rather than something to disguise or hide. It has a general concept of highlighting or emphasising imperfections, visualising mends and seams as additive, or an area to celebrate or focus on, rather than as an absence or missing pieces.

Using lacquer dusted or mixed with powdered gold, silver, or platinum as the restoring 'glue', the broken pieces are pieced together making beautiful golden, silver or platinum veins in the pottery. The veins are clearly seen in the restored work. Instead of taking away from the original design, the precious metals enhance the beauty of the ornament. Rather than disposing of the item, it now has added dimensions of beauty in its brokenness.

The word 'Kintsugi' means 'Golden Joinery' and is a perfect picture of what our master carpenter Saviour does with our lives, in the areas that have been damaged.[147] When the spiritual work of restoration takes place in our lives, it may leave no marks or at other times retain some, but only to demonstrate the finished work as a tribute to our master craftsman God who restored it.

---

[147] https://en.wikipedia.org/wiki/Kintsugi. Accessed 7/2/19.

Redesigned by the Master.

Only God knows how to take damaged vessels apparently beyond repair and rework them into a beautiful piece of art. Jeremiah the prophet spoke of God being like a potter who can remould a piece of clay and if it does not turn out right the first time, He can place it back on the wheel and make it a thing of beauty. Sometimes as in the case of Jacob, there is a Kintsugi 'limp' enhancing the beauty of humility in the restored vessel.[148]

My own story was a crazy roller coaster ride towards 'almost' destruction. The self destruct journey downward was very painful but out of tragedy came triumph. He lifts up the wounded and the fallen even if it has been by their own hand that their demise came. If like me you pressed that button and thought there was no way back, change your thinking, because to think that way is to reckon without God's glorious restorative intervention.

A bruised reed.

Few things are more fragile than a bruised reed. In Christ's day, children playing beside the river made music pipes out of them. They were hollowed out and holes bored in them. But afterwards when they were bruised, they became useless and were discarded.

It's sadly true, that people may disqualify you, the devil will condemn you, and your own heart will rehearse your failure over and over again, yet still come up with the same negative, soul destroying answers, but God is a restorer and He is looking for the opportunity to reinstate you.

It was when I came to the end of myself that God was able to step in and begin healing me. Out of the fire of failure came the amazing healing of God's grace. I began to understand grace as if I had never heard of it before. Slowly but surely, God brought me back to physical and spiritual health. I soaked in His grace every day. I began to understand that it is indeed *"not by might*

---

[148] Genesis 32:30,31.

nor by power" that my mountains would be moved but only by His empowering presence.[149] He is the only one who can make bruised reeds play tunes again and smouldering wicks burn brightly again.

Failure is not the last word.

Whatever has happened in your life, as I said in an earlier chapter, God says it is not over until it becomes good. He called you and set you apart.[150] He created you for His good works[151] and even though you may have been a prodigal, smelling of pig excrement, Father God welcomes you back fully into His house so you can take up your God-given position as a son to reign in life and serve His purpose for you.

God will turn around whatever mess you've gotten into. He knows the poor choices, reckless decisions and every wrong turn you've made. Just as He did with Peter,[152] He's already planned your restoration. If you've run away like Jonah, God is chasing you down right now to bring you back to your place of destiny. If He did it with Jonah, He'll do it with you. You may feel like you're in the belly of a fish right now, but God will get you back on the dry land of your call again.[153] If He has done it for all those 'heroes' of the faith, He will do it for you! If He did it for me(and He did), then He'll certainly do it for you. Watch out, He's coming after you.

Failure is not the last word in God's vocabulary. His grace is the last word. And grace always loves, always believes the best and never ends.[154] As we read from Daniel at the beginning of this

---

[149] Zechariah 4:6.

[150] Galatians 1:15.

[151] Ephesians 2:10.

[152] Luke 22:31,32.

[153] Jonah Chapter 1:17, & Chapter 2:10.

[154] 1.Corinthians 13:7,8.

chapter, God uses failure 'to refine us'. Grace removes the filthiness and dresses us in righteousness.[155] I am so glad Father God came after me, cleansed me and brought me back into His house to celebrate and feast with Him as a son.

Second chances and new beginnings.

> Second chances are not given to make things right
> But are given to prove that we could be better even
> after we fall.

Our God is the God of second chances and new beginnings. That phrase is one of my favourite prayers. I can't remember where I first heard it but it goes like this: *"Oh God of second chances and new beginnings; here I am again"*. I know He chooses not to remember our sins anymore once we have confessed them to Him, but there is something so true and humbling in this refrain. The good news is that God is always ready to give us a second, a third, fourth chance and so on. In fact, God is prepared to give us as many chances as it takes to enable us to move forward.

Now is not the time to give up because God has not given up on you. He'll never forget you: He is more compassionate than a nursing mother. He has engraved your name on His hands with the permanent ink of His son's blood.[156]

No one has fallen so far that God can't pick them up again, restore them and reinstate them. From Biblical flawed heroes to my own experience, I believe and know that whatever you have been through in life, whether it has been personal and private or public and punishing, God is the champion of the fallen and the broken. He is the one who believes in you. No matter how great your sin, His grace is always greater.[157]

---

[155] Hebrews 8:12, 2. Corinthians 5:19,21.

[156] Isaiah 49:16.

[157] Romans 5:20.

As we have observed, God says He cannot forget His children. Natural parents may forget but God never will. He who began a good work in you shall bring it to completion.[158]

Ring your bell of freedom.

In Leonard Cohen's song 'Anthem',[159] the birds sing to welcome in each new day. Like the birds, we should do the same, forgetting what lies behind and looking forward with hope and purpose.[160]

We are imperfect vessels, with cracks in many areas of our lives. However, as Cohen suggests in the same song, the only way the light gets in is through those cracks. They are the broken parts of our lives where self-sufficiency, pride and sin have been dealt a death blow.

It was painful, but through this brokenness I was humbled and yielded to God in a new way. It's how the light of His presence began to shine in. I began to breathe again, I began to live again, and I began to dream again.

This time, it is God's light that shines through, not ours. The Kintsugi Golden Joiner has healed our wounds with His grace. It is transparent so that the light of His love can shine through making us look more beautiful than before.

As your dream flourishes again, just like a drooping flower responds to the sun, the sunshine of His love and watering of His Spirit will revive, refresh and enable you to take faith steps again to achieve your God given dream.

---

[158] Philippians 1:6.

[159] "Anthem" from the album "The Future" 1992, by Leonard Cohen, Columbia Records.

[160] Philipians 3:13

Dream again like Joseph,[161] only bigger this time. Spend time under the rain (reign) of His Spirit. Believe again like Moses and see your dream to set captives free become a reality again. Call out again like Samson and see your hair regrow and His power released through you again. Know you are loved unconditionally by Jesus just as Peter discovered by the seashore[162] and go forward with boldness. Then, just as Peter experienced, see great fruit in your life and ministry again.[163]

Perhaps your dream got shelved because you stumbled more than once and think there is no way back for God to partner with you again. Sadly, I am aware there will always be some who don't want you to succeed ever, but God's New Covenant work is always redemptive, not punitive. God is the restorer of His children, always. He takes the discarded, the outcast, the damaged, and the broken, and empowers them to stand tall and burn brightly again.

During the Second World War church bells were ordered to remain silent in the UK but their peals[164] were heard again all over Britain following victory in Europe with Nazi Germany's surrender. Every Sunday all over the UK church Bells ring out as a regular call to worship from many church buildings. Ring your bell of freedom today. Your war is over and Christ has won, He has restored what was broken.

There has been a war raging in your life, the enemy has been trying to destroy you, but Jesus has won the battle. Learn to rest in Him. Come home to the Father, and enjoy all the benefits of His house, because they are yours also.

Let the sound of rejoicing flow from within you as His Spirit refreshes, renews and restores you. You may be a cracked bell but that's how His light gets in and stays in. Indeed, His light

---

[161] Genesis 37:9.

[162] John, Chapter 21.

[163] Acts 2:41.

[164] A loud ringing of bells.

and His touch will enable you to look and sound more beautiful than ever before.

Until God is satisfied that His predestined plan for you is flowing again, He will be relentless in His love for you. He wants to see you become all He designed you to be, and after that He will just keep on loving you forever. Your hair is indeed growing again! As my friend John Dabrowski says in his book 'Off the Wall',[165] *"it's not how you start out in life but how you finish that counts"*.

---

[165] The Solopreneur Publishing Co. ISBN 978-0-9932987-2-1 http://www.jdmindcoach.co.uk/

Chapter 12. Dreams and Adventures

Some men are mere dreamers, but those who act on their dreams are dangerous men for they may see them become reality.

Duke City.

When my journey first began, I had no idea how it would unfold. Looking back, I can see the divine encounters that were set up for my future. God knew the good plans He had for me even though I was oblivious to them. He's good at working things out perfectly.

Bumping into people on my spiritual journey has now become a recognised trait of God in my life. When I was introduced to Errol Faulkes in Fort Collins, Colorado, I never realised how important that connection would be for me.

Albuquerque, (or Duke City[166] as it is known locally), is where Errol and Brenda live, and it has become a second home to us. A safe place which God used as part of my restoration. The city is nestled against the 'Sandia mountains'. The name 'Sandias' in Spanish means watermelon and it is used here to represent the beautiful pink colour of the mountains at sunset.

Mountains have played an important part in my life, beginning with the Mournes in Northern Ireland, then the Himalayas in Northern India and Nepal. There is something reassuring about them as well as their majestic presence. It was at the base of the 'Sandias' in Albuquerque that my journey with this book began.

---

[166] The city was named for the Spanish Viceroy Francisco Fernandez de la Cueva, the Duke of Alburquerque. The first 'r' in the spelling was subsequently dropped. But it's named after a duke, thus "Duke" city.

Errol first brought me to the Vineyard church in Albuquerque where he was the pastor. A few years later, he introduced me to Alan and Gail Hawkins, who together with Errol and Brenda, founded a new Church in Albuquerque, called New Life City(NLC).

NLC played a large part in my healing. The love and acceptance of the pastors, as well as many within the fellowship, continues to be a rich well that I drink from as often as I can.

A part of being rebuilt is being loved and accepted, even when you are not in great shape. That was how I felt when I first visited NLC. I was brought in to enjoy everything that was a part of the Church. I've been given the privilege to minister there on a number of occasions which has always been of great personal encouragement, as well as encouraging the church. When someone believes in you when you are still struggling to believe in yourself, it has such an affirming effect within.

God will provide you with your own oases. I discovered an oasis in Albuquerque where I found refreshment. Wherever or whatever they are, you will find those healing places of His restoring love.

Bengaluru, dreams realised.

When I first bumped into Pastor Samson Paul[167] I had no idea that God was setting up events to fulfil a dream He had instilled in my heart. Samson's father, Pastor Arthur Paul established Grace Gospel church in Bengaluru, India, which has now grown to over 6,000 people. Samson and his wife Shiby support Pastor Paul as senior leaders of the church. I subsequently visited Grace Gospel church on behalf of RI[168] and within a short time I became friends with Pastor Samson.

The church has 6 meetings every Sunday, the first one begins at 7am and the last service ends around 9pm. Sunday is a busy day at Grace Gospel church.

---

[167] Chapter 8. See under, Return to The Far Pavilions.

[168] Release International

Over the years, I've preached on a number of occasions at these Sunday meetings, and it's a powerful experience to be with 1,000 plus people in each of the services. The praise and worship propels you into the presence of God as the congregation exuberantly expresses their adoration to Jesus.

On one occasion, Errol Faulkes came with me to minister in Bengaluru. As I was preaching at the second service. I didn't realise that Errol had taken a photo of me. He took the picture from behind me looking over my shoulder as I was standing before the congregation. When he showed it to me later, I noticed for the first time the mass of people in front of me, and I was suddenly taken back to a dream I'd had years previously. In my dream, I saw myself preaching to thousands of people, but the dream had dissipated while I was in my distressed state. The photo brought the dream back to me and now I saw it was actually taking place. Throughout each of the services, I had a renewed wonder at the goodness of God; He does indeed work out everything well.

Take your almost forgotten dreams, dust them off and bring them out into the sunlight of His presence. He will renew you in His love, and He will rejoice over you with singing. He will *"restore to you the years that the swarming locust has eaten"*.[169] He will grow your hair again. He will take what is in shreds and make a beautiful tapestry out of the tangled and broken threads of your life. He will never forget you or the plans He has for you.

A Child realises he is a Son.

On a recent visit to Albuquerque, I was fortunate enough to travel to Texas for a retreat at Mineral Springs which was hosted by Jack Taylor. Papa Jack, as he is affectionately known, is a well-respected Pastor and author of many books, including, 'The Key to Triumphant Living' and more recently, 'Cosmic Initiative'. I had been introduced to Papa Jack by Alan Hawkins a couple of years prior to this and a divine connection was established.

---

[169] Joel 2:25.

Papa Jack is developing a network of sons and daughters around the world. Around 200 people consider him to be their spiritual father. I am proud to be one of them.

The retreat was a fun time of sharing and building relationships with other leaders. As I spent time with Papa Jack, his fatherly affirmation and encouragement brought me to a fresh realisation of my sonship in Christ, and in a deeper way than ever before. I always knew I was a child of God but this was a new dimension in my understanding of who I am as a son.

From vagabond and slave to becoming a son once more, I have been on a journey and walked many treacherous roads, but God brought me through. I would love all of you reading this to come to the same profound awareness.

Friends in high places

Here in England, I am so thankful for friends who rallied around me in my dark days. Some are mentioned by name in this story, and some are not, but you are all in my heart. When I thought I was completely alone, I discovered, like Elijah did, that there were others ready to stand with me.[170] And like Aaron and Hur, they were there when I was too weary to continue and held up my arms when I couldn't even stand.[171]

Friends like these don't need to say much. They just come and hang out, treat you to dinner, invite you to stay over, watch a movie with you, or just laugh with you over the silliest things.

Yet when needed, they speak into your life with words from God to strengthen and encourage you. Because they spend time in the high place of God's presence, they carry His aroma with them when they speak. Those friends continue to be a safe place and I am so grateful for them.

---

[170] 1.Kings 19:18.

[171] Exodus 17:12.

There are friends there for you also, just let them in and allow them to lift your dropping hands and shine light into your darkness.

Dream again, only bigger.

Joseph dreamed a big dream when he was a young man but unsurprisingly it didn't receive a very positive response from his brothers. Joseph's problem was that he was the favourite son of his father Israel.[172] Being a favourite[173] can generate the problem of jealousy from others. Some people won't like it that you have favour with God and will try to put you down. Satan of course is the main enemy against our favour with God and unfortunately in my case he was successful to an extent in derailing me for a season.

It is interesting to note that Joseph was undeterred by the opposition he encountered and dreamed again but with even bigger dreams.[174] The outworking of his big dream took a lot longer than he anticipated. He learnt lessons about humility and was broken of pride. When Pharaoh finally asked Joseph to interpret the dream he'd had, his answer was, 'only God can interpret dreams'.[175] From that point on, with a humility of heart, everything changed for Joseph.

I had almost given up on seeing my dreams of serving God being fulfilled. There were days when it all seemed hopeless, but out of brokenness came humility. In humility I dared to dream again and in God's timing, all things came together for good.

Never give up on your dreams, keep dreaming and dream bigger, holding on to what is in your heart. He will work out all things for your good and for His glory. Your adventure is not over. Never doubt that.

---

[172] Genesis 37.1-8.

[173] Ephesians 1.6, we are 'accepted in the beloved'.KJV. Greek word for 'accepted' means 'highly favoured'. It is the same word used of Mary in Luke 1.28.

[174] Genesis 37.9

[175] Genesis 40.16. paraphrased.

A new season begins.

As I come to the end of this story, I am also coming into a new season of adventures. As we used to sing back in the sixties, 'got my motor runnin',[176] but my motor is fuelled by God's love these days.

About two years ago, God's Spirit began speaking to me about relinquishing my leadership of Charis Church. At first I was uncertain about what was happening, but more and more God pushed me to the edge of my nest. It was unsettling at first as I had led Charis from its birth almost sixteen years ago, and it was a wonderful family of friends.

God, however, kept speaking to me and specifically on two occasions through prophetic words.

Joe Ewen is a Scotsman and has been a prophetic voice to the Antioch church planting movement,[177] in Texas for 25 years. He also serves on the Antioch Board of Advisors. As we kept pondering our sense of direction, Joe prophesied over Linda and I one evening in Sheffield. He declared that it was time to let go; we were not to be concerned about the 'sheep' who were God's people in the first place.

Gradually I came to the decision to step away from leading the church and it was placed back in God's hands. A new phase had begun, and I was stepping out in faith for new adventures the Father had planned for this wild rover.

This summer, as I was about to finish this book, I received another prophecy while in Albuquerque. This time it was from Nick Gough, of Great Falls, in Montana, USA. Nick has a widely recognised prophetic ministry, not only in America but also in other parts of the world.

---

[176] Born to be Wild, Steppenwolf. CD. Steppenwolf, 1968, ABC Dunhill Records.

[177] https://antiochwaco.com/

His word to me was about Humpty Dumpty. That sounds funny at first but the essence of his word to me was very profound. He spoke of my ministry healing those who had fallen over like Mr. Dumpty, but unlike Humpty who couldn't be put back together again, I would see those broken ones restored.

He knew nothing of this story you have been reading, which made his prophecy all the more exciting to me. Even as I write this, new doors of opportunity for ministry are opening for me. I am also believing in some small way that this book will restore many a Humpty Dumpty.

And finally.

Those who have heard me preach will know how many times I use that phrase. My spiritual father Peter Fenwick often would say as he was concluding a message, "*I am coming in to land now, but I may circle the runway a few times*". I like it so much that I use it a lot myself. But now I will be brief!

The two questions I began my spiritual quest with have finally, after a long journey, been answered. I know who I am now. I'm a child, and a son of God who is loved unconditionally. It's in my heart now, not just in my head. I know the meaning of my life now. I'm called to serve as a son and fulfil the DNA He stored in my heart long before I was born. My seemingly silly, childhood, Lone Ranger dreams are being fulfilled now as I help those in need and give away what I have learned. My hair is growing again and it is so fulfilling.

Whatever is going on in your life right now, continue strong friends. God wants to answer your questions and heal your broken dreams. He is committed to making things good for you. Ragamuffins, vagabonds, prodigals, and even Humpty Dumpty can be put back together again to become royalty, and reign in life once again.

Connect with Barry

Facebook. facebook.com/HighVoltageMinistry

www.highvoltageministry.co.uk

Slow Travel
Retired and Loving It!

Baby Boomers Retirement Travel Series

Slow Travel
Retired and Loving It!

A New "How to" Guide for Retirees Visiting Europe

Lynn Michelsohn
and
Larry Michelsohn

**Cleanan Press, Inc.
Roswell, New Mexico
USA**

Slow Travel—Retired and Loving It!
A New "How to" Guide for Retirees Visiting Europe
(Baby Boomers Retirement Travel Series)

Copyright © 2017
by Lynn Michelsohn and Larry Michelsohn

All rights reserved. No part of this book may be reproduced or transmitted in any form or by any means, electronic or mechanical, including photocopying, recording, or by any information storage and retrieval system, without prior written permission from the authors, except in the case of brief quotations included in articles or reviews.

First Print Edition 1.0 CS (3/17)
ISBN: 978-1540372789

Also available as an ebook.

Cover photograph © 2015 by Moses Michelsohn. Used with permission. All other images are courtesy of Pixabay.

Published by
  Cleanan Press, Inc.
  401 West Vista Parkway
  Roswell, NM 88201 USA

www.cleananpressBooks.com

This series is not a comprehensive guide to touring Europe. We can only tell you how we have done it. You can use our choices and experiences as a model, but you should also inform yourself about travel through other books, personal contacts, travel organizations, US government travel alerts and warnings, and the good ole Internet.

Disclaimer: The information contained within this book is for educational and entertainment purposes only. The reader acknowledges that they are reading and using this information contained herein at their own risk, and that the author is not engaging in the rendering of legal, financial, medical, or any other professional advice. No warranties of any kind are expressed or implied. By reading this book, the reader agrees that the author, publisher, or anyone else affiliated with the production, distribution, sale, or any other element of this book is not responsible for any damages or losses, direct or indirect, which occurred as a result of the use of information contained within this book.

Table of Contents

Introduction to Slow Travel

1. Where in the World Is . . . ? Choosing a destination.	7
2. An Arm and a Leg? Costs, finding freebies.	11
3. Ready, Willing, and Able. Getting ready, passports, visas.	15
4. What to Take? Clothes, equipment, supplies.	19
5. Home Sweet Temporary Home. Accommodations.	25
6. Can I Drink the Water? Tap water, bottled water.	31
7. Eating our Way through Europe, Part 1: Buying Groceries. Foods, grocery stores, markets.	33
8. Money, Money, Money. Cash, credit and debit cards.	41
9. *Habla . . . Sprechen Sie . . . Parlez-vous . . .* English? Language.	45
10. There and Back Again. Crossing the Pond.	49
11. Trains, Planes, Trams, Trolleys. Transportation in Europe.	53

12. Attitudes—Pro and Con. What do Europeans think?	63
13. We're Here, Now What? Tours, tourist information, services.	67
14. Popular Entertainment. Music, sports, TV, movies, the Internet.	71
15. Highbrow Entertainment. Opera, concerts, theater.	75
16. Is That All? Museums, battlefields, family history.	79
17. Getting To Know You . . . Meeting locals and fellow travelers.	83
18. Eating Our Way through Europe, Part 2: Eating Out. Restaurants, street food.	87
19. Wet Your Whistle. Bars, pubs, alcohol.	91
20. Shop Till You Drop. Stores, products, hours, souvenirs.	93
21. An Apple a Day . . . Health.	99
22. Stay in Touch. Phones, the Internet, mail, news.	103
23. . . . And the Law Won. Laws, drugs, crime, terrorism.	105

24. And Did I Mention? 109
  Time, measures, restrooms, tipping.
**25. Slow Travel—How to Relax
  and See the World.** 115
  You can do it!

Afterword

Introduction

Do you want to travel the world?

Why not do it! We did.

We're a retired Baby Boomer couple, happy to be healthy and in good shape. Well, reasonably good shape. Well ... sort of good shape.

We are also fortunate in having had two well-paying professional careers— psychology and law. But we have always valued our free time and family activities more than money, so we didn't amass great fortunes. We consider ourselves frugal, although some of our relatives prefer the word "cheap."

After putting two children through college—and one of them through law school—we decided to fulfill our long-time dream of spending a relaxing summer in Europe, just getting to know the place.

"If it's Tuesday, this must be Belgium" package tours didn't appeal to us. Certainly that type of travel has its place. It can be nice to have someone else take care of everything while you just enjoy. But to get to know a place, and maybe some of its people, you need to LIVE there for a while.

A permanent move to a foreign country requires a major commitment. Instead, we chose something less drastic—Slow Travel—settling into a place for a week or a month at a time to experience

Europe

something different from our familiar surroundings without making life-shaking changes.

Of course, a week or a month only sparks a glimmer of real understanding, whether it be of a city or of a country. But the limits of time require compromises . . .

As retirees with few time constraints, we figured that as long as we were expending the money and effort to get to Europe, we might as well stay a while. Two months? Four months? Why not six months? One month here, one month there—think of all the places we could see, even with our Slow Travel approach!

And so our retiree adventure began. We have now spent our third summer in Europe, enjoying (almost) every minute.

We choose countries that sound interesting and relatively safe, and where a good number of people speak English, at least in the tourist areas. We travel by ship, plane, train, and other public transportation, and stay in apartments rented through Airbnb—all easy to arrange using the Internet.

Our Principles

- ◊ We put ourselves in positions to learn about new, or relatively new, places and their inhabitants.
- ◊ We settle in for fairly long periods of time—a week or a month. We want to see a variety of localities without getting caught up in a whirlwind tour. A month in each location generally seems ideal to us. This allows us to get to know the area at a leisurely pace but avoids too many hours spent on planes or trains—or more likely, waiting in train stations and airports—

and also reduces the effort of arranging for too many places to stay.

◇ We continue many of our usual daily pursuits—reading, writing, cooking, exercising, playing guitar, watching movies, chatting on Facebook. We just do them in a different setting, with a few additional activities thrown in.

◇ We live as much like locals as we find conveniently possible, but don't pass up experiences just because they seem "touristy." That usually means they are interesting or fun.

◇ We live reasonably frugally, but don't deny ourselves things we really enjoy. We'll (probably) only live (here) once! The only absolutely necessary expenses beyond those we encounter living in the US come from tickets to get where we're going and places to stay once we've gotten there. At home or abroad, we still have to eat, right?

◇ We look for enough adventure to spice things up—a little, but not too much. Pushing our boundaries staves off boredom, but each person has his or her own level of tolerance for "new" and "exciting."

◇ We don't wear ourselves out. We want our Slow Travel to be fun, not exhausting. We definitely don't want it to feel like a chore—*Tour one more magnificent cathedral? Really? Maybe next time . . .*

At the urging of friends, we created this series of books explaining our way of experiencing the world. This first book in the series lays out the "how to"—or "how not to"—aspects of the gentle adventure we call Slow Travel. Subsequent books chronicle our experiences putting Slow Travel principles into practice. These lighthearted travel memoirs come from correspondence with friends and relatives back home during our travels.

We hope you enjoy our books. And we hope they inspire you to try Slow Travel for yourself.

Going to Europe for a summer sounds hard. It really isn't if you prepare well, remain flexible in your plans and expectations, and maintain a sense of humor. It's easier and less expensive than you think—if we can do it, almost anyone can!

We almost always prefer Slow Travel, but you might only want to try it occasionally, or perhaps just for that "once in a lifetime" summer. Whatever works for you . . .

Does **Slow Travel** sound appealing?
Want to know more?
Let's get started.

Chapter 1.
Where in the World Is . . . ?

Choosing a destination

What interests you? Have you always wanted to see the sun rise at Stonehenge or learn to make authentic Spanish paella? Hike the Italian Alps or spend Halloween in Dracula's castle? Guide a dogsled across Lapland or sketch the Acropolis? Whatever it is, go for it! If not now, when?

Any new experiences usually interest us, rather than specific ones, therefore the exact location of our Slow Travel doesn't matter. It's almost all new to us.

Most of the time, we do want to be in cities with easy access to interesting museums, music, restaurants, and other activities. Although both of us love country living, we usually look for a summer of city life.

We want to be someplace relatively safe—no interest in hiking the Iraq-Iran border. We also like countries where a good number of people speak English. Although one of us studied French in her youth and spoke fluent Italian at one time, and the other one once spoke a little German in addition to fluent Hebrew and Aramaic (so useful for travel—if you live in the First Century), forty years of disuse takes its toll.

So, for our trips we have rather haphazardly chosen:

Barcelona: When we sailed to Europe, that's where the cruise ended.

Copenhagen: Another cruise ended here.

Vienna: Friends briefly traveling with us wanted to visit the city, and it fit in with our Austro-Hungarian Empire theme for part of one summer.

England: The language barrier is a little lower here.

> **London**: We have friends in the city, and find much to see and do.
>
> **Brighton**: Larry once lived in the Brighton Beach section of Brooklyn—and always wanted to be a pinball wizard—so, why not?
>
> **Salisbury**: Lynn hoped to explore some of the pre-historic and historic sites that surround it.

Ireland: One of our sons and his girlfriend praised its beauty and friendliness after a bicycle trip here.

> **Dublin:** The center of it all.
>
> **Galway**: Friends of friends recommended it highly as a contrast to Dublin.

The Netherlands: Both of us enjoyed brief visits here long ago and wanted to return.

> **Amsterdam:** Great museums, interesting lifestyles.

Utrecht: Larry graduated from New Utrecht High School, so he already had the jacket.

Haarlem: Lynn's great-great-great-great-great-great-great-great-grandmother, Marritjen, left here for Nieuw Amsterdam in the 1650s.

Bremen: A perfect place to break our train trip between Copenhagen and Amsterdam—and to seek out the Bremen Town Musicians.

Budapest: We were hoping to see a former Soviet-bloc country before it became westernized. Too late!

Prague: Ditto for Prague, plus everyone says it's a must-see.

Paris: Because—Paris!

What place interests you? Why not go there and check it out!

When to go

We take our trips during the spring, summer, and fall. Being retired, we can travel whenever we want, but we like the weather in Europe better during these months. And being retired, we live in Florida—not a fun place to be in the summertime, unless you really enjoy steam baths.

The tourist areas of Europe can certainly get crowded during the summer, especially in July and August. Crowds dissipate in the winter and rental rates go down, but we moved to Florida to get away from snow, and fourteen hours of darkness is just too much! Remember, much of Europe sits at the latitude of Canada—blissfully long summer days, but oh those winter nights! The Aurora Borealis can only make up for so much.

Chapter 2.
An Arm and a Leg?

Costs

Travel can be expensive—but it doesn't have to be. For us, the only absolutely necessary expenses, beyond those we would normally incur while living at home, are for places to stay and tickets to get there.

Of course, each person has his or her own level of "acceptable." One of our sons enjoys "couch surfing," that is, staying with people around the world who exchange a free couch or floor to sleep on for the experience of meeting people from other places. Not for us! Others we know always demand the amenities of a five-star hotel. Also not us! We only desire a clean one-bedroom apartment in a safe and convenient location with modern appliances, WiFi, and a washing machine.

Costs of living vary greatly from place to place. Generally, the farther east you venture in Europe, the less it costs to live. Cities are more expensive than small towns or rural areas. We don't avoid expensive locations, but finding inexpensive ones can sure be fun, and allows us to "live it up" a little more than usual.

Of the places we have stayed, we've found London and Vienna to be the most expensive and Budapest to be the least. For example, in June 2016, we rented a spacious and elegant, two-bedroom art deco apartment slightly past its prime in the heart of Budapest, close to stores like Prada and Lacoste, the Hard Rock Cafe, the Opera House, and St. Stevens Cathedral. With all fees and taxes included, rent cost us $1,000 for one month, just a little more than the price we paid for a similar but very modern place in Vienna for one week.

There in Budapest, we often ate delicious dinners in cafes or bistros near our apartment (NOT the Hard Rock Cafe) for $15 or so for the two of us, including a glass of wine each. Our host told us that this was considered expensive by Hungarian standards. Local produce in the grocery stores in that city cost about half of what it did at home, although meat was more expensive. Tickets to equally wonderful productions in the Budapest opera house cost about half of what we paid in Vienna.

Saving money

Tickets for transportation and for admission to attractions and events in Europe are often discounted for those over 60 or 65. It never hurts to ask about rates or special arrangements for seniors or retirees or pensioners, or the comparable word in the local language. We've never been asked to prove our age—don't know why; surely we don't look that old!—but we always carry copies of our passports for identification purposes anyway, so no problem.

We do spend more on entertainment when we travel than we would at home, but we have also enjoyed all sorts of free indoor and outdoor events throughout Europe: a violin, cello, and accordion performance in Barcelona's tiny cultural center; the drumming and Druid madness of summer solstice at Stonehenge; enthusiastic crowds in Wenceslas Square cheering on very tall, very white competitors at the Prague International Streetball Championship; a series of early music concerts amid the lush gardens of Utrecht Cathedral's cloister; a lively street fair in Budapest's Jewish Quarter; a fascinating tour of medieval buildings led by a Galway archeologist; and an all-day rock concert in Amsterdam's spacious Vondelpark, to name just a few free events.

We are easily entertained by simple activities, and often take pleasure in merely exploring new streets, admiring interesting architecture, browsing local shops and markets, searching out quirky statues or monuments, and enjoying scenic views—all absolutely free, and good exercise.

Free View of the Eiffel Tower, Paris

The types of free activities offered seem to vary from place to place. We attended organ concerts in spectacular churches throughout the Netherlands and France at no charge, but had to buy tickets for these in Prague. National museums in Paris charge admission fees, sometimes quite steep, but those in London and Dublin admit visitors for free. When we mentioned this to a chatty Irish cloakroom attendant, he explained the appealing local philosophy, "We own everything in the museum. Why should we have to pay to see our own possessions?"

In any location, we find both free and paid happenings online or by visiting tourist information offices. We always come up with more appealing activities than we have the time or energy to attend.

The Internet also provides wonderful opportunities for finding inexpensive tickets for ships, airplanes, and trains. For example, in the fall of 2016 we found a flight from Dublin to New York City for less than $300 per person in coach on a comfortable but no-frills airline. Of course, we did have to change planes once—in Oslo!

As frugal travelers, we find that bringing along our own food and water on train, plane, or bus trips saves substantially. Local bread, cheese, fresh or dried fruit, and chocolate (always chocolate!) make tasty lunches. And water bottles can be refilled easily in most any restroom.

Chapter 3.
Ready, Willing, and Able.

Getting ready to go

We can close up our condo in Florida easily enough. We make sure we have ways to contact the condo managers and for them to contact us.

Most of our check-depositing and bill-paying takes place online these days but we forward the rest of our mail to one of our sons.

We make sure our credit and debit card companies know we will be using our cards in Europe. We also check their expiration dates and take any steps necessary to keep them valid during the trip. Each of us takes a credit card and a debit card for two separate accounts. If something goes wrong with one card or account, we still have access to money.

We learned this hard lesson in Paris when a pickpocket lifted our only debit card. After a long morning trekking from one bank to the next, we finally found a place where we could get a cash advance—at exorbitant interest rates—on our one remaining credit card.

European countries require no specific inoculations for visitors arriving from the US, but both of us do keep our various immunizations up-to-date. We also have our routine medical and dental checkups before leaving.

Our medical insurance only covers emergencies, but we have decided to chance it. Travel insurance offers another possibility. Remember, Medicare only covers expenses in the US.

Getting our insurance company to cover six months of medications at one time has become our most difficult medically related preparation. Start early on that one, and expect to spend a lot of time on hold. You may have to pay for some of it out-of-pocket.

Passports, visas

Travel anywhere outside the US requires a passport these days. Although they are easy to obtain at most post offices, they do take a while to process—exactly how long changes from time to time. If you already have a passport, check its expiration date—you don't want any nasty surprises at a foreign border.

There must be some requirement somewhere for passport photos to make you look your absolute worst. Ours always do, although one of us thinks her driver's license looks even uglier.

You will need to show your passport when you enter a foreign country as well as when you check in to board a ship or an airplane, and to make certain bank transactions. Some countries, such as Germany, require that you present your passport to check into a hotel or rental apartment. Of course, you will need to show it to get back into the US.

Protect your passport carefully. Thieves supposedly prize them. We make multiple color photocopies of the main page of our passports and of our driver's licenses. We stash these copies in various places in our luggage, and email them to each other. This makes copies easily retrievable anywhere in the world.

Each of us also carries one of these photocopies with us at all times to use as day-to-day identification. We keep our actual passports safely tucked away in our apartment and only carry our passports on our person—never in luggage—when traveling between "permanent" locations.

Fortunately, neither of us has ever had to replace a lost passport. US embassies and consulates in most major cities have routine procedures for dealing with these problems. Expect the usual bureaucratic hassles.

Guidebooks all assure us that we Americans do not need a visa if we plan to stay in a European country less than 90 days. True—at present—but beware the Schengen Agreement!

At present, 26 European countries make up the Schengen Area. Many of them also belong to the European Union, that is, the EU (e.g., France, Germany, Spain, Italy, Sweden, Hungary) but some non-EU countries (e.g., Norway, Switzerland) have also signed the Schengen Agreement.

People and goods move freely among these nations. You need to show your passport to enter one of the countries, but then you never need to show it again when moving from country to country within the Schengen Area. Sometimes, you may not realize you have crossed a border.

When we traveled from Copenhagen to Bremen by train, the only way we knew we had crossed the border into Germany was that billboards and signs on local businesses changed from containing short words with lots of ø's and å's to incredibly long words peppered with umlauts.

The Schengen Agreement is important because it limits the time US visitors are allowed to stay within the Schengen Area. That limit is 90 days—90 days TOTAL, for the WHOLE area. To our great distress, we only discovered this startling fact four days before our Schengen time limit expired during our first European stay. We now know how it feels to be illegal aliens! Suddenly, those horrible two-toned European police-car sirens took on a whole new significance.

Extended visas for the Schengen Area can be obtained, but only if arranged beforehand—with the usual bureaucratic hassles. We now solve this problem by selecting both Schengen and non-Schengen countries for our extended stays—three months or less in the Schengen Area and the rest of our time elsewhere.

Chapter 4.
What to Take?

Take as little as possible! You need much less than you think—they do have both washing machines and stores in Europe.

Clothing

We pack lightly—one carry-on suitcase each, one daypack, and one guitar—but still take too much. Boy do those bags get heavy! Lugging them up and down train station stairways gets old fast (one advantage to being an old lady: eager young passersby always offer to carry a suitcase up or down the stairs for the Poor Dear). And then, there's hauling them up to that fourth floor apartment in elevator-deprived Europe!

Trying not to look like a foreigner? Forget that notion. We attempt to blend in with locals in our dress, but it never works. They can always tell . . . even before either of us opens a mouth. So we have decided to be comfortable in what we wear, without drawing too much negative attention. And with washing machines readily available, we really only needs three days' worth of regular clothing.

Acceptable dress in Europe differs little from that in the US and, like here, varies by location. More formal clothing appears in London, for example, than in Budapest but jeans, shorts, T-shirts, and athletic shoes seem to be the norm for locals and tourists alike in most places, especially for men. Most young women seem to prefer strikingly short skirts or even shorter shorts, but older women generally wear longer pants, skirts, or dresses. Tourists dress casually—and sometimes astonishingly badly—everywhere.

To our surprise, all sorts of clothing seems acceptable even in formal settings. When we attend the opera we see men in coats and ties but others in casual shirts and slacks, or even jeans. Occasionally, a woman sipping champagne will be attired in an elegant gown and extravagant jewelry, but more wear slacks and other informal clothing.

Lynn says . . .

For me, shorts and short-sleeved blouses usually suffice. In some countries, such as Spain, older women rarely wear shorts, but tourists of all ages wear them and are forgiven for not knowing any better. I also take several changes of underwear, a pair of socks, a nightgown, a bathing suit, one pair of long pants, a sweater, a light jacket, one outfit that can look reasonably dressy, a pair of good walking sandals, a pair of athletic shoes, a pair of ballet flats (although I tend to wear my sandals everywhere, even to the opera), eyeglasses, sunglasses, toiletries, and medications.

Leave most of your jewelry at home. It only causes extra worry. And what do you really need in the line of cosmetics? Take the minimum. I do always take a trip-long supply of Chapstick—just a personal quirk.

I don't bother with a purse—one less worry. I prefer cargo shorts. I pin a zippered mesh bag inside one front pocket to carry my ID and about $20 in backup cash—and a bank card only when I need to withdraw money from an ATM. Other deep pockets hold my keys, a little cash for the day, Chapstick, and a tissue although, actually, I carry a paper towel because it holds up better. Additionally, I usually carry a stubby pencil and an ibuprofen tablet. When new to a city or exploring a new area, I stuff a street map in my pocket. A smart phone would be even better.

Larry says . . .
I pack a similar list, including one nice shirt and a pair of walking shoes that looks OK with my one pair of slacks. Avoid jeans. They take forever to dry. After that all-too-common encounter with a pickpocket in Paris, I have given up carrying a wallet in favor of the mesh bag pinned inside a pocket.

Equipment

Once again, the less the better. What do you really need? Most electrical appliances are out because of voltage differences. You can rent sports equipment. Binoculars sounded good but we discovered neither of us used them.

Each of us brings a laptop computer—an essential! We rely on them daily, sometimes hourly, for entertainment and for staying in touch with the world. WiFi connections turn up almost everywhere these days.

We have decided to do without phones so we rely on Skype to stay in contact with folks back home. Video chatting is free to anyone with the Skype app. Calls through the website to landlines or cell phones worldwide cost ridiculously little.

Mobile phones, especially smart phones, could certainly make a trip easier. Check with your phone company and look online to understand the requirements for using your phone in Europe.

Cameras on mobile phones snap adequate, even good, photos. Unless you pursue serious photography, don't bother with a camera—less worry and weight. We prefer to travel without any camera and simply enjoy our moments in special places—no reason to add to those boxes and boxes of photos under the bed. We count ourselves fortunate that kind acquaintances occasionally snap photos of us on their phones and email them to us as happy remembrances of special times.

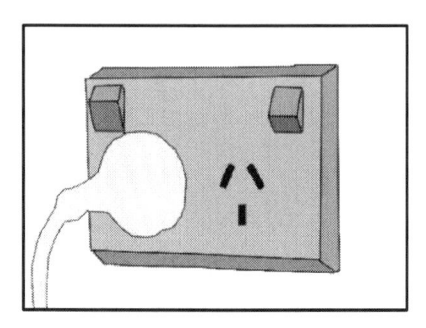

Electrical Outlet, England

We do carry water bottles and always find ourselves glad we packed scissors (very short ones, although airport security personnel sometimes even confiscate these—you never know what will strike them as dangerous; they took our peanut butter in Paris and a souvenir cobblestone in Prague), a tiny sewing kit, an extra pair of eyeglasses apiece, a flashlight, an alarm clock, umbrellas, electrical plug adapters, and several pens. Plastic rain ponchos work for some instead of umbrellas but we find them too hot and cumbersome.

Lynn says . . .

I always bring my Kindle Paperwhite, with its hundreds of books. Lightweight, it recharges easily from any computer. I can download new books—either from an online bookseller or from my local library's website—anywhere I find a WiFi connection, and I can read in direct sunlight or a darkened room. The Kindle's built-in light can even serve as an emergency flashlight.

Novels set in our chosen destinations add to my fun. Reading them on location enhances the visit—any Sherlock Holmes by Sir Arthur Conan Doyle in London, A Place to Die *by Dorothy James in Vienna,* The Da Vinci Code *by Dan Brown in Paris,* The Shadow of the Wind *by Carlos Ruiz Zafón in Barcelona, and* Ulysses *by James Joyce in Dublin—just kidding, nobody really reads* Ulysses, *although someone must have been familiar enough with it to install plaques around town marking spots where its scenes take place.*

I research our destination locations before leaving home—I find Lonely Planet and Rick Steves' guides the most useful—but don't carry heavy guidebooks anymore—all that information lives online these days.

Larry says . . .

In addition to our two laptop computers, I pack my CPAP machine for sleep apnea. Fortunately, all three operate on both 230 and 120 current so we don't need voltage converters.

I take a set of earphones so I can listen to music or shows on my laptop without disturbing Lynn. Additionally, I like to bring a crossword puzzle book—Kindle doesn't offer that . . . yet.

I also bring along my guitar—no electricity required. I can't imagine not playing for six months.

Supplies

We carry our prescription medications for our entire trip with us when we travel. We also pack vitamins, sunscreen, toothpaste, and a few over-the-counter medications, although European stores carry all these. They have most toiletries as well, but if you just can't do without a particular brand of product take it with you.

Stores throughout Europe sell batteries in standard sizes. Even though they're heavy, we still carry one replacement set each for the clock and the flashlight because they always seem to die at inconvenient times.

And one of us always throws in a roll of duct tape—invaluable! What holds the heel on a disintegrating athletic shoe for one more day? Duct tape. How do you re-attach a cracked shower head to an uncooperative water pipe? Duct tape. What pulls almost invisible thorns out of your wrist after a close encounter with a potted cactus? Duct tape. Take it!

Chapter 5.
Home Sweet Temporary Home.

Renting apartments

Airbnb (www.airbnb.com) has become a wonderful place to find a wide range of accommodations almost anywhere in the world. We find the website simple to use. Photos, descriptions, maps, and reviews make it easy to select just the right place. Vacation Rental by Owner (www.vrbo.com) provides a similar useful service. We have always found information on these websites to be accurate and helpful in choosing the right apartment for us. Many other such websites appear online but we have no direct knowledge of them.

We look for one-bedroom apartments, but have occasionally rented studios—like our surprisingly expensive 15' x 15' (that included a bathroom!) garret in the City of Light's historic Marais district. This choice led to our perennial laughing comment when we reminisce with our older son and his girlfriend who unexpectedly needed to share the place with us, "We'll always have Paris."

One-bedroom apartments seem to have plenty of space for the two of us. We select places close to the center of things—or at least close to public transportation—with WiFi, a washing machine (dryers are rare and often weird), and not too many stairs to climb. Remember, "first floor" means up one flight throughout most of Europe.

Weekly and monthly rates can reduce the "per night" charge substantially. Accommodations farther from central areas usually cost less and offer opportunities for exploring interesting, less "touristy" neighborhoods. They do create additional expense and effort in reaching central attractions, however. We have decided that we prefer to live within walking distance of "the action," even if it costs a little more.

Procedures

We try to make arrangements for accommodations six months in advance. This seems to offer us the best selection of places, but even last minute rentals can be found if necessary. Of course, by renting accommodations online from private individuals we always take the chance that something will go wrong—the description is false, the host disappears, the building burns down—but luckily we have never encountered such problems.

We have run into a few difficulties—a broken hot water heater, 7:00 a.m. hammering and sawing during renovations on a next-door apartment, WiFi that only worked in one corner, arriving at our supposed apartment building only to discover that we had been given the wrong address—but we managed to adjust. It's all part of the adventure.

After we choose our place, we contact the "host" (as Airbnb calls the owner) through the website to ask questions or make reservations. One host told us he likes renting to Americans and Scandinavians because they know what they want and book quickly, while the French ask endless questions and then often do not book.

The company handles payments, which it holds until the guest uses the reservation. It mediates any disputes—which we have never had. The host usually sends us a telephone number and often his or her personal email address for alternative channels of communication.

Through the website or directly by email or phone, we arrange with the host to obtain keys to the apartment and be shown around it. We usually request two sets of keys so that we can come and go separately if we desire. We also ask the host about the best way to get to the apartment from the train station or airport. Hosts often respond with useful hints for this and have occasionally offered to pick us up.

The host or a representative usually meets us at the apartment, gives us the keys, and explains all procedures. Getting clear instructions at that time for operating the stove, the heating and cooling system, and any dishwasher, washing machine, TV, or other equipment there is important. Before the host leaves, one of us always make sure we can connect to the WiFi.

We also ask about the closest grocery stores and get recommendations for restaurants, bars, shops, attractions, and tours. We check on hours of operation for businesses, especially on Sundays and any upcoming holidays. We find out what to do if the electricity goes off (i.e., the location of breaker switches) and whether to expect anyone coming to the door (e.g., deliveries, pest control, neighbors, people soliciting contributions).

One important bit of information we now make sure to get is what to do with our garbage—it's not always obvious and disposal procedures vary. We incurred the wrath of a next-door shop owner in

Utrecht when we tried to slip ours into his bin before we discovered the correct way to dispose of it.

In Barcelona, our host told us to set our garbage out on the street after 8:00 pm. That didn't sound right—trash up the beautiful Gothic Quarter?—but we followed his instructions anyway. Feeling somewhat guilty, we left our little bag of garbage on the side of the narrow lane outside our door and headed to a guitar concert in a nearby chapel.

When we returned home several hours later, we stood amazed. Our picturesque neighborhood had turned into a landfill! Bags of garbage, broken crates, piles of newspapers, construction debris, and cartons of rotting fruit filled the streets. But even more amazing, by morning, it had all magically disappeared!

On the other hand, in Haarlem, even the bin for garbage always stayed out of sight. We needed an electronic key card to open the below-ground neighborhood dumpster.

We also ask about the use of any outside amenities like courtyards or BBQ grills. We find out what to do with the keys when we leave and whether any safety concerns about the building or neighborhood exist.

Many hosts place a selection of guidebooks and brochures in the apartment. Some even leave a few welcoming snacks or a bottle of wine.

The kitchen usually comes stocked with basics like salt, pepper, and a few spices, along with various odds and ends left by previous guests. We often find tea bags, a box of spaghetti, or a bottle of olive oil. Likewise, previous guests often leave shampoo and laundry detergent. Some items we use. Others we feel more comfortable buying for ourselves.

Electricity, appliances, lighting

European electrical current comes as 230 volts, not 120 like in the US. Most American appliances won't work in Europe. Instead, they fry!

Some electrical equipment, designated as dual-voltage, operates on either voltage. The CPAP machine and our laptop computers (and their chargers) operate in this manner. Neither of us uses phones or tablets, so we don't know whether or not their chargers work this way. Surely, instruction booklets carry that information somewhere. We charge the Kindle from a laptop USB port, and assume phones could be charged the same way.

Some experts indicate that voltage converters allow use of American appliances in Europe. Others say they can damage appliances. We find it easier to leave anything other than the laptops and CPAP at home. If we should really need some appliance (perhaps a hair dryer, although many hosts furnish these) we could buy one for use there and leave it behind when we come home—European appliances don't work in the US.

By the way, American DVDs don't work in European machines either, and vice versa.

European electrical outlets require a different type of plug than American ones, and the type varies from region to region. Plug adapters are inexpensive and light. They can be purchased easily in most countries. You plug the adapter into the wall outlet and plug the appliance into the adapter (Warning! Warning! Warning! Make sure your appliance can run on 230 voltage. The adapter does NOT convert voltage!)

Often, apartments come furnished with plug adapters. Hotels usually have them to loan to guests. We carry adapters bought in the luggage section in

Walmart that easily convert to several different plug configurations.

Electrical outlets in European apartments, especially in older buildings, are often few in number and never where you want them. Time to smile and adapt. You can always buy an extension cord—just don't use one from home as the same voltage difference problem makes it iffy.

Speaking of iffy, the low wattage light bulbs often found in European apartments leave much to be desired. We could swear it got darker when we turned on the lights in one apartment. Once again, the best solution seems to be to adapt—and bring a Kindle Paperwhite for reading in dim rooms.

Other lodgings

Even with Slow Travel, the two of us occasionally stay in hotels, motels, or regular B-and-Bs for short periods. Like everything else, we find these easily on the Internet.

We have also rented university lodgings that open up when students leave for the summer. Dormitory apartments with several bedrooms, baths, a large central room, and a kitchen work well for families or couples traveling together.

While we have never tried it, friends who have stayed in monasteries and other religious institutions found them both inexpensive and interesting.

Chapter 6.
Can I Drink the Water?

Tap water

European cities have excellent water treatment systems. Tap water is as safe to drink there as in the US. Some cities, like Vienna where drinking water comes directly from alpine glaciers, even brag about the quality of their water. Of course, even in the US, standards differ from place to place and person to person.

Europe doesn't seem to believe in public drinking fountains, except occasionally as a part of a decorative fountain. More often, such features display signs warning against drinking from them.

Yes   No

In some cities, even if it's hard to find an actual drinking fountain, readily available public taps make it easy to refill a water bottle. For example, many public parks in Paris have permanent drinking-water faucets. In Budapest during the summer, workers fit fire hydrants with a clever mechanism that turns them into such taps.

Tap water in public restrooms (except on trains!) is almost always good for drinking, and thus for refilling water bottles. Airport security prohibits bringing water itself through, but our empty bottles pass scanners easily. We then refill them in a restroom on the other side.

Bottled water

Stores sell this usually needless commodity almost everywhere. Many of the brands familiar to Americans turn up in Europe. After all, that's where a lot of them come from.

Chapter 7.
Eating our Way through Europe, Part 1: Buying Groceries.

Shopping for food

For us, discovering new foods and new dishes adds to the fun of traveling. We do love to eat! The two of us cook for ourselves most of the time so much of our food comes from local grocery stores or markets.

Shopping in European grocery stores resembles shopping in the US but, like here, some stores carry more stock than others or organize it better. Most have shopping carts or baskets, although sometimes you must deposit a coin in a locking mechanism to get a cart—but you get it back when you return the cart. Like our grocery stores, those in Europe have separate aisles for produce and packaged goods, meat counters, and sections for refrigerated or frozen food. They usually sell toiletries, including many American brands, but often don't carry some items we normally expect to find there, like vitamins or flowers.

Grocery stores differ most in their checkout procedures, although these differences seem minor. Watch other shoppers to see what to do.

At the checkout stand, the cashier may ask you questions—about discount cards, payment choices, or other indecipherable things, but a shrug usually suffices. On realizing you don't speak the language, the clerk will probably switch to English or simply show you the amount due on the register. You can often pay either by cash or credit card.

You bag your own purchases in European grocery stores. And, you must bring your own containers or buy them at check-out. Free grocery bags are unknown. We learned this the hard way on our first trip to buy food in Copenhagen. We settled up with the cashier easily enough for a first attempt but when we began loading our groceries into a plastic bag lying on the counter, the gentleman next to us pointed out indignantly that he had just paid for that bag. Despite our profuse apologies, he left shaking his head, no doubt disgusted with these nervy foreigners.

European grocery stores carry the usual basic foods, although they may come in unfamiliar packaging. Items imported from outside the EU cost more, as imported items do everywhere. EU regulations require labeling of each item as to its country of origin, which provides an interesting geography lesson in itself.

We see many US brands, but usually stick with local products, both because of the expense and for the new experiences. We do look for a few American items—always expensive—that we particularly like. Hellmann's mayonnaise and M&Ms top our list, although to our shock and disappointment, the flavors of these vary by country.

When we buy local packaged foods, we rely on pictures on the box or bag to supplement our rudimentary knowledge of the language. Google Translate can really come in handy in these situations. Otherwise, expect occasional mishaps. We brought home confectioner's sugar for our coffee in Vienna and purchased buttermilk instead of skim milk in Copenhagen—after all, it did say *"0% fedt"* on the carton.

Recognizing fresh fruits and vegetables presents no problem, however, and most grocery stores carry the basics—apples, bananas, oranges, tomatoes, potatoes, cabbage. Local produce often costs less than in the US but problems can arise in trying to figure out prices. As in the US, grocers price some items by weight while they sell others by the piece or by some amount like a dozen. Abbreviations add to the confusion. *Do I want the "279 Ft/350 g" iceberg lettuce or the "349 Ft/db" leaf lettuce?* Careful study of signs, trial and error, or even asking someone, can all help.

We prefer to buy fruits and vegetables in farmers markets when we can. Pointing at selections and using hand signals to indicate numbers of items or sizes of slices works well. In addition to being less expensive, local in-season produce direct from the farm tastes better—ooh, those delicious tiny strawberries we found in Dutch street markets! Talking—or trying to talk—to venders usually turns into a fun exchange and occasionally leads to interesting insights, as well.

When we questioned a Budapest woman about suspicious smears on the eggs she was selling, she laughed and asked, "American?" When we nodded, she admonished us, shaking her finger, "No buy clean eggs here." At our puzzled looks, she added, "Always want dirt. With dirt, they are good." She then explained—we think—that washing eggs removes the natural protective coating that keeps out bacteria.

European eggs don't require refrigeration because they are never washed prior to sale. Once washed—as required in the US—eggs must be refrigerated to keep them from spoiling. Now we understand why European grocery stores display their eggs on regular shelves rather than in the refrigerated section—and why we find those occasional stains on them.

Fruits and Veggies
La Boqueria Market, Barcelona

To our surprise, produce and many other foods ship readily around the world these days. Who knew Old El Paso Fajita Dinner Kits would be so popular in Prague? And we found ourselves buying the same brand of Chilean red grapes we knew from home when we shopped in Barcelona's colorful La Boqueria Market, where, by the way, the misspent youth of one of us—not saying which one—finally paid off when addressing the grape vendor (*"Sin semilla?" "Si, señor!"*).

Browsing through produce sections of grocery stores or around farmers markets for new and interesting fruits and vegetables can also be fun—did we mention that we are easily entertained? Aside from all sorts of ugly new root vegetables, we discovered wonderfully sweet mangosteens in Vienna, pointy cabbages in Prague, and an incredible array of oddly shaped mushrooms in Budapest.

Meat costs more in Europe than in the US with beef being the most expensive, sometimes outrageously so. Chicken and pork generally cost the least. Butcher shops or meat sections in larger markets offer familiar selections, in addition to some that look quite odd to Americans. Fancy—and incredibly expensive—*ibérico de bellota* hams in Barcelona come with the black hoof still attached to prove their authenticity. Similarly, whole dressed rabbits still have their furry ears intact—to show that they are not cats, the butcher told us. Items rarely seen in the US, like chicken feet or beef innards, also appear regularly.

And don't miss specialty food stores in Europe. The aroma of baking bread draws everyone to wonderful Paris bakeries but those piles of gorgeous multi-colored macarons in its *patisseries* create a feast for the eyes as well as the taste buds.

We stopped often in Amsterdam cheese shops to sample new varieties and always came away with several paper-wrapped chunks for later devouring—so many choices, so much cheese! Smoked Edam became our favorite.

In Copenhagen we discovered a Middle Eastern bakery near our apartment that sold twelve kinds of baklava!

And in Barcelona, we lived two stories above a fine ham shop. The expert butcher in the window made a fascinating show of hand-cutting paper-thin slices of their $100-a-pound delicacies, flourishing his gleaming blade over the hams in their special cutting stands. The shop displayed a wide variety of cured yummies but their briskest business centered on take-away paper cones of less expensive ham cut into bite-sized chunks for munching on the street.

Our sampling in Amsterdam taught us to look for interesting cheeses in each city we visit—manchego in Barcelona, Clonmore in Dublin, Stilton in London, and Gouda in Gouda.

Cheeses, Paris

Local varieties of sausages also attract us—fat bratwursts in Bremen, juicy bangers in Salisbury, and that spicy *kolbász* in Budapest.

Even breads vary substantially from place to place, from heavy, heavy pumpkinseed loaves in Copenhagen to crusty baguettes in Paris to dense Irish soda bread in Galway. And then we come to the pastries! Brighton's Eccles cakes, Haarlem's *slagroomtaart* (ooh, the whipped cream!), Vienna's sachertorte, and so many more . . . Yum!

As we travel, we especially delight in sampling candy as it changes from country to country. Even the composition of US candy bars varies. The Milky Way sold in Budapest resembles a vanilla Three Musketeers.

Local candy interests us more and sometimes turns out to be delicious. When we left Hungary, both of us felt quite sad to say goodbye to Sport—a chocolate bar filled with dense rum-infused cocoa-fondant. By the way, European chocolate in all its forms and flavors deserves its own chapter—or book!

Weights and measures

In European grocery stores—except in the UK—the metric system rules. Grams (g) and kilograms (kg) measure weight. Liters (l) and milliliters (ml) measure volume.

It's easiest to think of a kilogram as being about two pounds, even though it's actually a little more. Halve the price of an item sold by weight to get a rough estimate of its price per pound, if you want to compare it with prices back home. Read posted charges for weighed items carefully. Venders often price meat, cheese, and other expensive foods by 100 gram amounts, which can add up quickly.

Thinking of liters as quarts also works well. Don't worry about exact conversions. The difference just gives you a slight bonus. You get a little more for your money than you expect.

UK folks still measure weight in pounds and ounces (and the "stone"—too infrequent and confusing to discuss, especially as Wikipedia also talks about a "metric stone"). They measure liquids in gallons, quarts, and pints, but each of these "Imperial" measures includes slightly more than the US equivalent. Again, just a little bonus.

Chapter 8.
Money, Money, Money.

Cash

Much of Europe uses the euro (€) for currency, which makes travel much easier. You don't have to learn a new monetary system every time you cross a border and you don't accumulate a pocketful of suddenly worthless coins left over from your previous stop.

It's surprising how quickly you can begin to think in terms of euros. If you don't mind being a little off, you can simply look at them as dollars. They're not that much different. The same holds true for pounds in the UK.

Unfortunately, even some EU countries still insist on using their own currency—Danish *krones*, Polish *zlotys,* Romanian *leus.* Converting them requires serious math and can easily get confusing.

Our first day in the Czech capital of Prague, we discovered a street market selling the most luscious cherries ever. A rapid calculation in the new currency indicated that they cost about half the price of cherries in the US, so we quickly purchased a box, and returned regularly for more.

After a few days, the more cost-conscious one of us started looking at the price a little more carefully and realized we had based our calculations on Hungarian *forints*—the currency of the previous country we had visited—and not on Czech *korunas*. Horrors! The cherries actually cost twice as much as in the US! The more profligate one of us claimed that he had known this all along but didn't say anything because he *really* liked the cherries. In the end, we decided to continue treating ourselves—a little splurging nurtures the soul!

Euros

Credit and debit cards

Merchants in larger population centers throughout Europe accept credit cards, especially Visa and Mastercard. They usually expect cards to have chips, although most machines can also accept those without chips. Discuss this with your credit card company in preparation for your trip. Also make sure your card isn't scheduled to expire during your stay. It is theoretically possible to have replacement cards sent to you in Europe, but we have never tried.

As mentioned earlier, we carry credit and debit cards for two different accounts. If something goes wrong with one card or account, we still have access to money. Make sure all your accounts know when and where you will be traveling in Europe.

We use cash for purchases in Europe as much as possible because all sorts of extra fees can apply to using your credit card there—foreign transaction fees and currency conversion fees (either from the merchant or the credit card company) being the most common. Check with your credit card company for details. And besides, everyone accepts cash.

We use our debit cards to withdraw local currency from ATM machines. We usually get enough cash each time to last several days or a week. These machines pop up everywhere and provide the easiest and cheapest way to get the money we need.

When we arrive at a train station or airport in a new country, we make the ATM our first stop. This immediately allows us to buy a snack or purchase tram tickets with our new currency.

While some—but not all—banks charge a withdrawal or conversion fee when using an ATM, these fees usually amount to less than the cost of using a credit card or of changing cash at European banks or at the money exchange bureaus that proliferate in tourist areas. If you insist on exchanging cash, compare the rates at several places first. Exchange rates and commissions often vary.

Using an ATM is certainly more convenient, and a lot safer than carrying enough cash to get you through the entire trip.

Traveler's checks have pretty much gone out of use—and don't even think about trying to cash a personal check!

Chapter 9.
Habla . . . Sprechen Sie . . . Parlez-vous . . . English?

Our Good Old Mother Tongue

An amazing number of people around the world speak English these days.

Lynn says . . .

Once, when we were trying to find our way out of the confusing basement of a large office building in an outer suburb of Paris, we came across a tattered cleaning woman at the end of a dim hallway scrubbing the floor on her knees. Desperate to escape and theoretically knowing some French, I ventured to try out my rudimentary language skills, "Boujour, Madame."

The weary-looking woman raised her head and smiled—so far, so good. Encouraged, I continued with what I hoped was a question about the exit, "La sortie, s'il vous plait?"

The cleaning woman immediately stood and shocked us by switching to heavily accented but excellent English. She pointed out the intricate route, "You go back the way you came, turn left at the glass doors, take the first stairway on the right, go up one flight, and follow the corridor to the door at the end, which will take you outside."

Wow!

English has become the Twenty-first Century language of global communication. These days, signs in airports and train stations almost always include an English version. Large and small museums in many European countries label exhibits in both the native language and English.

Other than the language of the country, we hear English on the street more than any other language in tourist areas, even if many of the speakers have obvious "foreign" accents—how else would you expect a young Russian man in Rome to try to pick up a Brazilian college student?

When you need help in a public place, asking anyone "Do you speak English?" usually turns up at least one eager nearby volunteer with good command of the language.

Even communicating in English can be tricky at times, however. Not only accents but word meanings can vary from one place to another. George Bernard Shaw supposedly said, "The United States and Great Britain are two countries separated by a common language." And remember, most European schools teach British English, not American English.

On a tour of a former concentration camp, our Czech guide told us that Nazis did not permit Jewish prisoners there to walk on the pavement, but made them walk in the street instead. This confused us greatly until later discussions revealed that in British English, "pavement" means "sidewalk."

On another occasion, we startled a British friend by commenting that few women seemed to wear pants in London. He explained that in England, "pants" refers to underpants. It's also helpful to know that "pissed" means intoxicated in British slang. And we won't even mention "fanny"—and you shouldn't either in polite company.

Local languages

It's always nice to learn a few phrases in the language of your host country, but often your attempts to use it will be met by locals raring to practice their English. What a blessing for language-challenged Americans!

In Western Europe we can usually make some sense of menus or signs because at least a few of the words look similar to ones in English. Our language shares many roots with other Latin-based or Germanic languages. Recognizing such familiar terms can be reassuring.

Eastern European languages extend no such comfort. We can probably all guess what *boeuf* or *Suppe* mean on a menu, but what about *jablečný koláč*? Unless you grew up with a Polish grandmother or one who spoke Finnish, expect to be completely lost with local languages when you venture very far east or north in Europe.

Google Translate makes life so much easier. We use the website most often to look up the names of foods we want in the grocery store or to translate frightening-looking warnings posted in apartment hallways, but we first discovered its usefulness in Germany.

Larry says . . .

I have an interest in military history (for some reason, Lynn uses the word "obsession"). Once, I tried to ask the aged proprietor of a small Bremen antique store about several interesting WWII relics on display. My shaky German—picked up from my Berliner father and a grandmother remembered best for her frequent comment, "Du bist zu dick!" (You're too fat!)—didn't get through to the non-English-speaking gentleman.

After several frustrating miscommunications, the elderly proprietor led me to his computer and opened the Google Translate website. Suddenly, perfect communication!

Only limited suitcase space prevented me from bringing home several of the items, especially after he brought out some of his "backroom" merchandise—German law forbids any public display of Nazi symbols.

Chapter 10.
There and Back Again.

Crossing the Pond

Cruising across the Atlantic Ocean sounds exotic, exciting, and restful, all at the same time. What a great way to start a Slow Travel adventure!

Many cruise lines reposition their ships twice a year, moving them to the Mediterranean or Baltic for the summer and to the Caribbean for the winter. Surprisingly, deals often allow us to travel to or from Europe on one of these repositioning cruises for not much more than the price of airline tickets! This includes their two weeks of elegantly presented food, fun entertainment, and all the other usual cruise amenities. Wow! Why not?

Admittedly, we book one of their cheapest inside cabins, which, despite vicious rumors, don't lie below the waterline. We do sometimes hear strange noises at night—the anchor chain rattling? Or maybe just ghosts. We spend most of our waking hours on deck or in public rooms anyway. The cabin just serves as a cozy place to sleep.

The two of us have also crossed the Atlantic in staterooms with balconies. Although pleasant and offering nice views, these cabins don't have much more room than inside ones—not worth the extra money to us. It's usually too chilly to sit outside, and how many hours can you really spend admiring the ocean? After a very short while, rolling blue waves all look the same. We did delightedly anticipate sitting on our balcony and admiring the Rock of Gibraltar as we sailed by it on one trip—until we discovered we would be passing it at midnight.

If you decide to go by ship, choose your cruise line carefully. Consider the cost of the cruise, its embarkation and landing locations, the dates it leaves and arrives, any stops it makes along the way, and the amenities it provides, as well as the "style" of the cruise line. Ships operated by different companies can differ substantially in all of these factors. Both of us prefer an informal atmosphere, but even cruise lines advertising more relaxed styles provide opportunities for "dress-up" for those who enjoy occasional elegance.

As with most travel-related activities these days, multiple websites carry reviews of cruises. If you decide to sail to Europe, be sure to read the information from the company carefully, and then check online for reviews, not just ratings. What causes one traveler to downgrade a cruise or a ship may be just the characteristic that appeals to you— "The pool area was always full of rock music and people partying" vs "The pool area was dead— nothing but old folks stretched out in the sun."

Two weeks on a ship? Don't you get bored? Not at all! Both of us enjoy solitary activities like reading, writing, and watching movies so we love the opportunity to relax—and let someone else cook and clean. Cruise lines always schedule a spate of free activities throughout the day for those more actively inclined—everything from a well-equipped gym to karaoke evenings to dance classes to game show contests to craft demonstrations to lectures about buying diamonds to table tennis tournaments to religious services to liquor tastings, and much much more. We enjoy the small venues around the ship that offer a variety of live music most evenings, in addition to the free Broadway-style, or at least Ed Sullivan-style, nightly shows in a larger setting.

Frugal travelers can have an enjoyable, exciting trip without spending an additional penny beyond the fixed price of the cruise, if they so choose. We fit that category and usually only buy an occasional alcoholic drink—such as wine with dinner—but have even found cruises that offer free unlimited alcoholic beverages. For those willing to spend a little more, spa services, art auctions, bingo games, specialty dining, casino gambling, and other fee-based activities abound.

But with all that delicious food, I'd gain ten pounds! Yes, that can be a problem. It does call for a little self-discipline. Fortunately, ships provide a wide variety of fresh fruits and veggies, healthy salad items, and lean meats. We try to load up on those but also manage a few indulgences—midnight chocolate milkshake, anyone?

Our trick of asking the waiter or waitress to remove the bread basket from our table as soon as we sit down helps. Otherwise we find ourselves scarfing down delicious fresh-baked rolls or cheese bread or sourdough muffins . . . all slathered in butter, of course. We do have to keep turning away other zealous staff members carrying bread baskets, though. They always think someone forgot to put bread on our table.

We also try to get a lot of exercise—walking once or twice around the ship before each meal, climbing stairs rather than taking the elevator, and visiting the gym regularly, well, at least occasionally.

Dining arrangements vary from cruise line to cruise line and should be a factor in choosing your ship. They can range from regimented formal service—eating at the same hour and same table, with the same companions and same wait staff at each meal—to informal self-serve buffets open much of the day, to ordering food from room service.

We usually eat breakfast and lunch at the buffet and dinner in a formal dining room—it's fun to be waited on occasionally. We personally prefer the less rigid arrangements for formal dining found on Norwegian Cruise Line ships. They seat us whenever we arrive, give us a table by ourselves or with others, depending on how we feel that evening, and only require reasonable casual dress.

Luckily, we enjoy researching cruises and book ours on the Internet—so easy these days. You can too.

Air travel

Flying always remains an option—less fun but a lot faster. We usually take a cruise on our way over to Europe but if we want to come back before the ships get ready to reposition, we fly home.

The Internet provides wonderful ways to find the cheapest airfares. Sometimes, improbable routes offer the best deals if you don't mind spending a little more time in transit. London to Atlanta with a plane change in Toronto? Why not.

Chapter 11.
Trains, Planes, Trams, Trolleys.

Public transportation

Both of us prefer using public transportation in Europe. It has developed much more extensively there than in the US and makes it possible to get to almost any town, however small, if not by train then by bus. Organized day tours often visit sites not otherwise easily accessible without a car.

We buy airline tickets online ahead of time but wait to buy train and other local transportation tickets until we get on location. Of course, rail passes and the like should be purchased in advance, but we don't travel around Europe enough to make them worthwhile for us.

Occasionally, strikes disrupt the availability of public transportation but most European unions schedule strikes and publicize them widely ahead of time. They last only specified periods—hours or days—so planning can avoid most of the serious travel problems strikes might create. They still inconvenience us at times though—how dare those people want better working arrangements!

We had just learned to use the Dublin city bus system when workers scheduled a two-day strike beginning on a day we had booked an out-of-town bus tour. Fortunately, a private bus company not subject to the strike ran the tour. Unfortunately, the bus departed from a location two miles from our apartment. No problem—we'll take a taxi. Funny, every single employed person in Dublin had the same idea that morning—not an empty cab in sight! So we got a little more exercise than planned, but we did manage to arrive in time to catch our bus to the spectacular Neolithic tomb at Newgrange.

Air travel

Europe has a number of inexpensive, no-frills airlines, all with safe, reliable air service between major cities. Often, flying costs less than taking a train. Once again, the Internet is your friend. Be sure to read the requirements for things such as luggage sizes, check-in procedures, and boarding passes carefully. Ryan Air, for example, charges a hefty fee if you do not arrive at the airport with a pre-printed boarding pass. They also insist on strict adherence to carry-on luggage limits—as we discovered to our dismay.

Airport terminals in Europe generally resemble those in the US. Security procedures are similar as well, and change about as quickly with each new terror threat. Minor differences do exist. For example, we have rarely had to remove our shoes to pass through security, and in Prague, security checks took place at each gate rather than in a central screening area.

We have found locations and directions within terminals to be clearly marked, with English always being one of the languages on the signs. Personnel have usually been responsive to our polite questions and requests for assistance.

Trains

Trains connect most large European cities and often stop at smaller towns along the route. Most long-distance trains provide convenient, fast, and comfortable travel.

Many trains have some form of food and drink service and free WiFi. Sleeping arrangements can be made for longer trips. All long-distance trains have restrooms, often marked "WC" for "water closet." Figuring out how to open or lock the doors to these can be tricky though. Clearly, someone with a dark sense of humor designs those inscrutable pictures explaining the procedures. And remember, water in on-board restrooms is almost never drinkable!

Trains charge more than buses to cover the same route, and even cost more than flying at times, but have other advantages. You can easily walk around on a train to stretch your legs, and dine or drink in comfort on some of them. You don't have to go through security or arrive two hours early to catch a train. You can board with as much junk as you can carry. With prior arrangements, you can often make intermediate stops of a few hours or days along the route at no extra charge. And train stations are usually located in or close to the centers of towns, making transportation to downtown apartments quick and inexpensive.

First and second class tickets are available for most trains but we have never found a reason to purchase a first class ticket. The numbers "1" or "2" on the sides of the cars clearly mark the different classes. Tickets often cost much less if purchased in advance, but may have restrictions as to the hours or days of travel. Return tickets are usually cheaper if you purchase them at the same time as the original ticket. Some trains seem to require reservations, while reservations are optional on others, and still others don't take reservations at all. Reserved seats may or may not cost extra.

Most train lines are government-operated and many charge seniors or retirees or pensioners (called different things in different places) less than the usual adult fare. Often the senior fare equals the student fare. Special deals, such as Eurail Pass or retirée discount cards, can also save money. As with everything else, this type of information shows up readily online.

Careful reading of this information can be important. On a cruise across the Atlantic to Barcelona, we met a couple who had only booked passage as far as Madeira, the ship's first stop in Europe. They explained that they planned to use their Eurail Passes to travel from there around the rest of Portugal, then on to Spain and France. Aghast expressions met the information that the Portuguese island of Madeira lies 400 miles off the African coast! Evidently, the geography skills of some Americans are just as lacking as their foreign language skills.

In many places, tickets can be purchased online or from vending machines at train stations. We prefer human ticket agents. Someone in these offices always speaks English, and kind, incredibly patient agents there explain fares and routes, help us select our tickets, direct us to the right track for our chosen train, and generally assist us often-confused tourists with our travel.

Some trains have open seating—you take any vacant seat. If you have a reservation on a train with reserved seating, your ticket will state the car number (posted on the outside of the car) and seat number. If you don't have a reservation, you may sit in any seat that does not have a reservation marker of some sort on it—or someone already sitting in it.

Sometimes a seat will only be reserved for a portion of the trip, which the marker will indicate. You can still sit in it during the non-reserved portion of the trip. If you cannot find a seat at all, you may have to stand or sit on your luggage or on the floor.

Prominent boards in stations usually show arrival and departure times, but you often need to know the origin or ultimate destination of your train to find its listing. Ask the ticket agent for this information when you buy your ticket. Also make sure you find out whether the entire train goes to your desired destination. Sometimes a train splits somewhere along the route, with some cars going to one destination and other cars going to another. If it does, choose your car carefully!

Public address systems in train stations often make announcements in English as well as in local languages. These are usually as understandable in Europe as in the US—that is, they aren't. Fortunately, fairly conspicuous sign boards somewhere in the station list most information, even about train delays or changes in platforms. As with most situations, asking fellow travelers for help in understanding instructions, announcements, or procedures almost always meets with enthusiastic assistance, or at least, with confused commiseration.

European trains run on tight schedules and usually arrive and depart on time. Trains that originate at a station often wait at the platform and open for boarding long before the scheduled departure time. However, trains originating elsewhere only make brief stops in stations along the route. These stops last anywhere from 30 seconds to five minutes. Be prepared to scramble on or off! If you're having trouble finding your correct car, just get on the cotton-picking train! You can always walk between cars once you are on board.

Train doors usually open automatically but sometimes you must push a button to make it happen. Actual door handles seem to have disappeared, at least in the modern parts of Europe.

As in most of the civilized world, allow disembarking passengers to get off before climbing aboard. The train will not leave as long as a group of people is actively boarding.

Buses

Networks of bus routes cover most of Europe quite thoroughly. Often, you can reach even the smallest town by bus if you are willing to work within the limits of their schedules.

A variety of private and public bus lines often provide multiple options for travel and can vary substantially in cost, scheduling, and amenities. Bus travel usually costs less than train travel but takes a bit longer. On the plus side, it sometimes provides a better view of small towns or of the countryside.

Buses traveling between cities almost always have restrooms on board. Some have drinking fountains and most provide free WiFi.

Organized bus tours offer pleasant and convenient ways to visit popular tourist sites. These can usually be arranged through city tourist offices or directly with the company, or even online.

Bicycles

Europeans commonly use bicycles for transportation. What a great way to get exercise, reduce pollution, and see a country up close, all at the same time!

Provisions for cyclists vary by country. Some, like Denmark and the Netherlands, have excellent networks of bike paths between and within cities. Others expect cyclists to take their chances on narrow roads shared with crazy motorists—pretty much like in the US.

Bike shops in most cities offer short-term and long-term rentals. Many cities have public bike rental stations throughout the downtown area with basic bikes available for temporary use at little or no cost. Buses and trains often carry bikes for free or for a small charge.

Always wear a helmet when you ride and if you plan on bicycling much, bring your own helmet for an assured fit. The problem of bike theft makes strong locks and chains necessary in most places—although in Ireland, we have seen people lean their bikes, unsecured, against shop fronts while they pop inside to make a purchase or two.

Rental cars

If you feel especially adventurous, you can drive yourself around Europe. It does give you more freedom than relying on public transportation. You can travel where you want, when you want, and make any interesting detours that suddenly appeal to you.

We choose not to drive. For us, the stress of dealing with different traffic patterns, road signs, laws, and customs—not to mention those places where people drive on the WRONG side of the road!—is more than either of us wishes to tackle.

If you plan to drive in Europe, make sure you understand and meet the requirements for renting a car, having a valid driver's license, and carrying proper car insurance.

Baby boomers need to be aware that some countries and companies set upper age limits for car rental. Supposedly, a car rental agent in France refused to rent to Senator John McCain's 93-year-old mother because of her age. Her solution? She promptly bought a car of her own and headed off on a road trip through Europe with her twin sister. Finland looks safe though. The Internet lists the upper age limit for renting a car there as 97.

More information about driving in Europe falls beyond the scope of this book. Make sure you inform yourself thoroughly before you undertake this activity and study the rules of the road carefully for any country where you plan to get behind the wheel.

City Transportation

Most cities have convenient, well-marked, fairly inexpensive bus, tram, subway, light rail, or trolley systems. Unfortunately, types of tickets, where and how to buy them, and procedures for using the system correctly vary substantially from place to place.

For example, in London you must insert your ticket or electronic card into a machine simply to gain access to the Underground system, while public transportation in Copenhagen operates on something of an honor system. There, you are supposed to validate your ticket before riding but nothing stops you from boarding buses or subway trains if you don't validate it, or even if you don't have a ticket. You do pay a huge fine if caught without a valid ticket, but figuring out how to validate it is not always easy.

Lynn says . . .

As you may have guessed, my motto about this and many other things is "Just Ask"—often to the embarrassment of "Directions? We don't need no stinkin' directions!" *Larry.*

Most places sell a variety of choices for tickets—single ride, multiple rides, unlimited rides for a specific period of time, rides plus admission to attractions, paper tickets, electronic tickets, and so on. Think about your options before you buy. Which will work best for the service you desire?

You will feel most comfortable if you familiarize yourself beforehand with the transportation system in the area you plan to visit. Such information always appears in guidebooks and online. Ticket sellers are usually patient about explaining all the details, and seem to be used to dealing with confused tourists. Once again, watch others or ask!

Public transportation may operate on different schedules on Sundays and holidays. Print and online guidebooks usually list holidays, and give some indication of usual business and transportation operating hours.

Most public transportation ceases operation late at night and during the early morning hours, although not always. Make sure you know whether you can get home again if you plan to stay out late. Also check what time that subway or bus system begins operating in the morning if you plan to depend on it to get to the airport for an early flight.

The Google Maps website gives excellent suggestions for travel routes. It even tells you which trams, trolleys, or trains to take to get to your destination, and when the next one will arrive!

Taxis roam all cities and most towns. Rates, systems for charging fees, ways of engaging a cab, and the honesty of drivers vary substantially from location to location. Again, specific information appears online.

Services such as Uber are rapidly making inroads in Europe where they operate in much the same way as in the US.

We prefer walking whenever reasonable. Besides being the best way to get to know a place, it provides excellent exercise. Each person has his or her own limits, but the two of us find it easy to walk to an attraction two or three kilometers away. Farther than that and we start looking for a tram.

Detailed street maps from tourist services or online websites make getting around much, much easier. For the technologically inclined, Google Maps on a smart phone seems invaluable.

Comfortable walking shoes make a great investment. Everyone, everywhere wears athletic shoes these days. Lightweight but sturdy walking sandals that give good support offer another possibility. Many familiar brands of athletic shoes show up in stores in almost any European city if you need a new pair—although duct tape can be a lifesaver.

Chapter 12.
Attitudes—Pro and Con.

Toward Americans

Do they hate Americans over there? Will I have to be worried about being harassed?

We have found attitudes of Europeans toward Americans to be favorable in general and have never encountered any direct antagonism, although as world situations and US policies change, this could occur.

Individuals have certainly voiced their dislike for behaviors of specific Americans—everything from dolts talking loudly in restaurants to someone (naming no names) suggesting he might drop an atomic bomb on Europe. Such criticisms usually lead to interesting exchanges of ideas rather than uncomfortable situations, however.

More often, our experience has been that when someone finds out we come from the US, they want to tell us about a cousin living in Chicago or their trip to Disney World.

Toward older folks

Europeans seem to treat older people, especially older women, with great respect and kindness. Aging does bring some advantages.

Lynn says . . .

As a young single woman, I often found travel difficult because of unwanted attention from men in public settings. Fortunately—or unfortunately?—for some reason, such problems no longer arise . . .

Age does have its benefits. Nowadays, young European men—and women—offer me their seats on public transportation. Someone always stops to carry my heavy suitcase up or down stairs in train stations.

For a long time, Larry amused himself by claiming this happened because they could see how old and decrepit I was. Therefore, I delighted in watching a young London Underground employee chase him up a flight of stairs one evening calling, "Sir, Sir, we have a lift you can use!"

Larry says . . .

Actually, many young folks also give me their seats, although I usually have to carry my own suitcase. I guess I don't look feeble enough . . . yet.

Toward travelers with disabilities

Travelers who have physical disabilities seem to be treated with respect in Europe. Accommodations for people with disabilities are available in some places but are not nearly as widespread as in the US.

Public transportation and large museums commonly provide alternative arrangements for those with limited mobility but restaurants and bars, as well as many attractions, frequently lack these. Imagine trying to install an elevator in some of those ancient castle towers!

Specialized guidebooks are available for anyone with a disability who contemplates a trip to Europe.

Toward minorities

Attitudes toward racial, ethnic, or religious minorities vary widely from place to place throughout Europe, even more so than in the US. As white Americans, we have very little direct knowledge about how Europeans treat visitors of other races.

We have never noticed any overt discrimination or negative behaviors toward those who appear "different," either because of physical characteristics or dress, although some countries have laws specifically forbidding some types of clothing in certain places.

Attitudes toward LGBTQ visitors vary substantially from location to location and individual to individual. Large liberal cities like Barcelona, Prague, Dublin, and Amsterdam accept alternative lifestyles more readily than do smaller communities, or countries in the far eastern part of Europe. Gay friends who travel extensively in Europe tell us that they rarely encounter problems.

Overt homosexual displays of affection—or heterosexual displays, for that matter—are best avoided in most public places, however.

Travelers with concerns about these issues should seek specific information in specialized guidebooks or online.

Chapter 13.
We're Here, Now What?

Tourist information

The primary activity of most tourists in Europe is sightseeing. The multitude of attractions in Europe seems limitless—breweries, gardens, caverns, castles, spas, zoos, churches, wineries, amusement parks, nature preserves, towers, and cemeteries. Find those that appeal to your interests and enjoy them!

Most cities have information offices for visitors at train stations, airports, and scattered throughout tourist areas. These make great places to ask all kinds of questions and to pick up brochures or to buy tickets for organized tours. Many tour companies sell tickets from strategically located offices or kiosks as well. The people who staff these can also answer related questions.

Friendly and helpful people seem to proliferate the world over. Local residents passing us on the street, sitting beside us in restaurants, or looking at produce next to us in grocery stores invariably seem eager to help confused foreigners. In Ireland, simply standing on a street corner and looking at a map elicited offers to lead us to our destination. Other tourists can also be great sources of information, especially about attractions, restaurants, and bars to visit or avoid. When in doubt, remember that motto and ask, ask, ask.

Of course, you can also find almost anything online. We discover all sorts of useful information about attractions at TripAdvisor.com and by googling "activities" or "free activities" and the name of the city.

Tours

As one of our first outings in a new place, we usually take an organized walking tour of the city. These tours serve as good introductions to the culture and geography of the area as well as giving us an overview of attractions to visit later in more depth. Bus tours of the city serve the same purpose.

"Free" walking tours seem to be especially popular. We have found them in every city we've visited, usually led by college students or other enthusiastic and well-informed young folks. The tours last from one to three hours and cover major locations of interest in the city's central area. Guides typically request payment "for what you think it's worth" at the end of the tour, but this remains entirely voluntary—if you really need to economize.

Many companies sell bus tours and paid walking tours. Specialized excursions cater to those with special interests—the Spanish Civil War in Barcelona, Jack the Ripper in London, Scandinavian cooking in Copenhagen, or canal-cruising in Amsterdam.

With Slow Travel, we have time to see places beyond the specific cities we visit. Organized day-long bus tours give us easy and often relatively inexpensive ways to visit interesting nearby sites. We always find the tour guides knowledgeable and often highly entertaining.

Our organized tours from Galway to the Cliffs of Moher, from Budapest to a wine tasting in caverns under a neighboring town, and from Prague to the former Nazi concentration camp at Terazin, called Theresienstadt in German, all left us with unforgettable memories.

Many companies also offer individualized tours. These can be expensive, but may give those with specific interests or needs a more satisfying experience.

We also often take side trips to nearby places of interest on our own, making use of Europe's excellent public transportation, along with travel and touring information found on the Internet. Such trips only require a little planning.

From Utrecht, the two of us absolutely *had* to take the short train ride to explore Breukelen—namesake of the hometown of the New Yorker half of us, which also furnished many of that borough's early settlers. Not surprisingly, we found the tiny town's gift shops laden with souvenirs touting the town's name and heritage. Evidently we weren't the first to make this pilgrimage.

From Dublin, a commuter train and then a tour boat carried us to seabird colonies on Ireland's Eye, a small island off the former Viking stronghold of Howth (not to be confused with the Ice Planet). A frisky seal with quite an array of whiskers and a gorgeous coat cavorted around the boat while Monty Python's expurgated gannets flapped and squawked their way along the cliffs.

From Vienna, we took a riverboat down the not-so-blue Danube to Bratislava, Slovakia—not just a new city but a whole new country. Along the way, we waltzed to Strauss' "Blue Danube," even though we had to hum it ourselves.

From Paris, a brief train trip—and a very long wait in line—brought us to the grand Hall of Mirrors at the Palace of Versailles. Those folks sure knew how to live—at least for a time!

We have also been fortunate to meet Europeans who wanted to show us some of their countries. Our convivial host in Dublin told fascinating stories of his childhood while he drove us through the working-class neighborhood where he grew up—now turning into a posh suburb.

He then took us to view Dublin Bay from its Great South Wall, and ended the tour with a stop in his favorite pub so we could share a few pints—and a lot of joking insults—with the other regulars.

Friends from London chauffeured us around the stone-and-thatch villages of Wiltshire, with a special side trip to see the centuries-old giant figure of stunning phallicallity carved into turf on the mountainside above Cerne Abbas. They wisely avoided being drawn into the playful debate that broke out among other tourists there as to the religion of the giant . . . Jewish or not Jewish?

In addition to all the sightseeing, Larry and I also enjoy both popular and highbrow entertainment, as well as Europe's many other attractions.

Chapter 14.
Popular Entertainment.

Music

Whether it's Kenny G, Lady GaGa, Bruce Springsteen, or your favorite gypsy punk rock band—you do have a favorite gypsy punk rock band, don't you? Ours is Gogol Bordello—you'll find world-famous pop stars performing in venues all over Europe. Buying tickets online or over the phone has become easy, with "Will Call" options usually available if you can't print out your tickets beforehand.

Fabulous local music and folk festivals—free and paid—take place frequently in Europe, especially during the summer. What a great way to become a part of the local culture for a day or two!

For the less adventurous, most cities have theaters with resident ensembles that present evenings of local folk music and dance for tourists. We have always found these an entertaining way to learn something of the history and culture of the cities we visit.

In most cities, music abounds. Just follow your ears. Who know what delights you will discover?

Spectator sports

Soccer is the game of choice throughout most of Europe. Of course, English-speaking Europeans all call it "football." Tickets to regular professional games are readily available online or at the stadium, often even on the day of the event. Just don't expect to get into championship matches.

People more commonly watch soccer in pubs crowded with cheering fans. Many establishments post upcoming games and their starting times on chalkboards outside the door to attract customers. Periodic loud cheers or unison groans echoing down narrow streets can also lead you to a popular match being shown on TV in the local pub.

Stopping to watch an amateur soccer or rugby game or practice can also be fun. Some of those kids have already become amazingly accomplished ball-handlers, or footers.

In Ireland, hurling and Gaelic football replace soccer as the national obsession. Friendly patrons at our local hurling pub in Dublin delighted in teaching us the intricacies of this sport—sort of like lacrosse played with hockey sticks. After a few pints, one family of fans even escorted us to a nearby park so their young son could demonstrate his stick-handling maneuvers.

Fervent supporters of the Tipperary team made up most of the pub's clientele, so you can imagine the joyous pandemonium the evening "Tipp" won the All-Ireland Hurling Championship.

Other local sporting events can also be fascinating. In Scotland, we spent an enjoyable day at a Highland games gathering. Brawny kilt-clad lads tossed enormous cambers and "put" huge stones. Nearby, a stage showcased a dance competition for young girls—highly reminiscent of beauty pageants with their elaborate costumes, perfectly styled hair, and pushy mothers.

Bicycle races take to the roads in various countries around Europe during the summer. While its finish line on the Champs-Élysées is usually mobbed, multiple roadside venues along the 2100-mile path of the Tour de France offer splendid opportunities to watch for the leader in his yellow jersey to whiz past.

And speaking of bicycling, while touring Ireland on his bike, our older son once happened upon a crowd of fans watching a road bowling match. Yes, they bowl—on the road! There's an Association and everything.

Sporting activities

Europe teems with opportunities for participation in active sports. Hiking, swimming, boating, climbing, biking, horseback riding—we're told they just call it "horse riding" in England, saying, "Where else would you ride?"—and similar activities rate as popular there as in the US.

The two of us no longer follow particularly strenuous pursuits, other than a lot of daily walking, so we can provide little further information on this subject. Once again, check the Internet for your favorite sporting activities in any location.

Movies, TV, the Internet

Movie theaters are common in Europe and show the latest films, both local and foreign, that is, American. Finding theaters that show films in English outside the UK presents a challenge, however. Most American films are dubbed into the local language.

The same holds true for television. American and British TV shows dominate the airwaves in Europe. Our host in Prague proudly informed us that the TV in our apartment got 22 channels—almost all of them carrying exclusively American or British shows. True—but as we discovered, all those shows came dubbed into Czech. You think *Game of Thrones* is difficult to follow in English!

The most likely channels to arrive over the airwaves in English are the BBC and CNN International.

For those of us who enjoy watching TV, the Internet becomes a lifesaver. So much American entertainment appears online these days. *Big Bang* and *Law and Order* reruns are always available on some website.

We watch Yankee games live, but only the day games. Night games begin after midnight in Europe—the time difference, remember? That time difference can be a good thing for those of us who like to sleep late. In Europe, we finally get to watch *Morning Joe*. It comes on at noon there. For folks who prefer Rush and his compatriots, talk radio also streams live online.

Larry says . . .

Watching movies is one of my passions. Luckily, I find Netflix and similar services throughout much of Europe, although this varies by country and changes regularly as services expand or contract. My headphones allow me to enjoy TV and movies on my laptop without disturbing Lynn, who prefers to read.

Chapter 15.
Highbrow Entertainment.

Opera

Despite occasional derision by our friends, we admit to enjoying opera. Before dismissing it completely, remember people once looked at opera as entertainment for the masses. Therefore its music had to be engaging, its staging spectacular, and its plots dramatic. Where do you think the term "soap opera" comes from?

An elegant evening at the opera can be a night to remember—the sparkling chandeliers, the chilled champagne, the fabulous music—and in some locations, it can be quite inexpensive.

Inside the State Opera House, Vienna

Cheap seats or standing room at a performance often cost less than tickets for a guided tour of the building. If the production doesn't enthrall you, can always leave before the fat lady sings. And even in such an elegant setting, surprisingly casual dress seems common. A few people always show up in jeans.

European opera houses stage wonderful productions, even during the summer, which is outside the normal "season." We have never encountered difficulty getting tickets for good seats. Usually, artists unfamiliar to us sing the leading roles but the house orchestra is sometimes famous.

And some buildings constitute impressive attractions in themselves—like Budapest's jaw-dropping State Opera House with the most over-the-top Neo-Renaissance decor imaginable. Velvet, marble, gilt, mahogany, or crystal covers every square inch of the interior.

Fortunately, most opera houses provide line-by-line translations of operas into English as well as into the local language. These translations appear on screens over the stage or on the backs of auditorium seats.

Our delight in this feature turned to amused frustration in Barcelona, however, when we realized that the only translation of the production of *Die Walküre* we were attending was into the local Catalan. Nothing to do but relax and enjoy Wagner's beautiful music, including the iconic "Ride of the Valkyries"—or as one of us better knows it, "Kill the Wabbit."

Concerts

Symphony orchestras and chamber ensembles perform in many European locations during the summer. Tickets, again frequently available even on the day of the performance, often cost little and free concerts take place regularly indoors and in the open air.

Pipe Organ, Notre-Dame, Paris

We particularly enjoy pipe organ concerts in spectacular cathedrals. Those in Notre-Dame always please us, and a special excitement comes from attending a concert in Haarlem's Grote Kerk to hear the same organ Mendelsohn, Handel, and Mozart once played. Herman Melville even mentioned it in *Moby Dick*. He compared the baleen of a whale to its striking array of pipes.

Theater

Formal and informal theater productions take place in every city. Unfortunately, our knowledge of the local language limits our ability to enjoy most productions. Theaters in the UK furnish wonderful opportunities for enjoyment, however.

London's West End is comparable to Broadway. Shows sometimes open there before coming to New York—with tickets costing just as much or more.

Who wouldn't enjoy seeing a revival of *My Fair Lady* in a theater located a mere hop, skip, and a jump from the play's setting in Covent Garden?

London also boasts the unique Globe Theater—definitely worth a visit, but take a pillow. The reconstructed venue is designed to recreate the Elizabethan theater experience, hard benches and all. And talk about appealing to the masses! What Shakespeare comedy couldn't be rewritten as an *I Love Lucy* episode? And probably has been.

Smaller venues with interesting productions flourish throughout the UK. We just missed seeing Gandalf and Captain Piccard perform together in a Harold Pinter play at the Royal Theater in Brighton but did manage to see a less highbrow presentation there that included a rousing audience sing-along to "It's a Long Way to Tipperary."

Chapter 16.
Is That All?

Museums

We find museums in Europe to be extremely educational and interesting—some more so than others, of course. A few "must see" ones spring immediately to mind, but we have also found many less-well-known museums to be charming. How can you not like the Musée des Arts et Métiers in Paris where an amazing 1897 airship hovers bat-like over the staircase, or Museum Speelklok in Utrecht with its wonderful array of antique street organs that fill the air with cheerfully syncopated music?

Prior to visiting a large museum that charges a substantial admission fee, we identify the highlights we want to see. Evidently, we're not the only ones. We marveled at the crowds elbowing their way into the *Mona Lisa* room at the Louvre while ignoring four other Da Vinci works hanging along the hall outside.

Naturally, the two of us prefer large museums that have free admission. There, we don't feel so pressured to see everything in one day. For example, we only discovered out-of-the-way but far from minor treasures at the British Museum because we could explore that storehouse of marvels at a more leisurely pace during repeat visits (It's the Rosetta Stone!—*the Rosetta Stone!*). Of course, you can always return anywhere. It's only money.

We have been delighted to discover English labeling in addition to labels in the local language on exhibits in almost every museum we've visited. Occasionally, other popular languages also appear but English is a constant.

Many larger museums and other attractions provide taped audio tours in a variety of languages, either for free or for a reasonable charge. Some even give live tours in English at certain hours.

Large museums have cloakrooms for storing backpacks or other paraphernalia and some insist you use them. Most are free—often a locker requires you to put in a coin to get a key but returns the coin when you return the key. Such museums also frequently have pleasant attached cafes with good food at reasonable prices. And they always have free restrooms.

Battlefields

Visiting historic battlefields has become a major tourist activity in Europe. It's not just devotees of military history who seek out iconic battlefields—from Marathon where the eventually triumphant citizens of Athens won their first victory over invading Persian troops in 490 BCE to allow the rise of Classical Greek civilization, to the beaches of Normandy, the D-Day landing sites for Allied forces as they began their final push to defeat fascist Nazi Germany.

Many visitors feel an emotional connection to these places where unknown combatants from the distant past, or more recent remembered heroes, fought and died for their beliefs.

Lynn says . . .

As Larry and I walked a windswept field on England's southern coast one misty afternoon, ghosts of ancient warriors rose up in my imagination. Here at the Battle of Hastings, William the Conqueror and his invading Norman infantry, cavalry, and archers vanquished Anglo-Saxon King Harold's native foot-soldiers in 1066, and determined the future of England.

I, like most modern British folks and Americans of British ancestry, probably had ancestors on both sides of that fight. Such visits push me to learn more about long-gone folks such as these who directly or indirectly contributed to who I am today.

Genealogy, family history

Speaking of family history research, this activity has become popular with Americans visiting Europe. Some countries—Ireland in particular—give visitors easy access to research resources, although serious endeavors take prior planning and sometimes require prior contacts with institutions, record repositories, and genealogical professionals.

We prefer exploring our family history in more informal ways. Walking the same Haarlem streets and admiring the same magnificent cathedral that a Dutch ancestor saw before she left to settle in Nieuw Amsterdam, or finding tiny Whittlesey Street in London, named for another ancestor, thrills us.

We always stay on the lookout for reminders of Larry's Jewish heritage as we explore Europe. Finding a *stolperstein* in Gouda memorializing a woman bearing our same last name sobered us.

Over 50,000 of these small brass "stumble-stone" plaques commemorating individual victims of Nazi persecution have been set into sidewalks throughout Europe since 1992.

Stumblestones

Chapter 17.
Getting To Know You . . .

For us, the joy of traveling includes meeting other people—either fellow travelers or local inhabitants of the countries we visit. Slow Travel provides many opportunities for these encounters. Some occur in the course of day-to-day activities. Others require more effort.

Meeting local residents

Some of our most pleasant memories come from contacts with residents of the countries we visit. Our most frequent local interactions come from contacts with our apartment hosts. Many rent out their lodgings because they enjoy getting to know visitors from other countries.

We learned a lot about the Czech film industry—who even knew there *was* a Czech film industry?—from our host in Budapest who works as a casting director in her day job. In Paris, we exchanged ideas about recent anti-Semitism with our host while he guided us on a personal tour of the Jewish quarter. In Dublin, we regularly invited our jovial host into our apartment for a chat. Our conversations ranged from commiserating about the intricacies of dealing with our respective adult children to solving most of the world's pressing problems.

Other contacts are more fleeting. In London, we exchanged ideas about politics with a British chauffeur and his wife while sharing a table with them at a rock concert. During an Early Music Festival dinner in Utrecht, featuring foods appropriate to the era, we learned from Dutch table mates about the anxieties of living below sea level at the mercy of a dike. Keeping a rowboat on the roof helps, they said. In the course of the meal we also learned that no one likes turnip tarts anymore—if they ever did.

Lynn says . . .

Sometimes opportunities for getting to know others arise unexpectedly. A chance meeting on the street in Amsterdam led Larry, the more adventurous one of us, to head off in a taxi with two questionable local characters and their dog in search of a Pirate Party rally and rave. Despite my worries that I would never see him again, he did return safe, sound, and well-fed.

Bars and pubs can be great places to meet friendly local folks. Who doesn't becomes more sociable after having a few? Choose your establishment with some care, though. Online review websites can give you a good idea of the type of clientele and level of openness to "outsiders" at specific establishments. A peek in the door can often serve the same purpose.

It's also helpful to have some knowledge of local rules and customs for bars and pubs—again, print or online guidebooks usually contain this information. Hint: buying a round for new friends is almost always welcomed.

Larry says . . .

I bring a guitar or mandolin with us when we travel. This frequently leads to new contacts and interesting conversations. An interest in music is universal.

Sometimes I've been invited to join informal music sessions. Our favorite pub in Galway welcomed all comers. Quiet strumming in a park often attracts like-minded folks. If nothing else, just carrying a musical instrument can lead to friendly chats with fellow travelers.

A guitar is a little awkward to manage, but European airlines—unlike American ones—usually allow it as carry-on baggage. I bring an inexpensive purpose-bought instrument so as not to worry about damage. At the end of our trip, I leave it—and, hopefully, a bit of goodwill toward Americans—with someone in the last country we visit.

Meeting fellow travelers

Sharing information and experiences with fellow tourists can also be fun. Organized tours often lead to enjoyable contacts with others interested in the same activities.

Lynn says . . .

On the way to and from a wine tasting in Budapest, I shared ideas about genealogical research with a Canadian couple while Larry learned a lot about Cold War document and artifact collections in Hungary from their chatty daughter, a curator in the state museum there. More than we expected to get out of a wine tasting . . .

Another evening, during a dinner centered around Irish folk music and storytelling in Dublin, we sat next to a couple from Arizona. Between courses, they explained their "Fast Travel" approach to seeing Europe. They rent a car and visit as many sites in as many countries as possible. We stayed in touch after that evening, in awe of their wonderful photos and all the ground they covered in just two months. We still prefer our Slow Travel though.

We don't see ourselves as overly social folks, so these brief contacts suffice for us. If you desire more in-depth connections with local people, all sorts of organizations exist to arrange such contacts. Check online.

Chapter 18.
Eating our Way Through Europe, Part 2: Eating Out.

Restaurants

We enjoy occasional fine dining in an elegant restaurant but we rarely get around to it during our travels. So many fascinating and less expensive local places pop up that we almost never get the chance to move on to the fancier spots. The most expensive meal the two of us ate during the entire summer of 2016—a trip that included one feast with so much food that the leftovers we took home fed us for two more meals, and another, a three course dinner featuring duck with appropriate accompanying wines, backed by a gypsy violinist—involved hamburgers, French fries, and milkshakes at a Hard Rock Cafe on the Fourth of July. Had to go American that day!

Procedures for visiting a restaurant in Europe seem much like those in the US. Systems for making reservations, seating, ordering, and paying are generally similar, although minor—but sometimes important—differences do exist.

Restaurants often furnish English versions of their menus in areas frequented by tourists. In especially "touristy" restaurants, which also have much higher prices, pictures of the dishes sometimes appear on the menus. In these areas, restaurant staffs will probably speak English and can answer questions about the food.

We find eating in less touristy neighborhoods more fun. Once again, Google Translate comes in handy. If necessary, we just point to items on the menu, or at a nearby table. If neither of us understands details—or anything at all—on the menu, we order anyway. What's the worst that can happen? If we don't like what we get, we simply don't eat it—we're looking at you, cold congealed pork *Grieben in Schmalz*! And frequently we discover something new and delicious!

Details do vary from place to place. In some restaurants, ordering a main dish also brings sides. In others, side dishes must be ordered separately. Additional charges may apply for bread or for extras like catsup.

Most restaurant menus list a few vegetarian dishes, although some cultures have a rather vague understanding of what "vegetarian" means—*"No beef, right?"* Vegan, kosher, and halal restaurants can even be found most places with some effort.

EU countries require fourteen major food allergens to be noted on menus, a real boon for those with difficulties in this area. Menus and packaged goods in grocery stores detail the allergens in each dish, from gluten to tree nuts to celery (people are allergic to celery?). One friend of ours carries a sheet with images of the items that give her problems. She shows it to the wait staff when ordering. If using this method, make sure you mark the items clearly with the "prohibited" sign—a circle with a line through it—so the waitperson doesn't think you actually *want* the items pictured.

Despite having good tap water, Europeans drink bottled water in restaurants. Your choice will typically be "still" or "sparkling," or some version of this. Water often costs about as much as other drinks on the menu, sometimes more. Don't even try to get tap water with a meal unless the waitperson offers it or you have also ordered another drink—cappuccino seems to come with a glass of water in Vienna, for some reason. You can probably argue successfully for a free glass of tap water, but surely that sets back international relations years.

Cappuccino and Water, Vienna

The "doggy bag" is not a common practice in most of Europe, although a kind waitperson will occasionally offer to wrap extra food for you to take home. So eat up—or order less.

In some countries, like Spain, the waitperson will not bring the check (called the bill in the UK) until requested to do so. You can sit and talk or sip a drink for hours. The universal sign for the check—eye contact followed by a check mark in the air—is understood most places.

The bill you receive in a restaurant may simply state the total amount due or may be extremely detailed. Check your detailed bill to make sure it is correct, which may be difficult. Taxes may or may not appear on it. Sometime restaurants add a fixed tip or service charge. You can always ask—or at least, try to ask—about any charges that you do not understand, and whether the total includes a tip. The word "tip" seems to be one of those almost universally understood. Guidelines for tipping in different locations can be found in guidebooks or online, like almost everything else.

Many restaurants accept credit cards. If you need to pay with plastic, make sure you ask before you eat.

If you're desperate for a fix of American fast food, all the usual chains show up everywhere—McDonalds, Burger King, Dunkin' Donuts, Subway, KFC (love their Dublin ads for their "O'Sanders Menu—it's Irish-ish"). And wherever we go, the proliferation of restaurants selling all kinds of good old American food—you know, like pizza and tacos—continually amazes us.

Street food

We especially enjoy "street cuisine" sold by small "take-away" stands throughout Europe—and the world. Not only is it quick and inexpensive, but it gives us another "taste" of local culture. It also creates so many wonderful gustatory memories.

Ah, the *lángos* in Budapest —rounds of fried bread dough topped with veggies, meats, cheeses, and sauces; the raw herring in Amsterdam (not a winner, by the way, although the somewhat related *kibbeling*—deep-fried chunks of fish that we snacked on daily in Utrecht—was unbelievably addictive); the spiral cinnamon-spiked chimney cakes in Prague; the paper cones of French fries with twelve kinds of sauces in Haarlem; the frankfurters in Hamburg (to our regret, we couldn't find a hamburger during our brief stopover); and the gelato everywhere—one of us prefers pistachio while the other *loves* Nutella.

Chapter 19.
Wet Your Whistle.

Alcohol

Alcohol features more prominently in everyday life in Europe than it does in the US. Legal ages for purchasing it are usually lower there and many European countries have no minimum age for drinking alcoholic beverages. People regularly consume beer, wine, and spirits on the street, in parks, on beaches, and in other public areas, although local laws may impose some restrictions on this.

The preferred alcoholic beverage varies from place to place, as does quality and price. France touts its wines while beer reigns supreme in many parts of Germany. Hard cider seems especially popular in England. Young folks flock to Prague for its cheap beer and lively "ruin pubs." Each location sings the praises of its own unique type of distilled spirits—*grappa* in Milan, *pálinka* in Budapest, and Scotch in Edinburgh.

To us, sampling the local preferred beverages constitutes an important part of getting to know a culture. We also enjoy learning and practicing the appropriate toast in the local language. And as the evening progresses, we get better and better at pronouncing those foreign words of the toast. At least, it seems that way . . .

In most of Europe, the usual glass of draught beer—what you should be drinking if you're in a pub

—contains 500 ml, that is, half a liter or a little more than one US pint. In England and Ireland, order a "pint" and you get even more because of the British system of liquid measures. Their Imperial pint glass (568 ml) holds 20% more than a US pint (473 ml). Cheers!

    A typical serving of wine totals 300 ml. Some bars and restaurants price it in 100 ml amounts, so the glass of wine may cost more than you expected. Menus usually make this clear, if you look carefully.

Bars and pubs

    Bars and pubs abound throughout Europe. Bars tend to feature cocktails and hard liquor while pubs focus more on beer, wine, and cider, although much overlap exists between the two. Many serve food in addition to alcohol—sometimes just snacks, sometimes full meals, especially in pubs. Both often attract customers with scheduled or impromptu live music. Often, proprietors tune at least one television to a popular sporting event—invariably soccer.

    Many pubs in places like England and Ireland seem to serve as community gathering spots for friends or families to spend a convivial afternoon or evening. And if you're partial to Irish pubs, you can find one in any European city.

Chapter 20.
Shop Till You Drop.

Stores

Shopping in Europe is comparable to shopping in the US. Malls look the same all over the Western world and contain many of the same stores everywhere—from Foot Locker to Prada.

Large department stores exist but most shops are small and carry only limited types of merchandise. Sometimes the selection seems odd—the liquor store in Budapest that also sold underwear and baby shoes always puzzled us. Finding exactly what you want may be difficult but you know what to do when you need something—just ask.

Proper etiquette becomes more important in small stores. Greeting the clerk when entering, and saying good-bye or thanking them when you leave a shop, is usually considered an important gesture. We find saying "Hello" upon entering satisfies this requirement. It also alerts the clerk to the fact that they must deal with foreigners—as if they couldn't tell—and that we use English. Repeating one of your memorized phrases of greeting in the local language serves a similar purpose. It is polite, and your accent lets them know they're probably going to need to find another language to communicate with you.

In some places, shopkeepers considers it impolite to pick up or even touch an item in a store unless you intend to buy it. "Just looking" should be only that. Other local customs sometimes arise. Guidebooks usually alert the tourist to important differences. Watching other shoppers always offers a good way to learn.

In large and small stores, you pay for your purchases in much the same way as in the US. Many stores accept credit cards but many others do not. As in the US, most stores that take credit cards display signs showing which ones they accept.

When paying for purchases in cash, bills in a foreign currency rarely cause confusion. Coins are another story. Rather than picking through unfamiliar coins, trying to find and read the sometimes-obscure numbers hidden on them, one of us usually just holds out a handful of coins to the clerk. Most clerks happily select the proper combination from our hand—it speeds up the transaction mightily. Of course, it's possible to get ripped off this way, but how much can you actually lose? We believe most people are honest, and have never noticed a problem.

Merchandise

You can find pretty much anything in Europe that you might buy back home, although not necessarily the same brand. But familiar company names do appear with some regularity—Converse, Head and Shoulders, Jim Beam, Levi, Apple—and the common electronic brands from Asia have flooded the world.

We usually buy local brands when one of us needs vitamins, hand cream, shampoo, or socks. If you do buy a local item, make sure you know what you are getting. Pictures on packages don't always convey enough information. As we discovered, conditioner doesn't work very well as shampoo, even though both have images of luxuriant heads of hair on the bottle.

If you absolutely *must* have some particular product of a particular brand, take it with you. We have never been able to find Chapstick in Europe.

Business hours and holidays

Most businesses in European countries keep hours similar to those in the US, although shopkeepers in Mediterranean countries occasionally close for a few hours in the early afternoon for "siesta." Most stores post hours on the door. Banks worldwide tend to have shorter hours than shops, but ATMs always stay open. We find retail stores often remain open longer in the evenings in Europe than where we live, sometimes until 10:00 pm. Perhaps this just happens during the tourist season.

Rules for shopping on Sundays vary drastically from country to country. The two of us found ourselves looking longingly—and hungrily—into the front windows of a tightly closed grocery store on our first Sunday in rigidly Catholic Austria. Stores in other places sometimes operate 24 hours a day, seven days a week. Our best advice? Check it out when you arrive, and plan ahead when necessary.

Holidays can also be tricky. When we confidently—and even more hungrily—returned to that same Viennese grocery store the next day—Monday—the same darkened windows greeted. What! A holiday? Something about Pentecost . . .

Gifts, souvenirs

We all want to remember our visits to special places. Somehow, simple memories don't seem enough. Photos are nice, but taking them can get to be a distraction. Sometimes, don't you want to yell, "Put down your smart phone and just experience the moment (and then get off my lawn)?" Instead of photos, we write to preserve our memories—and we also take home a few souvenirs. And, of course, there are always those gifts for folks back home to consider.

Stores selling souvenirs clog tourist areas. Most items look horribly tacky but treasures sometimes hide among the shelves of made-in-China junk. Flea markets are fun to visit, can also supply unique—or downright odd—souvenirs or gifts. We found a great Viking-horn bottle opener in a Copenhagen street market for one son. A decorative wooden "L," for a friend named Lisa, turned up a box of jumbled antique printer's typeface in a Barcelona market. We then spent a good while searching the box for a similar "K," for Katie, before remembering that the Spanish alphabet doesn't contain that letter.

If you ship your purchases home, the sky—or the wallet—is the limit. We don't ship, so we need to think small, light, and unbreakable.

How much you spend depends on your budget. Diamonds—small, light, and easy to pack—make lovely mementos of historic Dutch diamond-trading centers, but we enjoy our free souvenir placemats from Dampkring, our favorite Amsterdam coffee shop, instead. Their lovely swirling designs fit perfectly with our home decor—and the marijuana menu on the back amuses dinner guests.

Despite our best efforts, we always come home with a few coins and bills in foreign currencies—unintentional souvenirs. These, along with attractive stamps, also make good gifts for children or collectors. What grandchild wouldn't want a 1,000 Forint note, especially since it sports a great portrait of such a stern Hungarian leader? And it only costs about $4.00. (Actually, the guy on the 500 Forint note looks much more intriguing, with his long curly locks, his bushy hat, and his wonderfully evil moustache—perfect for twirling.)

We usually pick up a few picture postcards of special places for our own enjoyment and always come home with a small mound of ticket stubs. How do you throw away that ticket from the Springsteen concert in Copenhagen?

Photo books of specific locations look nice but really weigh down a suitcase, and can be purchased online from home—probably at less cost and from a wider selection.

T-shirts, although not very imaginative, are relatively inexpensive, easy to find, take little room in a suitcase, and don't break. Other small knitted or embroidered items can recall a special place every time they are worn or used.

We're partial to folk art. Small unique carvings are easy to carry. We still enjoy our little painting of Gaudi's Sagrada Familia Church purchased from a Cuban immigrant artist on the street in Barcelona.

Special local foods also appeal—oh, that Scottish shortbread! Just make sure you know the regulations about bringing foods into the US, and into any other countries you plan to visit along the way, before you stock up.

Jewelry is easy to carry. Charms for bracelets can match every budget. And although not exactly jewelry, rosaries from specific shrines make nice gifts for Catholic friends. Make sure you purchase any expensive pieces from reputable dealers and save the sales slips for customs. Shops can explain the requirements and procedures for refunds of the Value Added Tax (VAT) charged on such items.

Some international companies design items with traveling collectors in mind. One of our friends collects Hard Rock Cafe T-shirts. Another collects Harley-Davidson pins. In both cases, only the store in the location named on the item sells it, which adds to the pleasure of tracking it down.

Tourists find bringing home alcohol tempting but difficult—heavy, breakable, and limited by customs. However, anyone who visits the Heineken Brewery in Amsterdam usually comes away with enough free souvenir bottle openers to take care of several friends back home. Guinness doesn't give away anything at their Dublin brewery, but the city's pubs are happy to let you take home a few of their Guinness beer coasters, each with a different image.

We try to find interesting and distinctive items. Fossilized amber from the Baltic States always appeals. Some pieces even contain ancient creatures—Jurassic Park, anyone? In the same vein, the Bohemian region of the Czech Republic has been famous for its fossilized trilobites for centuries. One town even features a trilobite on its official crest. While loading a suitcase with heavy objects never sounds ideal, even these rocks can make great gifts or souvenirs, if collected in moderation.

We consider our reusable shopping bags from the British grocery store chain of Sainsbury to be one of our best finds. The bags are brightly colored, practical, and inexpensive. We can even present them to folks back home as "trip-used" gifts. After all, if game-used dirt from Yankee Stadium sells for a premium, don't the bags that carried our cheddar cheese and Wheetabix through the streets of Salisbury have extra appeal?

Chapter 21.
An Apple a Day . . .

Medical services

Most European countries have modern health systems. Standards vary widely from location to location, but first-rate physicians, surgeons, and dentists can be found with a little effort, and a little help from locals. We have been fortunate during our stays in not needing medical assistance, except for a tooth extraction in Barcelona—which turned out to be a surprisingly excellent experience even though most communication took place in rudimentary Spanish or English aided by hand gestures and, once again, Google Translate.

A friend who suffered a heart attack in Prague has only praise for the medical care he received there, and his wife celebrates its success by inviting friends in for a yearly "We're Glad You're Not Dead" party. Others we know have had sketchier but still effective treatments—one from a private physician in Belgium and one in the emergency room of a public hospital in Paris.

Finding a physician, dentist, hospital, or other medical assistance in a strange place can feel intimidating. Airbnb hosts supply much basic information, which can sometimes include medical referrals. Tourist offices usually have lists of English-speaking medical professionals. Concierges in large hotels have similar lists and will sometimes help you even if you are not a hotel guest. Pharmacists give medical assistance for minor problems in many countries and can make referrals for more serious conditions.

Americans usually must pay for medical care at the time it's provided. Paperwork for insurance reimbursement can be filed later, so get whatever documentation they offer. Travel insurance can be reassuring but we have decided to risk relying on our regular medical insurance, although it only covers emergencies. Medicare does not cover any services outside the US.

Pharmacies

Pharmacies in Europe operate in a way similar to those in the US. Some countries, Portugal for example, do have fewer restrictions on the medications that can be purchased without a prescription.

It's a good idea to carry copies of your prescriptions with you, but trying to fill a prescription written by an American provider will probably present problems in Europe. The two of us always take along all the prescription medications we will need. If problems arise, we plan to see a local physician, and hope that pharmacies in the country carry the medication we need.

Medication names, as well as medications available, do vary by country of course, but pharmacists can usually recognize the written generic name of a drug. Even in English-speaking countries, they may use different names for prescription or over-the-counter medications than in the US. We finally gave up looking for acetaminophen (Tylenol) in the

UK, and only later learned that they call it paracetamol there.

Staying healthy

Of course, staying healthy always remains a concern, wherever you find yourself in the world. All those things your mother told you become especially important when traveling. Get enough sleep, eat healthy foods, drink plenty of clean water, get regular exercise, wash your hands often, avoid those coughing and hacking folks on the subway, and so on. New places and new situations often raise your stress level, which can lower your resistance to illness, so pay extra attention to doing whatever works for you.

And always remember the most useful piece of advice for staying healthy in Europe: Know which way to look before you step off the curb! As Americans, our automatic impulse—to look left before crossing the street—works fine in much of Europe, but not in the UK or Ireland.

This has become such a problem that many cities have taken to writing "Look left" or "Look right" in bold letters on the sidewalk at street crossings in tourist areas. Popular spy novelist Daniel Silva even began one of his books with the death of a foreigner who steps into the path of an oncoming bus after carefully checking in the wrong direction for approaching traffic.

Be careful. Make a habit of looking *both* ways before crossing the street, wherever you are.

London Crosswalk

Chapter 22.
Stay in Touch.

Phones

We have chosen not to use cell phones in Europe in the past—mainly to avoid hassles and expense—but don't necessarily recommend this option. Cell phone use is rapidly becoming easier to arrange and less expensive. Worrying about loss, damage, or theft does add one more burden, but the convenience of having map and translation websites at our fingertips, and the peace of mind that comes with being able to contact each other easily, has started looking better and better.

The Internet

We have always relied on our laptops to gather information, access entertainment, and stay in touch with folks at home. Email is easy. Skype allows both free face-to-face visiting and calling any phone anywhere for a small fee, about two cents a minute at present.

We stay in touch with a 96-year-old cousin and usually call her several times during our trips to Europe. Each time, we have to keep reassuring her that the call isn't costing us a fortune. We understand. For those of us who grew up speaking to relatives only on very special occasions (Hurry up.

It's long-distance!), the modern technology that allows such easy and inexpensive contact remains a marvel.

For those even farther behind the times than we are—those who have no smart phone, laptop, or tablet—Internet cafes still exist and rent access to computers at reasonable by-the-minute rates. These and regular copy shops are also excellent places to print out tickets, boarding passes, and other documents when you need them in paper form. We always pack a USB-port memory stick to facilitate this.

Snail mail

We've never tried to use European postal services to receive mail, but we suppose it could be done. We do mail postcards home occasionally and have always found postal clerks to be helpful in purchasing the right postage and getting the cards in the correct bin. Stamps from foreign countries make attractive, easy-to-carry souvenirs, or gifts for those at home interested in such things.

News

When we want to stay in touch with world events, we find news on the Internet, CNN, or the BBC. Occasionally, the two of us track down an English-language newspaper, most often in airports, train stations, or even subway stations. Sometimes the odd newsstand in a tourist area will carry one.

We come across the *New York Times International* most often. We search it out mainly for the Wednesday, Thursday, or Sunday crossword puzzles—Monday's seem too easy and Saturday's border on impossible.

Chapter 23.
... And the Law Won.

The Law

Laws vary from country to country but are generally similar to those in the US in most of Europe. When in doubt, ask. We have always found police officers to be helpful and polite, as well as quite young...

One of the most obvious differences to travelers arises when checking into a hotel or rental apartment in some countries. Germany, for example, requires the visitor to complete a governmental registration form and present identification, such as a passport, at that time. Hotels usually follow these regulations carefully but apartment landlords treat them more casually.

Another obvious difference in laws relates to buying and consuming alcohol—usually more lax than in the US. On the other hand, civil rights appear much more limited. And some places frown severely on jaywalking—startling to the New Yorker soul that resides in one of us.

Fortunately, we have never run into any serious legal difficulties in Europe. Others have told us that dealing with police bureaucracy there is much like in the US but even more confusing and frustrating. If you become involved with the police, contact the US Embassy or Consulate. They may not supply much direct help, but can, at least, give you information.

Crime, terrorism

The crime rate in most European cities remains lower than in most American cities, and not much of a concern. Of course, you should stay alert, use common sense, and avoid "bad" areas or wandering down dark, lonely streets at 2 a.m., just like anywhere in the world. We've never encountered muggers or had anything stolen from cars, public transportation, hotel rooms, or apartments, but it happens—again—just like anywhere. Don't take obvious chances, but there is no need for paranoia.

Pickpockets present the greatest threat to most tourists. We have found that our money and small valuables stay safe in a small zippered mesh bag pinned to the inside of a pocket. We get the bags from the pharmacy department at Walmart, sold as containers for medicine. Other people like money belts or small pockets worn around the neck.

Most days, the two of us carry only the money we need for that day, our identification, and maybe one credit card. Everything else, including at least one more credit card, stays at our apartment or other lodging.

For identification we carry photocopies of our driver's licenses and the main page of our passports, with our local address and a list our emergency contacts written on it as well. We usually only carry one debit card at a time and only when we need cash from an ATM. When traveling between countries we always carry our passports and our bank cards on our person, never in a backpack or suitcase that might disappear.

Terrorist attacks can happen anywhere, any time. Avoiding war zones and riots always seems like a good idea, but other than that, no one can remain absolutely safe—anywhere. So, you might as well live your life doing something you enjoy—like traveling.

The United States Department of State regularly issues travel warnings and alerts for Americans considering international travel. These provide notice of serious long-term or temporary threats to the safety of travelers in the areas specified in the warning or alert. You should definitely check these before planning a trip and again before heading out. Find them online at www.travel.state.gov.

Drugs, legal and illegal

Tobacco use takes place much more commonly in Europe than in the US. Many countries allow smoking in restaurants and bars but others ban it or limit it to specific areas in such establishments. Some ban smoking in many public areas, and almost always prohibit it in stores, concert halls, and on public transportation. Regulations permit the use of e-cigarettes more places than regular tobacco, but often limit these as well.

Laws about marijuana and hashish vary by country, and sometimes by locality within the country, as they do in the US. Its use has become legal or semi-legal in some places, notably the Netherlands. In other places, like the Czech Republic, possession of small amounts has been decriminalized, meaning that punishment only amounts to a fine. Other countries continue to impose harsher penalties for possession of even small amounts of illegal substances.

Possession of hard drugs, such as cocaine and heroin, psychedelics, and other odd chemical substances, as well as excessive amounts of prescription medication, is illegal almost everywhere.

Don't take chances! If such activities interest you, know the laws and the practices of the countries or cities you visit. You have seen *Midnight Express*, haven't you?

Chapter 24.
And Did I Mention?

Time

The Prime Meridian runs through Greenwich, England (pronounced "GREN-itch," not "Green-witch" as one son's seventh grade geography teacher insisted). All time the world over derives from it.

England operates on GMT (Greenwich Meridian Time), which runs five hours ahead of—that is, later than—New York time. When it's 1:30 in the afternoon in New York, it's 6:30 in the evening in London.

Most of Western Europe operates on CET (Central European Time), one hour later than GMT. When it is 1:30 in New York and 6:30 in London, it's 7:30 in Paris, Rome, and Budapest. Farther east, time zones get more complicated. In all, Europe includes seven major time zones, some only appearing in certain seasons.

Most countries use some version of Daylight Savings Time in the summer. It's always a good idea to check the local time when you arrive in a new place—easy to spot on airport and train station clocks. You don't want to miss an appointment or a performance because you are on the wrong time.

Transportation lines, stores, and theaters in Europe usually use the 24-hour clock, rather than designating hours as a.m. or p.m. Anyone who has served in the military is already familiar with this system.

For the rest of us, the a.m. hours are easy—8:10 a.m. is 0810. The p.m. hours require a little more adjustment. In this system, 2:30 p.m. becomes 1430. We find that subtracting two hours and ignoring the first digit yields a number that has more familiar meaning to most Americans.

Weights, measures, sizes

Except for the UK, European countries use the metric system. Thinking in metric terms becomes surprisingly easy, especially if you forget about exact conversions.

As mentioned earlier, units of weight include kilograms (kg) and grams (g) in the metric system. One kg (1,000 g) equals a little more than two pounds. The UK uses pounds and ounces to measure weights.

Liters (l) and milliliters (ml) measure volume, with 1000 ml making up a liter, which approximates a US quart. The UK uses pints, quarts, and gallons, although these are bigger than in the US.

Distances, measured in meters (m) and kilometers (km), pose a little more difficulty. One meter can easily be thought of as a little more than a yard, but kilometers usually take more real conversion. A km contains 1000 m, which equals a little less than two-thirds of a mile, actually 0.62 miles. A traveler going from Paris to Prague covers 890 km but only 550 miles.

We don't drive in Europe so we don't have to think much in terms of long distances. If you do drive, when your speedometer reads 100 kph—a common speed limit on four-lane highways—you are going 62 mph.

Distances in meters come up more often for us because we walk a lot. Directions often read something like, "Turn right after 50 m and your destination will be 200 m on the left." Again, we just think in terms of yards.

Europeans use the Centigrade scale for measuring temperature, rather than Fahrenheit one. Water freezes at zero on this scale and boils at 100 degrees. Centigrade temperatures in the teens are chilly (50° F to 67° F). The twenties are warm (68° F to 85° F) and the thirties are hot (86° F to 102° F).

Sizes for clothing and shoes in Europe differ substantially from those in the US. A US women's size 8 1/2 shoe equals a size 6 in the UK and a size 39 in the rest of Europe, but a men's size 8 ½ equals an 8 in the UK and a 42 in the rest of Europe . . . more or less. Clothing sizes are even more complicated.

Don't even try to understand sizes. It's not worth the frustration, especially because they can also vary from country to country. Additionally, sizes vary from manufacturer to manufacturer, exactly as they do in the US. Just try items on before you buy them.

Tipping

Tipping customs also change from one country to the next. In some countries, like Spain, wait staff, taxi drivers, and such folks receive little or no tip. In most countries, service providers expect tips, usually about 10% to 15% of the bill.

In some places, restaurants automatically include a service charge in the bill so the wait staff does not expect an additional tip—but may hope for one from uninformed tourists. Guidebooks—online or in print—usually indicate the custom of the country.

Restrooms

What a wonderful surprise to find great restrooms in Europe, especially after remembering the state of such things many years ago when each of us first visited the Continent!

Directions to the Facilities

Public toilets in airports, train stations, malls, restaurants, and museums in most European countries these days are clean, modern, and well equipped—with toilet paper even! The old-style hole-in-the-floor toilet thankfully seems to have disappeared, but probably still lurks in some backward rural areas, especially as you go farther east.

Flushing mechanisms vary but usually require an obvious action—pull a chain, depress a handle, or push a button (the small button produces a little water, the larger button produces more).

Those self-flushing mechanisms that startle the heck out of you also lie in wait in some stalls.

Urinals look and function pretty much the same in Europe as in the US but one of us (guess which one) found some amusing art in a Prague restroom. A mural backed the wall of urinals. In it, women were pointing and laughing while looking through magnifying glasses aimed at the lower anatomy of urinal users.

Public restrooms often charge a small fee to enter, especially in train or bus stations, so carrying coins for this is wise. Sometimes you put the coin in a machine. Other places, surprise!—a bored-looking male or female attendant—never mind the "gender" of the facility—waits to take your money.

When you're desperate, you can always find restrooms in bars or restaurants. Making a small purchase in the establishment avoids any hassles.

The most universal method for finding the facilities seems to be to seek out someone who looks like they might know and greet them with a plaintive, "Toilet?" If you want to appear more sophisticated or genteel, you can murmur instead, "*La toilette?*"

Signs for the WC help in some countries. (School children in Italy once requested a bathroom break by raising two fingers in the "Victory" symbol so closely associated with Winston Churchill—get it? it's his initials.) Avoid asking for the "bathroom" or "restroom" as these terms will likely lead to confusion.

Separate-gender restrooms—not always present—are usually labeled clearly. Surely you know how to say "men" and "women" in the language of the country. If not, it's worth making the effort to learn the words well enough to recognize which is which on the signs. Just hope they don't use clever alternative terms for the two genders—imagine the confusion of poor visitors to the US encountering the cutesy signs for "Does" and "Bucks" or the canine-themed "Pointers" and "Setters."

Often, symbols appear on the doors as well. In case you're not sure, the figure wearing the skirt indicates the ladies' room—even in Scotland.

Chapter 25.
Slow Travel—How to Relax and See the World.

You now understand our approach to Slow Travel—a fun and easy way for retired Baby Boomers to see the world, or some part of it.

As we explained, we started with one vague goal—to spend a relaxing summer in Europe, just getting to know the place and some of its people. We wanted to live there for a while without making any long-term commitment to permanent relocation.

We have reached that goal—and so much more. Our approach worked so well for us that we have now repeated it for three summers in three different parts of Europe.

Each time, the two of us chose interesting and relatively safe countries where a good number of people speak English. We traveled by ship and plane, and then by train, subway, bus, tram, trolley, and the occasional taxi. We stayed in rented apartments arranged over the Internet.

Our decision to settle in for a week or a month in a variety of locations each summer has worked well for us. We've gotten to know something about each place and some of its inhabitants at a leisurely pace while being able to maintain a bit of our usual, familiar daily routine. Our decision has also reduced the hours spent in less pleasant activities—actual travel and tracking down places to stay.

On each trip, we've lived reasonably frugally and as much like locals as possible, but have also enjoyed some interesting and fun "touristy" doings and occasional splurges on special activities. We've found just enough "new" and "exciting" endeavors to spice things up a bit without getting in over our heads.

Our Slow Travel is fun but not exhausting. We see a lot of Europe but pass up additional sights and sites when visiting them begins to feel like a chore. Sure, we miss a few "important" things, but we gain so much . . .

No reason YOU couldn't do the same. You might even want to try Slow Travel in another part of the world . . . Asia . . . Australia . . . South America . . . or perhaps even in the United States. What do you really know about Santa Fe, Charleston, or Portland?

Leaving home for a summer sounds hard. It really isn't, *if* you prepare well, remain flexible in your plans and expectations, and maintain a sense of humor.

Why not give Slow Travel a try?

You can do it!

Afterword

You've now read the first book in our series for retired Baby Boomers so you understand how we undertake this gentle adventure we call Slow Travel.

Our next book, *Lynch the Swan*, chronicles our experiences putting Slow Travel principles into practice. We compiled it as a lighthearted travel memoir from emails sent to friends and relatives during our travels to Eastern Europe, England, and Ireland during the summer of 2016.

We hope you enjoy our books. And we hope they inspire you to try Slow Travel for yourself. It's easier and less expensive than you think. And as we said before, if we can do it, almost anyone can!

Acknowledgments

Friends and relatives in the US and abroad have greatly enhanced our travel experiences. Several—especially Dorothy James, Madeline Havas, and Nina Justman—also encouraged us to write about our travels, and added a slew of helpful suggestions.

Barry Sumeray and Gerry Nicholas offered us room and (fabulous) board in London while serving as our tour guides and experts on all things British—and some things Irish.

Susan and Michael Karlson's description of their Fast Travel journeys helped us give a name to our very different approach to seeing the world—Slow Travel.

Our sons and their significant others have always been supportive of our traveling—perhaps they prefer having us out of the country. They also continually enrich our writing, and our lives.

Moses took the photo on the book cover during a visit to Jamaica. His wry comments have always helped shape our thinking. Lisa's good humor, even under difficult conditions, brings joy—and she's still kind enough to smile when we remind her about our time together in Paris.

Aaron's vigilant editing greatly improves our manuscripts. He also takes care of our mail during our trips. Katie's globetrotting inspires us—although we can never hope to see as much of the world as she already has.

Our Airbnb hosts over the years have made our travel adventures both possible and enjoyable.

Throughout Europe, innumerable strangers have helped carry our luggage, given us directions when we've found ourselves lost, suggested interesting activities, shared information about their countries, interpreted incomprehensible tickets or signs or menus, and chatted with us about their lives and ours. Their kindnesses always made us feel welcome in their homelands.

Critiques and suggestions from members of the Melody Lane Writers Guild—especially Linda, Bryon, Etya, Gerald, Elaine, Bill, Eva, and Janet—shaped this book. Their encouragement continually helps with the sometimes frustrating business of writing and publishing books.

And as usual, Robin Angel favored us with her extraordinary proofreading skills. Any errors are ones we introduced with our last-minute changes.

To all you wonderful folks, we say . . .
"THANK YOU!"

About the Authors

As youngsters, both Lynn and Larry set out to see the world. Lynn spent a year in Italy as an American Field Service high school exchange student. Larry backpacked around Europe after college—wasn't that required in the 70s? Now in their retirement years, they have once again set off to see the world—and to write about it.

Lynn grew up in the South, the daughter of a Methodist minister and a primary-school teacher, both with long family histories in America. After attending college in Vermont and Montana, she quickly headed for warmer climes.

Larry is Brooklyn born and bred, the son of a German Holocaust survivor and a first generation Polish Jew. He moved west after completing law school.

The two met in New Mexico where they married, raised two sons, and spent most of their working careers. Both maintained successful private practices—Larry in general law and Lynn in clinical and forensic psychology.

Now, when not traveling or visiting those sons and their significant others, they divide their time between Santa Fe and their home on Hutchinson Island, Florida. There, Lynn enjoys writing, beachcombing, and researching family history. Larry spends his days perfecting his guitar-playing skills, catching the latest movies on Netflix, and dreaming of following the Grateful Dead.

Other Books by the Authors
(available in paperback or as ebooks)

Baby Boomers Retirement Travel
Next in the series (coming soon) . . .

Lynch the Swan
A Lighthearted Travel Memoir

Slow Travel to Barcelona, Vienna, Budapest, Bratislava, Prague, London, Brighton, Salisbury, Dublin, and Galway

Carolina Lowcountry Folklore

The Galapagos Islands

The American Southwest

. . . at Amazon.com or your favorite bookseller